CW00555835

Making
Patton

Making *Patton*

A Classic War
Film's Epic Journey
to the Silver Screen

**Nicholas Evan
Sarantakes**

University Press
of Kansas

Published by the University
Press of Kansas (Lawrence,
Kansas 66045), which was
organized by the Kansas
Board of Regents and is
operated and funded by
Emporia State University,
Fort Hays State University,
Kansas State University,
Pittsburg State University, the
University of Kansas, and
Wichita State University

© 2012 by the University Press of Kansas
All rights reserved

Library of Congress Cataloging-in-Publication Data

Sarantakes, Nicholas Evan, 1966–
Making Patton : a classic war film's epic journey to the silver
screen / Nicholas Evan Sarantakes.
p. cm. — (Modern war studies)
Includes bibliographical references and index.
ISBN 978-0-7006-1862-0 (cloth : alk. paper)
1. Patton (Motion picture) I. Title.
PN1997.P375S27 2012
791.43'72—dc23
2012016530

British Library Cataloguing-in-Publication Data is available.

Printed in the United States of America

10 9 8 7 6 5 4 3 2 1

The paper used in this publication is recycled and contains 30
percent postconsumer waste. It is acid free and meets the minimum requirements of the American National Standard for Per-
manence of Paper for Printed Library Materials z39.48-1992.

For my wife, Patricia

CONTENTS

A photo section appears after page 97.

ACKNOWLEDGMENTS

Many people over the years have expressed an interest in this project. I am fairly certain this reflects interest in the subject rather than my skill as a writer. A common question I have gotten is do I want to write screenplays. Having watched this process and studied a really good script, I have no doubt I could write in this venue. It would be an interesting challenge, but I was struck during my research at the similarities between book publishing and filmmaking. Historians do not use every document available to them. They cannot tell their readers everything that happened; they must be selective. This situation was the same in the making of *Patton*. The film was a fictional representation of two and half years of George S. Patton Jr.'s life. The film could not and did not cover everything. *Patton* was innovative, and history also requires creativity. I will readily admit that originality of thought is a skill that one is far more likely to find in a screenwriter rather than a historian, but students of the past are well served in having that skill.

It is clear that filmmaking is a collaborative medium. So is book writing. That was one of the biggest surprises I learned in getting published. A good writer—and I try to be one—realizes this fact and uses it to advantage. As a result, they accumulate a lot of debts, and this is an opportunity to acknowledge those obligations. If the reader finds this book at all entertaining, it is because a number of people helped me along the way. The author's name might go on the dust jacket, but others have input as well.

This book began by accident, but the seed was planted long ago. In 1995, I saw Carlo D'Este on the C-Span program *Booknotes* talking about his new book *Patton: A Genius for War.* I even accidentally happened to be at a book signing that he did at Borders bookstore near the Pentagon. I was a poor grad student at the time, busy writing my dissertation. I did not have the money to buy the book or the time to read it, but it intrigued me. I eventually bought a copy for my brother as a Christmas gift, and then, after listening to him talk about the book, I bought a copy for myself. There were several references to the film in the biography, and D'Este cited the papers of Frank McCarthy, the producer of the film *Patton*, which were at the Virginia Military Institute. I thought there might be an interesting article about the film and its historical accuracy.

I did nothing with that idea until 2000. That year I was busy doing research for a book on the end of World War II in the Pacific. It was published in 2009 as *Allies against the Rising Sun: The British Nations, the United
States, and the Defeat of Imperial Japan*—buy a copy, it is brilliant! Work on
that project took me to VMI to examine the papers of General of the Army
George C. Marshall, Chief of Staff, U.S. Army. During a lull, I asked to
look at the Frank McCarthy papers. I knew that McCarthy had been the
producer of *MacArthur*, and I was looking for documents on that movie for
a conference paper I was writing on film and the Korean War. I did not
find the material I was looking for until I returned on another trip in 2010,
but I found a treasure trove about *Patton*. I was amazed at what was in front
of me, and I quickly decided to write an article on the making of that film.
A one-day trip became a two-day trip became a three-day trip.

By the time I left, my project had grown from one to two articles, then
finally a book project. I figured I had enough to write a book, but I visited
Lexington three more times. Each visit was more enjoyable and profitable
than the last.

Needless to say, I am grateful to D'Este for his Patton biography. I rec-
ommend that anyone interested in becoming a biographer read *Genius for
War* to understand this art form. After finishing the book, I felt like I had
actually met George S. Patton Jr. A year later, I stumbled upon D'Este
when we were both at the U.S. Army Military History Institute in Carlisle
Barracks, Pennsylvania, and had an opportunity to thank him in person.
Eight years later, in 2009, I was in California visiting my mother's brother,
Colonel David E. Thompson. At dinner, my uncle stared a conversation
about military history. He said there was a historian that he liked and the
two had grown up together in Berkeley, California. There was an eight-
year age difference between the two, so they had not been all that close.
My uncle was eighteen and going off to college when he last saw this future historian. The next time he saw him was in Vietnam, when this neighbor from California jumped into his helicopter. Had I read anything, my
uncle asked, by Carlo D'Este?

The world is a small place sometimes.

I am also indebted to Frank McCarthy. This book, and the quality of the
research that has gone into it, was made possible because McCarthy saved
almost every scrap of paper associated with the making of *Patton*. Despite
Hollywood's relative youth, the film industry has done—and continues to
do—a horrible job of preserving its history. Studios are good about saving

the things that matter to them, like physical artifacts—props, costumes, and sets—but not the less-than-sexy written records that explain how decisions are made. McCarthy saved these documents—letters, telegrams, memos, focus group reports, film treatments, scripts—and they discussed all sorts of issues like casting, marketing, dramatic structure, public sentiment, and popular opinion. His material also included other items like oral histories, reviews from media outlets in every part of the country, and correspondence from people, be they influential or average. I also want to thank film historian Lawrence H. Suid for depositing his research files at Georgetown University. This material proved useful for reconstructing early efforts to make the film.

Research at other institutions proved useful. The McCarthy papers collection is so extensive that much of what it contains I had already seen at VMI, but while this collection is both deep and broad, no collection can ever have everything. I thank Christopher Raab, the archives and special collections librarian at Franklin & Marshall College, for his help in gaining access to material in the papers of Franklin Schaffner, the director of *Patton*, particularly audio recordings that were available only in antiquated media formats. May Haduong, public access coordinator of the Academy of Motion Picture Arts and Sciences Film Archive, was helpful in giving me access to the Pickford Center for Motion Picture Study. While there, I was able to watch a recording of the Oscar ceremonies for 1971. Watching the video was extremely useful in reconstructing that evening's events.

I even had an opportunity to help other scholars. While at VMI, I found a letter that Ronald Reagan wrote McCarthy in which the governor of California discussed the film. I gave a copy of this letter to Martin Anderson, who was editing a volume of the former president's letters. Anderson was acting in the role of historian as detective. He had found many letters that Reagan sent to people for which there was no copy in the Reagan Presidential Library. When I mentioned this letter to him while we were at the annual conference of the Organization of American History, he told me he wanted a copy. I got the document to him, and it ended up in *Reagan: A Life in Letters*. The letter also ended up being reproduced in full in the September 29, 2003, issue of *Time* magazine.

During the writing of this book, I had the opportunity to give several talks about *Patton*. At a research-in-progress seminar, the chair of my department, John Maurer, asked a particularly useful question about the influence of the film on the historical literature that I incorporated into this account. During this session, I also learned about the consumer price index inflation adjustment website that the Bureau of Labor Statistics in the Department of Labor maintains. Since inflation changes the buying power of money, this website was useful for putting the dollar figures quoted here into context. Maurer also arranged for me to give talks to local civic groups, which was a lot of fun.

I want to thank several people for taking a look at early drafts of this book. They include Michael Creswell of Florida State University, David Kaiser of the Naval War College, and Galen Perras of the University of Ottawa.

My friend Mike Bell has been an important sounding board on this project. We have known each other since we were in the eighth grade and we both worked on the *Grisham Grizzly*, the school paper at Noel Grisham Middle School in Austin, Texas. Even back then he planned to pursue a career in film. I starred in one of his student films when we were at the University of Texas. Today Mike is a member of the Directors Guild of America and makes a good living in the entertainment industry. Conversations that the two of us have had over the years informed this book even while I was doing the research and writing.

I would also like to thank Frank McAdams of the USC film school for his commentary on earlier drafts of this study. They proved quite useful.

Laptop computers are wonderful because they allow writers to write even when they are traveling. I was really grateful for this tool because I got a chance to write while I was at the Philmont Scout Ranch—a place of special importance to me. I wrote in other places as well, and I hope these changing locales did not diminish the final product.

With all the assistance I have received along the way, whatever defects remain are mine and mine alone. It is an old saying, but it is true.

NEΣ

Spring 2012
Waterville Valley, NH
Cimarron, NM
Portsmouth, RI
Newport, RI
Chicago, IL
San Diego, CA
Commerce, TX

ACRONYMS

The following terms and initials appear in the text. Many of them appear in the original documents, and instead of using punctuation that would make for troubling reading, they appear here for reference.

AFI	American Film Institute
BEF	British Expeditionary Force
CBS	Columbia Broadcasting System
CP	Command Post
DDE	Dwight D. Eisenhower
DOD	Department of Defense
DVD	Digital video disc
DZ	Darryl Zanuck
ESPN	Entertainment and Sports Programming Network
G.C.M.	George C. Marshall
G.I.	Government Issue (nickname for U.S. soldiers)
GSP	George S. Patton Jr.
LSU	Louisiana State University
M	Sir Bernard Montgomery (Viscount Montgomery of El Alamein)
MGM	Metro-Goldwyn-Mayer
NAACP	National Association for the Advancement of Colored People
NBC	National Broadcasting Company
P	George S. Patton Jr.
P	The president of the United States
UCLA	University of California at Los Angeles
USAA	United Services Automobile Association
USAR	United States Army Reserve
VC	Victoria Cross (highest British military medal)
VCR	Videocassette recorder
VMI	Virginia Military Institute

Introduction

It was a warm summer's day in Madrid, Spain. The set was simple: a stage that stood in front of a giant but old version of the U.S. flag. (It had forty-eight stars instead of fifty.) The flag was painted on a backdrop. "It was as big as it looked on the screen—*enormous*," Fred J. Koenekamp, the director of photography, explained. Two cameras were locked down so the stripes would not produce a strobe effect.

Ten months later, on March 7, 1970, a powerful collection of middle-aged men and women sat in a movie theater to watch the Washington, D.C., premiere of *Patton*. The audience was full of senators, admirals, and generals, men who had fought under or alongside the real George Smith Patton Jr. in World War II. They wore tuxedos and uniforms, displaying awards for bravery and merit that they had earned in the war and during the semipeace of the Cold War. The cinema went dark, and the huge flag appeared on screen. A voice bellowed, "Ten-hut," and the audience watched the forty-one-year-old George Campbell Scott walk on to the stage from stairs directly behind the platform. "Reveille" played while Scott saluted. The camera cut in for a series of close-ups on the actor—his hands, his uniform, his helmet.

It was the last day of shooting on the film, and George C. Scott was less than happy. Early in his life, Scott had enlisted in the United States Marine Corps, earning the rank of sergeant. In Spain, though, he was wearing the uniform of an officer, a U.S. Army officer—a general, to be more exact. He was playing the role of Patton, the commanding general of the Third U.S. Army, and he was wearing a uniform that the actual Patton had worn only once. On display were reproductions of the medals—not the ribbons—of awards bestowed on the real Patton.

Scott was unhappy not with the uniform, the role, or even the speech that he was about to deliver, but with where the scene was scheduled to appear in the film. He had balked at using it as an introduction. He thought that it would start the film on such a high emotional level that it would be difficult to maintain. Studio executives, the producer, and the director disagreed and refused to change the film. Scott's anger and frustration at not getting his way were evident to the crew on the set.

"Be seated," Scott told the crew, repeating lines that screenwriter Francis Ford Coppola had penned four years before.

"Now, I want you to remember that no bastard ever won a war by dying for his country. He won it by making the other poor dumb bastard die for his country. Men, all this stuff you've heard about America not wanting to fight, wanting to stay out of the war, is a lot of horse dung. Americans"— with those words, the camera cut into a tighter focus on Scott, giving his words more power—"traditionally, love to fight. All real Americans love the sting of battle."

The introduction was the work of the film's screenwriter. "That was all Coppola's genius," producer Frank McCarthy observed. According to Coppola, he designed the scene to show Patton's character. He combined several speeches that Patton actually gave. Coppola also used two other events. The first was an occasion where Patton gave a talk in front of a giant U.S. flag. The second was a private moment when, as a four star general, he posed for a family picture wearing all his decorations and medals. The opening was in many ways a surreal moment in the film. "The idea was to see him at his zenith," the writer explained, "show him at the very height of his career."

McCarthy could vividly remember the enthusiasm Coppola showed when he suggested the scene. It was the first idea he brought to the producer. "The very first thing," he recalled. "The very first day."

Scott delivered his lines in his distinctive gravelly voice: "When you were kids, you all admired the champion marble shooter, the fastest runner, the big league ball players, the toughest boxers. Americans love a winner and will not tolerate a loser. Americans play to win all the time. Now, I wouldn't give a hoot in hell for a man who lost and laughed. That's why Americans have never lost and will never lose a war. Because the very thought of losing is"—Scott paused briefly, and then said with a slightly slower pace—"hateful to Americans.

"Now, an army is a team. It lives, eats, sleeps, fights as a team. This individuality stuff is a bunch of crap. The bilious bastards who wrote that stuff about individuality for the *Saturday Evening Post* don't know anything more about real battle than they do about fornicating.

"Now, we have the finest food and equipment, the best spirit, and the best men in the world. You know . . ." Director Franklin Schaffner then cut to a tighter focus on Scott's face. The actor was smirking as he delivered his next lines: " . . . by God, I actually pity those poor bastards we're going up against." The smirk faded, but a lighthearted lilt entered his voice as his Patton showed a degree of compassion for the enemy. "By God, I do."

All humor departed as Scott delivered the next lines with a combination of anger and disgust: "We're not just going to shoot the bastards. We're going to cut out their living guts and use them to grease the treads of our tanks. We're going to murder those lousy Hun bastards by the bushel." The camera cut back to an immediate focus. "Now, some of you boys, I know, are wondering whether or not you'll chicken out under fire. Don't worry about it. I can assure you that you will all do your duty." Volume grew as he delivered the next lines: "The Nazis are the enemy. Wade into them. Spill their blood. Shoot them in the belly."

The camera returned to a tight focus on the actor's face and hands, giving more emphasis to the words he was about to deliver: "When you put your hand into a bunch of goo that a moment before was your best friend's face"—his volume dropped instantly as he gestured with his hands— "you'll know what to do."

The emotion of Scott's delivery ebbed, and he paused for a second. Schaffner cut back to a wide focus to show him pacing back and forth across the stage. "Now there's another thing I want you to remember. I don't want to get any messages saying that we are holding our position. We're not holding anything. Let the Hun do that. We are advancing constantly and we're not interested in holding onto anything . . ." Schaffner returned to a closer focus on Scott and the actor delivered his next lines with emotional force that grew with each word: " . . . except the enemy. We're going to hold onto him by the nose, and we're gonna kick him in the ass. We're gonna kick the hell out of him all the time, and we're gonna go through him like crap through a goose!"

Scott paused again, and Schaffner moved to a tighter focus. "Now, there's one thing that you men will be able to say when you get back home, and you may thank God for it. Thirty years from now when you're sitting around your fireside with your grandson on your knee, and he asks you, 'What did you do in the great World War II?'—You won't have to say, 'Well,'" he said with a sigh, "'I shoveled shit in Louisiana.'"

In the tightest focus of the monologue, Scott said, his voice growing softer and softer, "All right now, you sons of bitches, you know how I feel." The cinematic general glanced down for a brief moment, which emphasized the vulnerability and sincerity of his next words: "Oh, I will be proud to lead you wonderful guys into battle anytime." He paused, and then added, "anywhere."

He paused again, began turning, and said, "That's all."

The screen went black after Scott walked back down the steps. The audience in Washington broke out into applause. After five years of a confusing conflict in Southeast Asia, after years of social turmoil, after the public questioning of their leadership, here was a reminder of what made these generals, admirals, and politicians great. It felt good. The applause in the room was thunderous.

Those who knew the actual general had different reactions to this scene. "After the first sentences, I knew what was coming. I had heard that speech before," Edwin H. Randle observed. A retired brigadier general himself, he had seen Patton deliver those remarks to the combat team that Randle commanded. The real speech, he reflected, was bloodier.

Omar Bradley, on the other hand, said his former colleague's words were "never quite so dramatic as the galvanizing opening scene." The language he used was more foul and "would not be suitable for a family film."

Back in Spain, Schaffner wanted to shoot the scene from different camera angles. Scott was none too happy about delivering the lines again. He agreed, but he refused to pick it up in the middle. It was the entire scene or nothing. After Schaffner moved the cameras, Scott began a second time, then a third time after another relocation of the cameras. "He never flubbed once. *Never once!*" Koenekamp declared. "We were done by the middle of the afternoon. It didn't even take a full day."[1]

Coppola was pleased with how his idea had translated to film. "I am very proud that the director, Franklin Schaffner, was to take the screenplay literally in this case, it's a very unusual scene, it's a great performance of Mr. Scott, and it was really a very surrealistic idea. I love especially the way the director had his feet actually walk on the bottom of the floor as though we're looking up at him on a stage before us."

Schaffner, for his part, knew what he and the rest of the production owed Coppola: "It should go without saying that had it not been for your skilful and inventive work on the screenplay that the project might never have got off the ground."[2]

Why study this film? The simple answer is that the production and success of this film can tell us many things about American society. In *Patton*, students of history have before them a useful prism to examine the past, and a good place to start is with the introduction—it captures an interesting contradiction. The film appealed to simple but strong national myths—or perhaps they are better described as ideals—while exposing more complex truths about power. Neither is wrong, and both deserve consideration.

For many—be they the filmmakers or the audience—*Patton* contained a powerful statement about the importance of self-reliance and the providential mission of the United States, and at the same time it stressed the importance of strong leadership. These notions attracted people regardless of their politics because this fictional representation of a real historical figure spoke to the basic vision most Americans had of their nation and seemed to confirm what they believed about the republic. In examining this period, it is clear that there was little, if any, dreary resignation to a diminished lot in life or cynicism about the workings of power, which many associate with the 1970s.

The introduction captures well the film's metaphors and the contradiction between complex truths and simple ideas. The words that Scott delivered—like the words that the real Patton had delivered—discussed the power of the team, but Schaffner's use of visual imagery stresses the importance of the individual.

At the same time, this film is useful to the students of history as a means to examine the changes that took place in American society in the middle part of the twentieth century. The Japanese film critic Hazumi Tsuneo observed, "To comprehend America, one cannot cast one's eyes away from American movies." To Hazumi, Hollywood films reflected a society that blended different peoples and cultures into a democracy.[3] He has a point. Far more people were involved with this film—in its production, or later as members of its audience—than in any of the social or political movements that have garnered attention in the literature of postwar America.[4] In a real sense—to steal a phrase from the era—the whole world really was watching.

There is an important story to be told about this film, which also happens to be a fascinating one. This book is relevant to historians of both mass media and popular culture.[5] As a film history, this book falls into both fields. Studies of film history usually fall into one of three camps. The first is material that entertainment journalists have written. These reporters are excellent at telling stories, but their research often rests on interviews that repeat unsubstantiated stories.[6] The second comes from communication and film schools. The scholars writing these books are mostly interested in explaining what appears on the screen and in using cultural analysis and film theory to explain movies.[7] Discussions of history and biography are normally absent, and clarity of expression often falls victim to cuteness with the tools of punctuation.[8] The third group is made up of a few historians who have offered studies that get behind the production process. It is an exceptionally small group. Despite the importance of the motion pictures in modern American society, historians have largely ignored Hollywood, and for good reason. The film industry does a horrible job of preserving its own history. Studios may hold on to costumes and props for decades, but they show far less interest in organizing or preserving the documentation that historians require to do their jobs.[9]

This book falls into that third category. This study is the product of research in studio archives, the records of the Academy of Motion Picture Arts and Sciences, contemporary newspaper and magazine articles, oral histories, the personal papers of the director and producer, and a number of films available in various media formats. Websites like Wikipedia and the Internet Movie Data Base have also been useful, offering up interesting facts while being more suspect when it comes to interpretative information. One site that has been used repeatedly is the U.S. Department of Labor's Consumer Price Index inflation calculator. The adjusted figures appear in parenthesis after the historical figure.[10]

The purpose of this account is to offer the reader a well-rounded, clear study that explains the origins, production, marketing, reception, and legacy of *Patton*. What follows is both social and film history.

One last thing is worth noting: ultimately this film was a work of fiction. It should be judged as such, not as a work of nonfiction. As history, it is better than most theatrical films, but it is still rather poor. What is unique about this movie, though, is that given the amount of time that it took to turn the life of George S. Patton Jr. into a theatrical production, the film opens a window onto American society in the postwar era, which allows us to see ourselves as we were and how we wanted to be.[11]

1. The General

Who was George S. Patton Jr.? When most Americans think of the general, the image that immediately comes to mind involve George C. Scott, a forty-one-year-old former Marine with a gravely voice, rather than the sixty-year-old general who spoke with a thin voice and a slight Southern accent. As a result, any study of the film bearing his name should take a moment to consider the real individual. The real Patton was a diligent military professional. His success—which was legendary—was no accident. Patton worked hard at his profession and had real intellectual gifts and leadership skills. He was no rebel against the system. The man behind the legend was an exceptionally interesting individual, and it was his larger-than-life personality that attracted filmmakers to the Patton project in the first place.

Despite his many intellectual abilities, Patton was dyslexic. Like many others with this learning disability, he saw words and letters backward, a problem that complicated his academic progress. His slowness in completing his education often obscured his intellect. One of his biographers remains skeptical, arguing that Patton's scholastic problems resulted from laziness.[1]

There is, however, little doubt about his religious nature even if it was at odds with itself. Wounded in World War I, he contemplated the meaning of Scripture, convinced he was dying—which was almost the case. At the same time, he believed in reincarnation. In his first life, Patton was convinced that he had been a cave dweller who hunted for mammoth. Then he was at Troy, where he died in combat. Patton returned as a Greek hoplite and fought against the Persian emperor Cyrus's invasion. He was also a Carthaginian soldier in the second century B.C. Mortal again a century later, he served as a Roman soldier in Gaius Julius Caesar's Tenth Legion. Patton waited a millennium before becoming a Viking warrior, and he could recall the stench of Nordic ships. He returned as a Scottish Highlander and fought the desperate cause of the House of Stuart. He could also recall riding a horse behind Napoleon during the march back from Moscow, his arm numb from the cold. Patton also fought in a New York regiment during the U.S. Civil War. At times, he could accurately take people to Roman ruins that he had never seen before. Patton also believed his ancestors were guiding him and directing him toward his ultimate mission. They, apparently, were not to be reincarnated.[2]

Although Patton's interest in religion was riddled with contradictions, it was serious. He read the Bhagavad-Gita, the key religious text of the Brahmins of India. While awaiting Operation Torch, he read the Koran to make sure that he and his men did not offend the Moroccans. In 1945, a German priest came upon Patton while the general was visiting a medieval church in Bad Wimpfen am Berg and found that he was sketching the stained-glass windows into a notebook.[3]

Patton was also a living contradiction when it came to his personal behavior. He never made off-color remarks or told dirty stories, but he used profanity on a regular basis to make a point. James H. Polk, who later became a general himself, recalled one incident when they were playing polo at Fort Riley, Kansas. Polk missed a shot and began cursing. Patton rode up to him and said: "Lt. Polk, you will not use profanity on this polo field, but it's a goddamned shame you can't hit the ball."[4]

Patton understood the professional importance the army gave to socializing. During one of his assignments in Washington in the early 1930s, he became friends with Secretary of State Henry L. Stimson. They rode horses together, and the Stimsons attended the debutante party of Patton's daughter, which was a social success for her parents. Patton, though, could make an odd impression. At one party, he grabbed a wine decanter and told Henry Cabot Lodge Jr.'s wife, "Did you know that a decanter, if properly used can be a lethal weapon? My grandfather killed the governor of the Bahamas with one."[5]

A study in inconsistencies, Patton knew early on in life that he wanted to be a military professional. The military ran in his blood. He was a direct descendent of Brigadier General Hugh Mercer, who was one of Major General George Washington's main subordinates. Mercer was killed at the Battle of Princeton during the American Revolution. Another relative, his uncle, Waller Tazewell Patton, died at Gettysburg, fighting for the Confederacy. Patton's goal was to attend the United States Military Academy at West Point, New York, but his dyslexia and poor education made achieving that ambition unrealistic. He enrolled instead at the Virginia

Military Institute. He was in Virginia for two years before he finally won an appointment to West Point. Despite the extra schooling, he still had a difficult time in New York. It took him five years to graduate. When he finally finished with the class of 1909, he entered the cavalry.[6]

Patton first made a name for himself in the army when he agreed to compete in the modern pentathlon at the 1912 Stockholm Olympics. The pentathlon was a contest that involved mastering a number of semimilitary skills: pistol shooting, fencing, swimming, the steeplechase, and cross-country running. Nervous about competing in the games, Patton did poorly at first, coming in twenty-first out of forty-two in pistol shooting. He recovered his composure and did well in the remaining events, eventually placing a respectable fifth in the overall contest.[7]

Advancement in the U.S. Army during the Progressive Era was slow. Yet Patton stood out. After returning from Sweden, he set out to redesign the cavalry saber. Weight distribution had been a major problem in previous versions of this weapon, a flaw that made it tough to use. The saber was most effective when horse riders hacked at individuals who were standing and lower than them. Patton's new design had a tapered sharp point, making the weapon an extension of the cavalryman's arm. It was also lighter and easier to handle. Many in the cavalry branch objected to this new weapon, saying it was a sword rather than a saber. Patton, however, in a series of articles, used military history to argue that the point was more difficult to parry than the edge. The recent experiences of the U.S. Army in fighting the Moros in the Philippines and that of the British Army against the rebellions of the Scottish Highlanders in the seventeenth and eighteenth centuries were perfect examples. The War Department agreed and adopted the Patton design in 1913.[8]

Patton's achievement was impressive, but the days of the horse soldier were numbered. The young officer quickly proved he could adapt to more modern technology. During the Mexican expedition of 1916–1917, he stood out from the other junior officers. "The most engaging personality of my Mexican service was my tent-mate, George Patton," Hugh S. Johnson, head of the National Recovery Administration, stated in the mid-1930s when Patton was still an obscure, middle-ranking officer. Patton, according to Johnson, would practice both right- and left-handed trigger pulling with a pistol fitted with a spring and a rod. He also had a bit of the theatrical showman to him. He refused to use automatic weapons and instead carried two pearl-handled .45 revolvers.[9]

It was in Mexico that Patton developed a close relationship with Brigadier General John "Black Jack" Pershing. When the raids of the bandit Pancho Villa finally provoked U.S. intervention in Mexico, Patton was determined to go even though his regiment had not been selected for this deployment. He lobbied friends whom he knew on the general's staff for recommendations. When Pershing heard of these efforts, he called Patton to see if he was serious. The young lieutenant used that opening to appear at the general's quarters, telling him he would take any position. The next morning, Pershing called to tell Patton he would be going. Expecting such a call, Patton had already packed his bags and said he was ready to go. Impressed, Pershing later told Patton that his efforts reminded him of the efforts he had had to make to get to the Philippines, and he made the young officer one of his aides-de-camp. Patton biographer Carlo D'Este also notes that the budding relationship with Patton's sister probably played a role in his selection. The general's wife and children had died in a fire, and his sorrow was still an open wound when Patton's sister, Nita, visited her brother at Fort Bliss, Texas. Pershing was instantly captivated, as was she. That this relationship helped her brother there can be little doubt, but George S. Patton Sr., their father, also played a role. The senior Patton was back in California waging a tough and tight race for a seat in the U.S. Senate. Pershing's previous father-in-law had been a U.S. senator who had helped advance his military career. Pershing knew the importance of having a political patron, and he thought that the elder Patton might fill that role.[10]

The relationship Patton had with Pershing was critical in the young officer's professional development. "Pershing's influence on young Patton cannot be overemphasized," D'Este observes. "He was the very model of a military commander, whose ideas of duty and discipline meshed perfectly with Patton's own conceptions." While Pershing was mentoring Patton, his relationship with his protégé's sister was becoming serious. He proposed, and Nita accepted. Despite his close relationship with the general, Patton was less than thrilled that Pershing was about to become his brother-in-law. He wanted to prove himself on his own and did not want others saying he owed his career to nepotism.[11]

The First World War destroyed the romance between Nita and Pershing. The general went off to war, and the relationship never recovered from the separation. Her brother, on the other hand, thrived professionally during the conflict. When Pershing became the commander in chief of the American Expeditionary Force, he took Captain George Patton with him. In Europe, Patton met a number of important people and made strong impressions on them as well. In one example, Field-Marshal Sir Douglas Haig, the commander in chief of the British Expeditionary Force, recorded in his diary after meeting Pershing: "The ADC is a fire eater, and longs for the fray." Haig's assessment of Patton was basically correct. The young American wanted to get into the fight and saw a real opportunity with the development of the tank. He had developed the best saber the U.S. Army ever had, but Patton was not attached to the past. He understood the opportunities this new technology offered in both an operational and a professional sense. He saw senior but less capable officers get promoted. Moving into tanks would allow him to set up the training school, which would also make him a likely candidate for assignment as one of the commanding officer of a new tank battalion that the school produced. Using his influence with Pershing, he became the first officer assigned to the U.S. Army Tank Corps. Although he was not the commander, he was a key figure. After consulting with British and French officers, he developed the organization, tactics, equipment, and training to be used in combat. It was testimony to his genius that he created workable, practical ideas and plans before he had the actual equipment on hand.[12]

In 1918, the army promoted Patton to major and then lieutenant colonel. He also became the commanding officer of the 1st Light Tank Battalion. The unit eventually became the 304th Tank Brigade. The U.S. Army spent most of World War I preparing for combat. Individual units fought under British and French commanders, but as a fighting force, it spent most of the year and a half between the U.S. declaration of war and the armistice preparing for combat. The Americans finally got into the fight in September 1918. Patton commanded the 304th during the Saint-Miheil offensive. During this operation, he briefly met the commanding officer of the 84th Brigade, Brigadier General Douglas MacArthur. They were standing on a little hill as a creeping artillery barrage approached. Patton wanted out of there, but was afraid to say so. He stood in front of MacArthur as the barrage walked over them, but "it was very thin and not dangerous."[13]

Saint-Miheil was an American victory, and the U.S. Army retook French territory the Germans had held since 1914, but Patton was disappointed. The power of his tanks had not been tested. Patton got that opportunity, though, in the Meuse-Argonne offensive that quickly followed. The attack on the Germans took place in a fog, which, when combined with the smoke from a rolling artillery barrage, made it easy to get lost. A body of about 100 men accumulated in a railroad cut in front of Patton. Taking command of this loose collection of soldiers, he held them together and then led them in an infantry charge up a hill, but they ran into a German machine gun nest and Patton was hit in the thigh. Only one of his men, Private First Class Joseph Angelo, survived the engagement without being wounded or killed. Angelo stayed with Patton, making sure he got medical attention, and saving his life in the process. Patton spent the rest of the war in the hospital. He, however, received the Distinguished Service Medal, the Distinguished Service Cross—the second highest award in the U.S. Army—and a promotion to colonel. He was thirty-three years old.[14]

After the war, Patton retained command of the 304th Tank Brigade. During this time, he met and became friends with one Dwight D. Eisenhower. Patton and Eisenhower were stationed together at Camp Meade, Maryland. Although Eisenhower was an infantry officer and Patton cavalry, both men believed the tank was the weapon of the future. They spent much of their time together, developing ideas on how to use the speed, maneuverability, and firepower of the tank in ground operations.

This effort was dangerous personally and professionally. On one occasion, a cable stretched taut between two tanks snapped and came within a few inches of their heads as it cut through the nearby brush. "We were too startled at the moment to realize what had happened but then we looked at each other," Eisenhower later wrote. "I'm sure I was just as pale as George." Another time a .30-caliber machine gun they were testing "cooked off." The heat caused the weapon to advance on its own, firing the bullets in the feed. The two future legends decided that discretion was the better part of valor and ran off for safety.[15]

Such results are understandable—weapons are dangerous—but they were attempting to develop new methods and procedures on how to use mechanization. "These were the beginnings of a comprehensive tank doctrine that in George Patton's case would make him a legend," Eisenhower explained. "Naturally, as enthusiasts, we tried to win converts. This wasn't easy but George and I had the enthusiasm of zealots." One of the reasons it was not easy was that this effort challenged the institutional interests of the existing branches. Each wrote articles that appeared in military publications that managed to anger higher-ranking officers. In 1920, Eisenhower received instructions to go to Washington, D.C., where the chief of infantry told him that his ideas "were not only wrong but dangerous and henceforth I would keep them to myself." If he did not, there would be repercussions to his career. "George, I think was given the same message. This was a blow. One effect was to bring George and me even closer."[16]

Although Patton and Eisenhower were genuine friends, they disagreed fundamentally on the issue of leadership. Patton believed it was the key, the vital element, whereas Eisenhower thought it was significant, but just one of many elements, along with alliance management and logistics.[17]

Despite this difference, they understood how the U.S. Army worked as a bureaucracy. When Congress—based on the recommendations of Pershing—reorganized the service and decided to fold the tank corps into the infantry, both realized that there was little professional future in tanks. In 1920, Patton reverted to his Regular Army rank of captain but was promoted to major the next day. These actions were part of the downsizing taking place in the army after World War I, but it was also a message to the two men. If Patton wanted to get promoted, he had to become a horse soldier again. Eisenhower would have to go back to the infantry. Tanks would simply not get the appropriations, equipment, or manpower necessary to do any meaningful training. Patton was no rebel, and looking to the future, he rejoined the cavalry.[18]

This decision was the right one professionally. After a period of slow advancement during the interwar period, Patton became a brigadier general in 1940, beating his friend Eisenhower to that rank. At the time of Pearl Harbor, he was wearing the two stars of a major general. A major element in his command style was his war face. To motivate his men, he often delivered outlandish remarks on purpose. Before departing the Desert Training Center in Indio, California, to take his troops to North Africa, he told them: "And where we can do the most good is where we can fight those damn Germans or the yellow-bellied Eyetalians. And when we do, by God, we're going to go right in and kill the dirty bastards. We won't just shoot the sonsabitches. We're going to cut out their living guts—and use them to grease the treads of our tanks. We're going to murder those lousy Hun bastards by the bushel."[19]

This fiery language was an act. When Richard N. Jensen, his aide, died, Patton was distraught. He had known Jensen's mother growing up, and they had briefly dated. "Had Dick been my own son I could hardly feel worse," he wrote Echo Jensen, his aide's mother. "You should not so much feel regret that he died as give thanks that you are the mother of such a gallant Christian soldier." He sent her a lock of her son's hair and kissed him on temple in lieu of his mother. "Truly Echo it is just awful. I can't realize it. Words fail me when I try to express to you my sorrow and sympathy." For days afterward, his staff found him weeping without reservation in his office.[20]

This sentiment was hardly reserved for those he personally knew. Patton had a strong attachment to the men serving under him: "I don't give a damn who the man is. He can be a nigger or a Jew, but if he has the stuff and does his duty, he can have anything I've got. By God! I love him. You've got to love them. You've got to be proud of them. You've got to give them loyalty when they give you loyalty."[21]

That type of speech earned Patton the nickname "Old Blood and Guts." It was as accurate as it was misleading. It was in response to the language he used, and critics said it reflected his monumental ego and disregard for those that served under him. When the nickname made it into the newspapers, men who had served under him objected, saying it obscured the real man. His troops could not have asked for a better commander to take care of them and lead them wisely and well.[22]

Omar Bradley was not one of those admirers. The two were hardly as close as most people think. They first met when they lived across the street from one another in Hawaii. "Patton's style did not at all appeal to me," Bradley stated years later. He knew when Patton was putting on an act but was highly ambivalent about these theatrics. In North Africa, the general told his staff: "Gentlemen, tomorrow we attack. If we are not victorious, let no one come back alive." Patton then retired to his room to pray. Bradley said these actions were "hammy" and "bewildering" to others. "I still could not accustom myself, however, to the vulgarity with which Patton skinned offenders for relatively minor infractions in discipline," Bradley observed. "Patton believed that profanity was the most convincing medium of communication with his troops." Bradley clearly disapproved of these methods, as he made abundantly clear, but he did concede that they were effective, which to him was their only saving grace. "Patton chose to drive his subordinates by bombast and by threats. Those mannerisms achieved spectacular results. But they were not calculated to win affection among his officers or men."[23]

In North Africa, Patton reunited with Eisenhower. The two had kept in touch over the years. In fact, just before Patton became the commanding officer of the 2nd Armored Division, he offered Lieutenant Colonel

Dwight Eisenhower the position of division chief of staff or the command of a regiment. "It would be great to be in tanks once more, and even better to be associated with you again," his friend replied. Others in the army, however, noticed his talent as a staff officer, which eventually led to his promotion to general officer. As it was, Eisenhower pinned Patton's third star on him. Even though the two were close, Patton often was critical of his friend's leadership style. "I was disappointed in him. He talked of trivial things," he observed. He worried that Eisenhower was pandering to the British, and he noticed that his friend was using the king's English. "I truly fear that London has conquered Abilene." Eisenhower, for his part, had equally mixed feelings about his old friend. The two had frank conversations about matters that Eisenhower could not share with others. While Eisenhower needed a friend to talk with, Patton was often long-winded and wanted to talk more than his friend did.[24]

One of Eisenhower's main goals in the war was ensuring that the U.S.–British coalition functioned effectively. Many Americans, particularly veterans of World War I, feared that the British were going to manipulate the United States into pursuing objectives that serviced British foreign policy interests, much the same way many believed they had done in the 1910s. The British, on the other hand, welcomed American assistance but also believed that their experience fighting the Germans counted for something, and that their allies were ignoring their expertise out of misplaced nationalism. Patton, for his part, was less than impressed with his British allies. "All of us think that if there ever were any pretty women in England they must have died," he wrote to his wife, Beatrice. "They are hideous with fat ankles." He also had little regard for the likes of Winston Churchill. He found the prime minister "cunning rather than brilliant." He also thought the politician was "easily flattered." Eisenhower made it clear to Patton that he would brook no criticism of their allies. He gave this warning to many of his generals, but with his old friend, it was merited. Patton often vented in public about the British. Eisenhower privately conceded to Patton that his criticisms had a constructive impact. Patton, though, steadily grew to resent his friend's treatment of him. It is hard to avoid the conclusion that at times Eisenhower unfairly directed anger toward his old friend when he was unable to do so against the British. It is also clear that Patton often deserved these tongue-lashings.[25]

Patton took command of II Corps immediately after its humbling defeat at the hands of the Germans under Field Marshall Erwin "The Desert

Fox" Rommel. He made immediate changes in the organization. He wanted discipline. Breakfast had been served at 9 A.M. Under Patton, that changed. The mess hall closed at 6 A.M.[26]

Omar N. Bradley came with the job. He was in II Corps to act as an observer for Eisenhower. Bradley had mixed views of the new corps commander. "As a soldier, a professional officer, Patton was the most fiercely ambitious man and the strangest duck I have ever known," the general reflected many years later. "Although he could be the epitome of grace and charm at social or official functions, he was at the same time the most earthily profane man I ever knew."[27]

Bradley was impressed with Patton's results. He realized that the strange duck had been put into a bad situation, assigned individuals with whom he had little familiarity or knowledge. "He had restored discipline to the corps and to a large extent its self-confidence."[28]

A major problem that Patton faced in Tunisia had nothing to do with II Corps itself, but rather the relationship he had with the American and British air forces. Neither wanted to provide close air support to ground units, preferring instead to wage strategic bombing campaigns. Patton complained instantly, and Air Marshal Sir Arthur Coningham, the commanding officer of the Northwest Africa Tactical Air Force, objected to his use of the "discredited action of using Air Force as an alibi for lack of success on ground." The feud grew quickly, and it got so serious that Eisenhower considered resigning his command. Fearing that Patton and Coningham were about to do serious damage to the U.S.–British alliance, Lieutenant General Carl Spaatz and Air Chief Marshal Sir Arthur Tedder met with Patton to convince him to contain his anger. During the meeting, as Patton listed to what he considered empty rhetoric about air superiority, three or four German Focke-Wulf 109s strafed the street outside of the office wall, dropping small bombs. Plaster flaked from the roof, and the concussion from a bomb jammed shut the door to the room. Spaatz turned to Patton and, shaking his head in disbelief, asked, "Now how in hell did you ever manage to stage that?" Grinning, Patton replied, "I'll be damned if I know, but if I could find the sonsabitches who flew those planes I'd mail them each a medal."[29]

Coningham and Patton met again the next day. The delay had done nothing to soothe tempers. The two were yelling at one another before they each realized that the disagreement was getting out of hand. Coningham apologized, saying he had many cables that day and had let the stress of the moment get to him. Patton accepted this explanation, but he also asked him to apologize in writing. Coningham agreed and did so. Both men ended up respecting one another. "I like him very much," Coningham wrote. "He is a gentleman and a gallant warrior." Patton later stated, "Personally, while I regret the misunderstanding, for which I was partially responsible, I cannot but take comfort and satisfaction from the fact that it gave me an opportunity of becoming better acquainted with you, but to me you exemplify in the most perfect form all the characteristics of a fighting gentleman."[30]

General Sir Alan Brooke, chief of the Imperial General Staff—the title accorded the head of the British Army—met Patton about this time. "A real fire-eater and definite character," he wrote in his diary. He had been looking forward to meeting Patton—the American's reputation had preceded him. After the war, the caustic Lord Alanbrooke added to this entry: "His swash-buckling personality exceeded my expectation. I did not form any high opinion of him, nor had I any reason to alter this view at a later date. A dashing, courageous, wild and unbalanced leader, good for operations requiring thrust and push but at a loss in operations requiring skill and judgment."[31]

In North Africa and Sicily, Patton developed a one-sided rivalry with General Sir Bernard Montgomery—one-sided in that the British general did not realize that he was in any competition with the American. Montgomery could be—and often was—arrogant, but he was not one to waste the lives of his men. He had seen too much of that in World War I. In Sicily, it was clear to him that there was no way his units could get to Messina, so he made way for Patton's.[32] Later in the war, when they were in France, Montgomery was quite pleased with the success Patton was having. As the overall ground commander, he had far bigger issues to worry about than the fame and accolades that went to any one general. There are indications that Montgomery thought Omar Bradley was inexperienced, and he was unusually diplomatic with the American. The problem was that Bradley harbored a grudge against Montgomery that had began in Sicily. Uncomfortable around these men of independence and creativity, Bradley frequently enjoyed advancing the rivalry between the two, neither of whom he particularly liked.[33]

The invasion of Sicily followed the campaign in North Africa. Patton became the commanding general of the Seventh U.S. Army on July 6, 1943. The Sicilian campaign did little for the reputations of the allied generals.

Patton and Montgomery pursued widely divergent courses of action thanks to the weak leadership of General The Honourable Sir Harold Alexander, general officer commander in chief, 15th Army Group. Patton's main goal was to take Messina, a legitimate strategic objective. Alexander's weak control made the drive to Messina a race between Montgomery and Patton. The American pushed his men to take the city, but Major General Lucian Truscott, commanding general of the 3rd Infantry Division, objected. Patton had a stormy meeting with Truscott at the division's command post. According to Patton's account:

> I said, "General Truscott, if your conscience will not let you conduct this operation I will relieve you and put someone in command who will." He replied, "General, it is your priviledge to reduce me whenever you want to." I said, "I don't want to. I got you your DSM and recommended you for Major General, but your own ability really gained both honors. You are too old an athlete to believe it is possible to postpone a match." He said, "You are an old enough athlete to know that sometimes they are postponed." I said, "This one won't be."

The operation went forward. Another incident showing Patton's drive occurred on a small bridge when a farmer was unable to move two mules blocking a column of Americans. The general walked up to the animals, shot them in the head, and had their bodies dumped over the side of the bridge. With the two allied armies pursuing different objectives, there was little concentrated pressure on the Germans. As a result, the defenders managed to extract all their men and equipment before surrendering the island to the allies. Patton, though, did reach Messina on August 17, before Montgomery.[34]

Despite this success, things had already started to go wrong for Patton. On August 3, 1943, when he was visiting the 15th Evacuation Hospital outside of Nicosia, he encountered Private Charles H. Kuhl, Company L, 26th Infantry Regiment, 1st Division. Kuhl had no visible wounds. When Patton learned that the private was suffering from shell shock, the general exploded. He swore at Kuhl, called him a coward, and ordered him out of the tent. The private did not move, which only angered Patton more. He slapped Kuhl with a glove, grabbed him by the collar, pulled him to his feet, shoved him out of the tent, and kicked him in the rear.[35]

A week later, Patton visited the 93rd Evacuation Hospital and went from cot to cot, talking briefly with each man. The fourth man he visited with was Private Paul G. Bennett of the 13th Field Artillery Brigade. Bennett was shaking and told Patton he could not take the stress of combat anymore. Patton began yelling and demanded that the soldier repeat himself. Bennett said, "It's my nerves, I can't stand the shelling any more."[36]

"Your nerves, Hell, your [sic] just a goddamned coward, you yellow son of a bitch," Patton replied in his high-pitched voice. "Shut up that goddamned crying. I won't have these brave men here who have been shot seeing a yellow bastard sitting here crying."[37]

After telling one of the officers assigned to the hospital to get rid of Bennett, he turned to the artilleryman and continued his rant: "You're a disgrace to the Army and you're going back to the front to fight, although that's too good for you. You ought to be lined up against a wall and shot. In fact, I ought to shoot you myself right now, God damn you!" He then pulled his pistol out from his holster.[38]

The commanding officer of the hospital arrived at the scene, and Patton told him: "I want you to get that man out of here right away. I won't have these brave boys seeing such a bastard babied." He then slapped Bennet and cursed him.[39]

Patton turned to leave. Just before he departed, he looked back and saw Bennett still quivering and in tears. The general walked back to the man and hit him a second time, with such strength that Bennett's helmet fell to the ground. After leaving the hospital, he bragged about the incident to Bradley.[40]

After word of these two incidents spread through Sicily, Eisenhower wrote a letter of censure to Patton. He required that Patton apologize to the individuals involved in the incident. Patton did so, including both men and the hospital staff members. On the advice of Major General John P. Lucas, Eisenhower's deputy commander, Patton apologized to the entire Seventh Army.[41]

There the incident might have stayed, if not for the efforts of syndicated newspaper columnist Drew Pearson. Eisenhower had worked out an agreement with war correspondents not to publish word of "l'affaire Patton." Pearson, however, had his own agenda. He had claimed earlier that the United States was delaying a second front in Europe in order to bleed Russia dry. He specifically blamed Secretary of State Cordell Hull for this policy, but Hull had about as much influence on U.S. strategy as Pearson.

Angry at these accusations because they fed Soviet paranoia about the United States, President Franklin D. Roosevelt lashed out at Pearson, calling him a liar at a press conference. Someone had leaked word of Patton's actions to the columnist, and with Pearson's own patriotism under attack, he reported the incident on his radio show. Other journalists who had known about the event began adding details. Eisenhower, Stimson (who was now secretary of war), and George C. Marshall, the U.S. Army chief of staff, were all determined to keep Patton because he was too valuable to the war effort to lose. Eisenhower explained why:

> His emotional tenseness and his impulsiveness were the very qualities that made him, in open situations, such a remarkable leader of an army. In pursuit and exploitation there is need for a commander who sees nothing but the necessity of getting ahead; the more he drives his men the more he will save their lives. He must be indifferent to fatigue and ruthless in demanding the last atom of physical strength. All this I well understood, and could explain the matter to myself in spite of my indignation at the act. I felt that Patton should be saved for service in the great battles still facing us in Europe.

The important point to note, though, is that Patton needed the help of all three to survive. As it was, the incident ended his relationship with Pershing. The old general refused to reply to any of the letters Patton mailed to him.[42]

After this incident, the U.S. Army moved Patton and his headquarters to duties of marginal importance. As Patton's biographer, Carlo D'Este, points out, this incident had enormous ramifications. There were only a few candidates for the position of ground forces commander for D-Day with the experience of fighting Germans. Basically, the choice came down to Patton or Bradley, but the slapping incidents cost Patton any chance at that command. He would spend four months in exile before Eisenhower ordered him to Britain to take command of the Third U.S. Army. At his first public appearance afterward, he said, "I thought I'd stand here and let you fellows see if I am as big a son-of-a-bitch as you think I am." The assembled troops cheered.[43]

In England, Patton prepared the Third Army to be a follow on unit to the Normandy invasion. He was also involved in a deception campaign aimed at convincing the Germans that the invasion would come at the Pas de Calais, the closest point in France to England. Patton was supposedly the commander of the fictional First U.S. Army Group. No effort was made to hide the fact that Patton was in Britain, just that he was actually in command of Third Army. While in England, Patton got a dog, a bull terrier he named Willy. The dog had once belonged to a deceased Royal Air Force pilot who had taken the animal with him on six bombing missions over Germany. As a result, Willy loved to fly, but he hated loud noises. He was rather smelly and, by canine standards, a bit of a coward.[44]

During this time, Patton managed to get himself into more trouble, this time in Knutsford, England. He made a few comments at the opening of a Welcome Club. The part that created an uproar: "I feel that such clubs as this are a very real value, because I believe with Mr. Bernard Shaw, I think it was he, that the British and Americans are two people separated by a common language, and since it is the evident destiny of the British and Americans, and, of course, the Russians to rule the world, the better we know each other, the better job we will do." The statement was fairly benign, but it came at a time when Republicans were looking for an issue to use in the 1944 elections. It also did not help that the Roosevelt administration had just sent Patton's name to Congress for promotion to the four-star rank of general.[45]

Eisenhower told Marshall he intended to relieve Patton. The chief of staff told him the decision was his. "My view, and it is merely that, is that you should not weaken your hand for Overlord. If you think that Patton's removal does weaken your prospect, you should continue him in command." A few lines later, he added, "Consider only Overlord and your own heavy burden of responsibility for its success. Everything else is of minor importance."[46] Marshall's cable swayed the balance; it was something of a gentle rebuke to Eisenhower.

Patton and Eisenhower met, and each left very different accounts of their conversation. Patton was unsure if he would be kept, while Eisenhower recorded that he made it clear he would stay. The official documentary record shows that Eisenhower cabled his old friend two days later and informed him he would be staying. Patton was grateful, to a degree. "Sometimes I am very fond of him and this is one of the times," he observed of his old friend. He told his wife, "Everything is O.K. because divine destiny [Patton's less than complimentary nickname for Eisenhower] came through in a big way."[47]

When Patton arrived in France after the allies had established a beach-head in Normandy, Patton's Third Army scored impressive victory after impressive victory and led the breakout out of this confined position. On the eve of battle—Operation Cobra, in which Patton's field army would be Bradley's strategic reserve—the general delivered a pep talk to his staff. "I don't want to get any messages saying that, 'We are holding our position.' We're not holding anything! Let the Hun do that. We are advancing constantly and we're not interested in holding on to anything except the enemy. We're going to hold on to him by the nose and we're going to kick him in the ass; we're going the kick the hell out of him all the time and we're going to go through him like crap through a goose."[48]

The Third Army was at a pivot point where it could attack to the east into southern Normandy or turn south, or even west into Brittany. It did all three. Patton conducted these operations at Bradley's direction. He insisted on them because of the logistical importance of the ports in Brittany. That was the plan, and Bradley was sticking to the plan, but in doing so, he passed on a fleeting opportunity. The German army was cracking under the stress of the allied advance, and a focused drive east could have forced it out of France entirely. The rampage was in the wrong direction. To his credit, Patton did not think much of this conservative plan, but in the wake of the slapping incidents and Knutsford, he was reluctant to challenge authority. After a failed German offensive, the Third Army turned to the east and began its advance into Normandy. Using the XIX Tactical Air Force to cover his flanks, Patton's command made a rapid advance in an effort to close the Falaise Gap, in which thousands of Germans were still located. It was too rapid for Bradley. After some hesitation, he ordered a halt, fearing that the U.S. Army could not sustain its positions against a German counteroffensive. This move was typical of Bradley's indecisive and conservative leadership. Patton thought Bradley had lost his nerve.[49]

Despite this hiccup, Third Army continued its mad dash across northwestern France towards the German Reich itself. Then a fuel shortage developed, which was the product of Eisenhower's broad-front strategy and a logistical system that lacked the resources to sustain the advance at the pace Patton was setting. "Damnit, Brad, just give me 400,000 gallons of gasoline and I'll put you inside Germany in two days," he begged of Bradley. In frustration, he ordered the Third Army Chaplin, Monsignor (Colonel) James H. O'Neil, to write a prayer for good weather so his army could advance. There are two very different versions of this incident, but the version that takes place in *Patton* is faithful to the account that one of Patton's staff officers, Paul Harkins, provided.[50]

The high point of Patton's military career came during the Battle of the Bulge. In December 1944, Adolf Hitler made a reckless operational gamble. In a vain effort to repeat the success his armies had enjoyed in 1940, he ordered an offensive through the Ardennes. The goal of this operation was to split the allied advance, reach the vital port of Antwerp, and force his opponents to sue for peace. It is testimony to the skill of the German fighting man that this offensive came as close to working as it did. Other factors in their initial success included weak U.S. Army intelligence and no allied reserve forces. Early German success made mid-December a grim time for Eisenhower. He held a conference with his subordinate unit commanders in a French army stone barracks on December 19 in Verdun. The atmosphere was somber, and the cold of the room only added to the tension. Patton was prepared for the meeting, though. While others at the command conference had vague ideas on what to do, his staff had come up with three plans.[51]

"When can you attack?" Eisenhower asked.

"The morning of December 21, with three divisions," Patton said without any hesitation. His old friend misread the response, thinking he was being boastful and theatrical. The time was not right for such antics.[52]

"Don't be fatuous, George," Eisenhower replied. "If you try to go that early, you won't have all three divisions ready and you'll go piecemeal. You will start on the twenty-second, and I want your initial blow to be a strong one! I'd even settle for the twenty-third if it takes that long to get three full divisions."[53]

Patton responded calmly with a map, showing the plans that he and his staff had developed. He gave rehearsed answers to questions he had expected. His presentation took roughly an hour. When he was finished, it was clear to Eisenhower and the rest of the men in the room that he and his men were ready to go.[54]

The Third Army pivoted to the north from its westward advance and raced to relieve the 101st Airborne Division, which the Germans had surrounded. Bradley called the move "brilliant." He went even further, describing it as "one of the most astonishing feats of generalship of our campaign in the West." Patton made this turn because of the high caliber of his staff organization. These men made the advances of the Third Army possible. Bradley, though, thought they were a below-average lot. After the advance into the Ardennes, he did not abandon this view, but grudgingly conceded, "Patton can get more good work out of a mediocre bunch of staff officers than anyone I ever saw."[55]

When the war ended, Patton became the military governor of Bavaria, a duty that suited him poorly. Keeping the economy going, repairing roads, bridges, sewers, and waterlines, caring for refugees, and arresting Nazi war criminals were important jobs, but Patton was far better at preparing for and conducting kinetic operations than he was in helping the conquered lands recover from the devastation of war. During a brief encounter with reporters, one asked the general a loaded question about the retention of Nazis in governmental positions. Patton responded: "The way I see it, this Nazi question is very much like a Democratic and Republican election fight. To get things done in Bavaria, after the complete disorganization and disruption of four years of war, we had to compromise with the devil a little. We had no alternative but to run to the people who knew what to do and how to do it. So, for the time being we are compromising with the devil." After that statement, there was no saving Patton. Six days later, Eisenhower called him to his headquarters—seven and a half hours away by car—and relieved him of command of Third Army. He made Patton the commanding general of the Fifteenth U.S. Army, but this unit existed only on paper. Its only mission was to write a history of the war in Europe. No one was fooled. PATTON FIRED was the headline in *Stars and Stripes*.[56]

Eisenhower might not even have bothered. Three months later, Patton was in an auto accident that proved fatal. The accident was due to the reckless driving of the general's driver, Private First Class Horace Woodring, who thought the four-star flag on the car's bumper absolved him from obeying the laws of the road, and the other driver, Technician Fifth Grade Robert L. Thompson, who was still hung over from a night of drinking. Thompson was behind the wheel of a two-and-a-half-ton truck and turned left onto the road that Patton and his party were taking. Woodring took his eyes off the road for a second in response to a comment from Patton. Returning to the road, he had just enough time to realize they were going to hit the truck. The car hit the truck at a 90-degree angle. Patton flew forward. His forehead struck the steel frame of the partition separating the front and rear seats, driving his head back and snapping his neck. He was the only person seriously injured in the wreck. Neither driver nor Major

General Hobart Gay, who was in the car with Patton, had more than cuts and bruises. Patton lingered for twelve days before dying in his sleep on December 21, 1945.[57]

Such was the life of General George S. Patton Jr., United States Army. It was also enough to inspire the efforts of some men who were middle-tier officers during the war to make a theatrical production about his life.

2. The Producer

Patton had become a success because of his hard work as a military professional. Fame, though, can be fleeting. Winfield Scott, Winfield Scott Hancock, George Dewey, and John Pershing were all venerated for a time after their great victories, but they have attracted far less attention in the years since. One of the major reasons Patton has remained a major figure in the history of World War II and in the public's understanding of that conflict has to do with the efforts of the man who produced *Patton*, Frank McCarthy.

The future film producer was born in 1912 and raised in Virginia. He was a member of the John Marshall High School Corps of Cadets, a program similar in many respects to Junior ROTC. His father had died, and an uncle was willing to pay his college bills. He strongly suggested that McCarthy attend the Virginia Military Institute because the program at John Marshall had been modeled after the one at VMI. McCarthy agreed. "I wanted to go to the University of Virginia. But he sent me to VMI. I liked it," he explained in an interview. He was the editor of *The Bomb*, the school's yearbook, and graduated in 1933. Since VMI is a military school, he also obtained a reserve commission in the U.S. Army as a second lieutenant in the field artillery.[1]

Like many young college graduates, he remained uncertain about what to do in life: "There were four things that interested me when I graduated from college, from VMI. One was the Army, regular Army. Another was the theatre, a third was newspaper work and the fourth was teaching. So I decided to test each one." He initially stayed at VMI as an instructor. After two years, he became a reporter for the *Richmond News Leader* before returning to his alma matter to run the alumni association. He then left Virginia to work as a theatrical press agent in New York. McCarthy was leaning toward an academic career. He returned to his home state and spent two years earning a master's degree in political science from the University of Virginia. He planned to return to VMI and teach. "Just as I was getting the degree the British evacuated Dunkirk and it looked to me as though we were going into the war right away. So I jumped the gun and went into the Army instead of going back to VMI to teach."[2]

Already having a commission in the U.S. Army turned out to be "very handy to have," he observed. By his own admission, he had hardly been serious about meeting his military duties, but the war changed matters quickly. Brigadier General John Magruder, a former commandant at VMI, was head of the military intelligence division of the general staff and requested McCarthy when he learned he was available. McCarthy was soon writing a daily bulletin, "Tentative Lessons of the War," and the quality of this reporting impressed another VMI alumnus, George C. Marshall, the chief of staff of the U.S. Army. Needing another assistant, Marshall requested McCarthy. The two had never met.[3]

This position put him at the center of the U.S. war effort. "I went everywhere that General Marshall went. I went to Hyde Park every weekend that President Roosevelt was there to brief him on what was going on in the war," he explained. He received a promotion to captain after less than a year on active duty. In 1942, he received two promotions: one to major, then another in December to lieutenant colonel. The next December, he became a colonel. A month later, in January 1944, he was assigned to be the secretary of the general staff, which is to say Marshall's own chief of staff. (McCarthy never received this title because it would be a bit confusing for Marshall, as chief of staff of the U.S. Army, to have his own chief of staff, but the basic point is that McCarthy was Marshall's main subordinate.) He was thirty-one years old at the time. McCarthy later observed that he "received very rapid promotion because General Marshall gave me responsible things to do and promoted me accordingly. I was very lucky in that."[4]

In the course of these assignments, McCarthy met regularly with many of the major figures of the war: Stalin, de Gaulle, Eisenhower, Roosevelt, and Churchill. He also met Patton on several occasions. "I saw him training his division at Fort Benning. I saw him in training at Indio [California]. He was really rough on those troops at Indio." According to McCarthy, there was a bond between Marshall and Patton. During a tour of front-line positions, the generals were presenting medals to various officers and men. Patton began to break down as an adjutant read the citation for the action that the general had personally witnessed. McCarthy noticed that Marshall had tears in his eyes as well. The only other time he saw Marshall with tears was when his stepson died in Italy. McCarthy later recalled that Patton was "the one and only officer whom General Marshall called by his first name."[5]

During the war, McCarthy did exceptionally important staff work, although Marshall allowed him a brief combat assignment during the amphibious invasion of southern France in 1944. Most of his work was less dramatic, although it was of crucial importance. Marshall had him plan Roosevelt's funeral, and he worked directly with the first lady, Eleanor Roosevelt. "I wish to express my deepest appreciation for the wholehearted cooperation and help rendered by Colonel Frank McCarthy," she wrote Marshall.[6]

He had a bright future at war's end. The army awarded him the Distinguished Service Medal, an honor usually accorded to general officers. The British government made him an honorary officer of the Order of the British Empire. On occasion, his name appeared in newspapers and magazines like the *New York Times*, the *New York Sun*, the *New Yorker*, and the *New York Post*. He was the subject of a profile in *Contemporary Biography*, and the U.S. Junior Chamber of Commerce also listed him as one of the Ten Outstanding Young Americans for 1945, an honor he shared with future U.S. Supreme Court justice Abe Fortas and with Henry Ford II, who ran Ford Motor Company. Another honor that probably mattered more to him than most others was a cover story on him in the *Virginia Military Institute Alumni Review*.[7]

During the war, he had gotten to know a number of important people well. He had briefly dated Churchill's daughter, Sarah, and had spent time with Patton's aide, Dick Jensen, altering the labels of cheap cigars they acquired for Churchill when they were unable to find his usual brand. The prime minister quickly noticed the poor quality of the tobacco and went without smoking on that occasion. One of the influential figures that McCarthy met was James Byrnes. A former U.S. senator, Byrnes had mentored Harry S. Truman when the Missourian first arrived in Washington. When Truman became president, he made Byrnes his secretary of state. Shortly thereafter, Byrnes offered McCarthy a position as an assistant secretary of state. McCarthy accepted and was sworn in after confirmation by the U.S. Senate. He was all of thirty-three at the time.[8]

A few weeks later, his life fell apart. McCarthy had been working long hours for four years. Twelve- and fourteen-hour duty days were normal. Saturday and Sunday were regular workdays. The stress of this schedule caught up with McCarthy, and he had a nervous breakdown. His doctor's recommendation was simple: rest—months and months of rest. McCarthy quickly tendered his resignation, which was noted in major newspapers. In accepting his resignation, Truman wrote, "I understand your position, and I cannot ask you to do anything that would in the opinion of your physician and in your opinion delay your recovery." McCarthy had been in office for less than two months.[9]

McCarthy had retained his commission in the reserves, but after he recovered his health, he decided to find a new career as a civilian. Marshall had always liked film, believing it was a good medium for instruction and propaganda aimed at developing and maintaining the morale of the U.S. Army. He authorized commissions for many studio executives and directors in the Signal Corps to make films for the army. The most famous of these efforts was the *Why We Fight* series that Frank Capra directed. The first film in this series, *Prelude to War* (1942), won an Academy Award as best documentary. Many, like Darryl F. Zanuck of Twentieth Century-Fox, took their duties seriously; others, like Jack Warner, did not. "So I got to know a lot of people in Hollywood," McCarthy explained, "and eventually, several years later, went to Mr. Zanuck and asked him for a job, which he gave me." That was in 1948. For the previous two years, McCarthy had been working in Europe for the Motion Picture Association, trying to liberate the foreign currency accounts that belonged to the studios. "At the time most foreign currencies were frozen. You couldn't take francs out of France, you couldn't take lire out of Italy, because those countries didn't have the dollars to up for the foreign exchange." It was only with the development of the Marshall Plan that McCarthy started having success. Marshall was glad to hear that his efforts were helping his former aide, but he also told him it was not exactly what he had in mind when he gave the 1947 commencement speech at Harvard University announcing the new program.[10]

Zanuck respected McCarthy and the administrative work he had done in the war. He knew McCarthy had little experience in the film industry, but his skills were too valuable to pass up. He offered the reserve colonel a one-year apprenticeship. McCarthy could spend a year observing the various departments at the studio, learning the film industry. "So for one year I wandered around the studio. I worked with the electricians, with the carpenters, went through the Story Department, story conferences. I went through the cutting of a whole picture which was *Twelve O'Clock High*—

looking over the cutter's shoulder." Before the end of the year, Zanuck made him coproducer, along with director Anatole Litvak, of the film *Decision Before Dawn* (1951). The film was nominated for an Academy Award as best picture.[11]

McCarthy appreciated the studio executive's creative abilities. "He just had the surest eye in the world," he recalled. "Zanuck had a big input into every movie that was made in that studio, and he was a wonderful supervisor."[12]

McCarthy had found a new career. "I loved working in the old studio system," he told several journalists just before he died. "People don't usually think of the producer as being creative, but I think he has to be—because if he's not there's no way he can supervise creative people like writers, directors and actors. He must understand the creative process to be effective and successful."[13]

McCarthy had developed a new career just at a time when his skills and experience became even more valuable to studios. The war film—particularly those set in World War II—had moved into an era of realism. Pioneering films in this regard included *Twelve O'Clock High* (1949), *The Sands of Iwo Jima* (1949), and *Battleground* (1949). All three of these films were commercial and artistic successes. Veterans of the war, in an effort to make sure people remembered what had happened, were crucial in the development of these epics. In addition to his proven administrative and managerial abilities, McCarthy was a witness to the strategic direction of World War II—just what studios needed and wanted.[14]

The new filmmaker also retained his commission in the U.S. Army Reserves and eventually was promoted to the rank of brigadier general. His duties were primarily in intelligence, then later public relations. McCarthy retired in 1963, receiving the Legion of Merit, an honor that normally goes to flag officers but rarely to reservists. According to U.S. Army tradition, every retiring general officer has a parade in their honor. The service agreed to his request that his retirement parade take place at VMI with the cadets, rather than an active-duty unit. Thirty years before to the day, he had received his commission on the same parade ground. "It was a very happy occasion for me," he stated afterward.[15]

Not only was his background unusual for a film producer, but so were the drive and focus that McCarthy showed in making the film. His vision became the dominant force in the making of *Patton*. For a producer rather than a director to dominate a film in this manner is unusual. "Schaffner directed it, but I think that picture's heart was Frank McCarthy," Karl Malden said. "I think the heart of that picture belonged to Frank McCarthy." George C. Scott agreed: "Frank McCarthy, in my estimation, deserves an incalculable amount of credit for his dream of a number of years. His devotion to the assembling of it. The enormous painstaking work involved over a long, long time. Not just a few months but literally years of perpetration."[16]

Zanuck was a long and strong advocate of *Patton*. He had enormous input into the production. McCarthy admitted after the film was finished and had won its Oscars that Zanuck had been his main asset in making the film. Studios can often be like government bureaucracies. There is often resistance to change, but when McCarthy talked to various divisions and departments of the studio, he quickly received cooperation from their heads. Everyone knew that the head of the studio was behind the project.[17]

One of Zanuck's biographers has described him as "Hollywood's Last Tycoon," which is basically true. Zanuck arrived in California after the First World War after having served in the U.S. Army as an underage private. "I had grown up, learned a helluva lot and fought for my country." His early career ambition was to be a writer. One of his biggest literary influences was O. Henry, and many of Zanuck's films reflect the style of the short story writer: well-developed characters, a strong emphasis on action, and unexpected turns in the plot building to a "socko" finish.[18]

The first major achievement in Zanuck's career came when he joined Warner Bros. and developed scripts for the canine actor Rin Tin Tin. The commercial success of the dog star's films and the energy that Zanuck put into their making impressed Jack and Harry Warner. In 1925, he was involved in writing eight of the thirty films that Warner Bros. released that year. Working in the film industry at a time of flexibility in the divisions of production, Zanuck learned the elements of filmmaking. As a result of his broad background, he moved up the corporate ranks, becoming a studio executive. In 1933, he was head of production at Warner Bros. when he quit over deceptive pay cuts that the two brothers were trying to impose on studio employees.[19] The Warners decided to use the difficulty all studios were then having in honoring their paychecks as an excuse to cut salaries. Zanuck refused to have anything to do with this effort and resigned when the Warners refused to reverse themselves.[20]

Zanuck was not long in looking for employment. Within forty-eight hours, he was having meetings that eventually led to the creation of Twentieth Century Films. Two years later, this studio merged with the Fox Film Corporation to become Twentieth Century-Fox. Zanuck was making $260,000 ($4,159,601 in 2010), got 10 percent of the company's gross profits, and had stock options. He was thirty-three years old.[21]

The new studio had a distinctive air to it. Because he had started off as a writer and had even published some short stories, Zanuck always liked writers, and as an executive, he created an environment conducive to their efforts. His studio was no different than others—many individuals would have a voice in shaping the script, and writers had to be prepared to revise and revise again—but Zanuck always treated this written document as the foundation of his productions. Once he had signed off on the screenplay, the revision process was done. Zanuck also had his way with numerous actresses. Although a sexual relationship with him was never a requirement for appearing in a Twentieth Century-Fox film and Zanuck employed many women whom he did not bed, many actresses believed that they had no other choice.[22]

Although Zanuck's sexual behavior and ethics left much to be desired, there was no question about his patriotism. He joined the U.S. Army Reserves nearly a year before Pearl Harbor, this time as a lieutenant colonel in the Signal Corps. He volunteered for active duty in April 1942. As a Signal Corps officer, his main job was to oversee the development of training films. This duty made sense and took advantage of his civilian job skills and proven administrative ability. Zanuck was not one to simply sit in an office; he made sure that he got overseas. George C. Marshall sent him to London to observe how the British were making their training films. During this time, he met Vice-Admiral Lord Louis Mountbatten, who allowed him to join a British commando raid in Nazi-occupied France. After returning to the United States, he asked Marshall's primary aide, Frank McCarthy, for a combat assignment. The result of this effort were orders to observe and film the invasion of North Africa. He came under fire and, according to the journal he kept, was thrilled with the experience. He met major figures in the war, including Roosevelt, Marshall, Patton, Eisenhower, and Mark Clark. Zanuck's energy and enthusiasm for the war effort led him to cut corners in his efforts to get films made. These actions, and the fact that he still drew his studio salary for several months while on active duty—he refused his army pay during this time—led him to be the subject of two investigations. Marshall had to intervene and argue that Zanuck's actions had been productive and proper. Despite these complications and his junior rank, the U.S. Army awarded him the Legion of Merit when he left active duty.[23]

With this background, it is no surprise that Zanuck was interested in hiring McCarthy and in making a film about Patton. The two former colonels were not the first ones in Hollywood interested in the life of the flamboyant general. In 1950, Columbia Pictures expressed an interest to the Department of Defense in making a movie about the general. The Pentagon suggested they contact Patton's widow, Beatrice. She had no interest in the project, and Columbia quickly abandoned the effort. Warner Bros. also attempted to gain Beatrice Patton's support for a film about her husband but also failed. "She was a very sweet, attractive, charming lady but she didn't like the media, didn't like the movies and had a grudge against the press. It was her feeling that the publicity given to Patton during his career had contributed to his downfall," McCarthy explained. With her in direct opposition, the studio made no effort to move forward.[24]

Twentieth Century-Fox became interested in the project in 1951. On October 23, McCarthy proposed to Zanuck that the studio make a film about the general. Zanuck agreed. They both knew that war made for good drama. "You see, war is a very fascinating subject dramatically because the minute you use the word 'war' suspense is built in," McCarthy explained to a soldier in the U.S. Army. "All you have to say is 'The enemy is approaching' and you don't even have to set up the scene. Everybody knows what that's all about. It furnishes, in my view, the most dramatic situations that can be found in human life." Patton was also the type of personality who would translate well on film. "As a field commander he was enormously theatrical," McCarthy explained. "He was theatrical in his speech, theatrical in his manner of dress. He was flamboyant." McCarthy found the same thing that Columbia had come across: the opposition of Patton's widow. Still in the reserves at this time, he learned that the army was also less than eager to highlight the life and career of a rebellious general.[25]

Then, in October 1953, Beatrice Patton's death seemed to change everything. A film producer called the family on the day of her funeral in an attempt to enlist the support of the general's children. Needless to say, the timing of this phone call ensured its failure. Warner Bros. went forward nonetheless. Less than a week later, the studio obtained a permit from the Department of Defense that gave it priority over other Hollywood productions. Brigadier General Frank Dorn, then head of army public relations, met with Warner Bros. executives. He hoped that the studio would work with the Patton family on this project. Twentieth Century-Fox put in a request for a permit, but the Warner Bros. request had arrived at the Pentagon first. After several days of trying, W. L. Guthrie, Warner Bros.' liaison with the military, talked with Patton's son, Captain George S. Patton IV, on the phone for half an hour.[26]

The context of this conversation was less than promising. Beatrice Patton had been dead for less than a week, and her son shared his mother's hostility toward the film industry. Captain Patton said he wanted a "dignified" portrayal of his father and that there was no living actor who could play the part in that manner. He said, according to Guthrie's record of the conversation, that "his little baby could portray his father better than John Wayne," the actor who was reportedly set to play the lead in the film. Patton admitted that his father's life was in the public domain, but he and his family would nonetheless refuse to cooperate in any fashion with any production.[27]

His sister had similar views. "The movies cheapen everything they touch," Ruth Ellen Totten observed. "Ma was *dead set* against a movie, so are we." She even considered suing Warner Bros.[28]

Zanuck and McCarthy had been outfoxed. Warner Bros. had beaten them to getting a priority for assistance from the Department of Defense. While that studio was attempting to convince the Pattons to cooperate, Twentieth Century-Fox limped out of the Pentagon with a second priority, which would be good only if Warner Bros. failed to make a film. Darryl Zanuck, however, was hardly one to accept defeat so readily. He quickly instructed McCarthy to register the title *Blood and Guts*—Patton's nickname—with the Motion Picture Association of America. Warner Bros. had attempted to do the same, but the MPAA's title bureau had turned them down on matters of taste. When McCarthy approached the association on behalf of Twentieth Century-Fox, the bureau told him they would do the same to his studio. A conversation ensued, and when the officials of the association learned the historical background of the phrase, they agreed to allow the title to be registered, but only for a film about Patton. For good measure, McCarthy also registered *Old Blood and Guts*.[29]

A stalemate ensued. Neither studio could move forward on a Patton film without a concession from the other, and neither wanted to give up on the project. The Department of Defense was also making it clear that it would not cooperate without the consent of the Pattons, and the family had no interest in seeing any film made.[30]

The most obvious next step was to contact the family and see if they would change their mind. General Mark Clark approached Totten and her brother to see if they would be interested in supporting a movie. His involvement hardly swayed the Pattons since they thought he was simply trying to make a buck. They had no more interest in supporting him than anyone else.[31]

McCarthy took an indirect approach. He wrote Major General Paul Harkins, whom he knew from his days in the army. As a colonel in World War II, Harkins had served on Patton's staff, and a decade later, he remained close to the family. McCarthy told Harkins that legally, the family could not prevent a Patton film from being made. They might be able to stop a studio from making a film with the support from the Defense Department, but there were other ways around that assistance, like using news footage. It would be cheap, but it was possible. His studio would never do that, but others in Hollywood had less interest in the professional quality of the product they produced. The best way the Pattons could control the general's public image was to cooperate with a "first-rate company."[32]

Harkins wrote back to McCarthy and offered some hope. George S. Patton Jr. was an American hero and belonged to the entire nation. His story deserved representation on film. He had told Patton's children the same thing, but they were still bitter at how the news media had portrayed their father. He enclosed a copy of a letter he had received from Fred Ayer, Beatrice Patton's brother. Ayer, a lawyer, was handling estate issues for the Pattons. With Harkins's handwritten notation "CONFIDENTIAL" scrawled at the top of the unfilled blank space at the end of the letter, McCarthy could see the deep opposition of the family. "As far as a movie of the General goes," Ayers told Harkins, "all I can say is that Beatrice never wanted it and both Ruth Ellen and George are violently opposed to it and have stopped several efforts to produce one including Warner Brothers whom, I think, have been quite decent about it." In the letter, Ayer also explained that he had told Mark Clark "nothing doing." George IV had told Clark the same thing. Despite this strong opposition, Harkins told McCarthy that he thought Patton's children would mellow with time. McCarthy realized that the only way to change the family's attitude was to talk to them directly, but he also knew that they did not want to talk to him. His immediate decision was to do nothing, which was all he could realistically do at the time.[33]

A few months later, McCarthy attempted to wrest Department of Defense approval from Warner Bros. when the authorization came up for renewal in 1956. Officials in the Pentagon saw no reason to revise their sanction, and the stalemate between the two studios continued.[34]

McCarthy made a move early the next year when one of his colleagues in the Department of Defense told him that if the Pattons would support the project, the Pentagon would award the permit to Twentieth Century-Fox. On February 8, 1957, he sent a letter addressed to George Jr., which was actually his father's name. George IV never responded. Three months later, McCarthy contacted Ayer. The lawyer never responded either.[35]

McCarthy then waited and waited. Two years went by and he kept himself busy doing other work for the studio. In 1959, he arranged a meeting with Ruth Ellen Totten while she was visiting Pasadena. He had no expectation of changing her mind, but he believed that he should explain himself to her. According to two records McCarthy made of that meeting, she was polite and civil, but she remained strong in her opposition to any film. She was also honest about her reasons: the family wanted nothing to do with the publicity that would come with a Hollywood production.[36]

Totten also made it clear that efforts to enlist the support of the Patton family had also made them angry and bitter. She made some rather harsh comments about Frank Dorn and Mark Clark, claiming that both had attempted to blackmail her brother. There was clearly some exaggeration in these comments. Clark's actions were clearly suspect, but Dorn had insisted on family consent—a requirement that had hamstrung all Hollywood efforts. A year later, McCarthy met with her husband, Brigadier General James W. Totten, in his office at the Pentagon. Since the two were of the same rank, they could talk as equals, but General Totten offered McCarthy no encouragement.[37]

Tired of seeing no progress on the film, studio executives assigned the Patton project to others. This move was the result of studio infighting after the departure of Darryl Zanuck. The studio head was exhausted with both the Hollywood rat race and his wife. His solution to both problems was simple: move to France. He stepped down as head of production at Twentieth Century-Fox, set up his own company, DFZ Productions, and left the running of the studio to others. Despite claims to the contrary, work on the Patton film continued after Zanuck left, but he had been McCarthy's main patron in this effort. His absence made progress much more difficult for the producer. Spyros Skouras, the studio president, seeking to assert his own authority, assigned the Patton project to producer Frank Ricketson and director George Sherman. A prolific director, Sherman had worked on nearly 200 films and televisions episodes. Most of them were westerns. Despite this volume, none had much enduring appeal or artistic merit. Skouras had also bought the film rights to a book titled *Blood and Guts Patton* (1961) by Jack Pearl. McCarthy was not impressed with the quality of work of Ricketson, Sherman, or Pearl.[38]

Skouras played McCarthy and the Ricketson–Sherman team off one another—a common tactic in Hollywood. Ricketson and Sherman claimed that they could obtain the support of George IV.[39] When that effort failed, McCarthy made a move using his contacts in the army to obtain a priority from the Department of Defense. The stalling tactics of the Patton family fell apart when Brigadier General Frank McCarthy, USAR, received a different duty assignment: assistant to the chief of information, United States Army. His immediate supervisor, Major General William W. Quinn, was responsible for army cooperation with the media. This assignment was no accident. General officers have more influence than junior officers in determining their duty assignments. Then again, the assignment also worked to the advantage of the U.S. Army. McCarthy's civilian background gave him an understanding of the media in general and the entertainment industry in particular that other officers of his rank simply would never have. On July 18, 1961, McCarthy told Quinn that the Pentagon could not make their support conditional on the Patton family's consent. By this time, Warner Bros. had let its priority lapse, and Quinn indicated that he thought the army could offer support with or without the Pattons' approval.[40]

Later that month, Skouras presided over a confusing meeting at the studio. Both Ricketson and McCarthy attended. Throughout that conference, the two battled for control of the project. McCarthy talked about giving the directing job to Richard Brooks, who had *Blackboard Jungle* (1955), *Cat on a Hot Tin Roof* (1958), and *Elmer Gantry* (1960) on his directing résumé. He also wanted to give the lead role to Burt Lancaster, but Skouras said no; John Wayne was under contract to the studio, and he would be perfect to play Patton. Ricketson added that if the role went to Wayne, James Edward Grant would be the best writer to assign to the project. A prolific writer, Grant had written, cowritten, or contributed to the screenplay for a number of Wayne films, including *The Sands of Iwo Jima* (1949) and *The Alamo* (1960). McCarthy responded saying the script for *The Alamo* was one of the worst he had ever seen on the silver screen. When Skouras asked him who he would like to write the screenplay, he had no ready answer, but he said journalist Robert Allen would do for writing a film treatment or outline.[41]

The meeting ended with a good deal of uncertainty. The only decision seemed to be that McCarthy would offer a contract to Allen and that Wayne would play Patton. Who would oversee the project remained unresolved, but McCarthy's work with the Defense Department was speaking volumes. Wayne was not McCarthy's first choice. At that point in time, he preferred Lancaster or William Holden or Gregory Peck over Wayne. McCarthy hoped to change the casting decision, but that was a battle for another day.[42]

Lawyers from the U.S. Army agreed with Quinn. A few days later, when Twentieth Century-Fox formally requested a priority from the Department of Defense, the army's position led the Department of Defense to give the permit to the studio. McCarthy had reached the end of a long, long road.

Twentieth Century-Fox could now move forward on the Patton project. On September 5, 1961, the studio issued a press release announcing it was going to make a motion picture based on the life of George S. Patton Jr. McCarthy would be the producer. A full paragraph discussed McCarthy's own military background.[43]

The Pattons responded immediately. Arvin H. Brown Jr. of the San Diego legal firm of Luce, Forward, Hamilton & Scripps sent a letter to Skouras making it clear that the family in no way approved of this production. Copies also went to McCarthy, the secretaries of defense and the army, and the vice chief of staff of the U.S. Army. An underlying tone of this letter was an assumption that the Defense Department could not grant a priority without the consent of the general's surviving relatives.[44]

McCarthy tried to reach out to the family. On September 13, he wrote his friend Hancock Banning, a cousin of the Pattons. He explained that the Patton project was moving forward with or without the family. He regretted their absence from the undertaking because their insights and advice would make the film that much more authentic. "Anyhow I want you, as my friend, to know that I am approaching the subject with the determination to make a film which will reflect great credit upon the Army, although unfortunately I have no way of determining what the Pattons' personal sensitivities and sensibilities may be."[45]

The family responded with another lawyer. Josiah A. Spaulding of the

Boston legal firm Bingham, Dana & Gould wrote Assistant Secretary of Defense Arthur Sylvester, on December 13, 1961, and stated, "The Patton family has objected to the production of these pictures because they believe that as contemplated they would not properly portray the General but would tend to stress some of the more misleading and dramatic incidents in his life." He also added, "We believe that the interests of the Defense Department and of the Patton family in this proposed picture are the same."[46]

When Sylvester demanded to know what was going on with this project, the chief of his audiovisual department told him that Patton was a public figure and that there was little the family could do to stop a film from being made. The Department of Defense would cooperate only if the film reflected well on the military. Despite these clear facts, Donald Baruch, the head of the Pentagon's film office, agreed to meet with representatives of the firm to hear their argument.[47]

In that meeting, Spaulding and an associate, Thomas Wiley, tried to stall the film with offers to make General Patton's diary available for use in a production. Baruch explained that the source material was a matter for the studio. He also added that McCarthy was a dependable producer because of his military background. He then shared all of this information about the meeting with McCarthy.[48]

What Baruch did not share was Spaulding's observation that something smelled rotten about the relationship between the studio and the military. The lawyer wanted to know what role McCarthy had played in the approval process of Twentieth Century-Fox's request for a Defense Department permit. The deputy general counsel for the Pentagon, in a two-page response, noted there was no policy requiring the consent of surviving family members when the department was making decisions about which film productions it would support. He added, "Frank McCarthy has at no time served in the Office of the Secretary of Defense." As a result, "he has not been instrumental in bringing about a change in Department of Defense policy with respect to consent of families of historical figures, because a requirement for consent of surviving families has never been a policy of the Department of Defense." His military background was important, though, in determining that he would make a film that would reflect well on the U.S. Army. That was an issue with which the Pattons could hardly object.[49]

The letter was accurate only in a technical sense. The evidence does indicate that McCarthy used his army connections to his own personal advantage. In short, he came much closer to skirting the ethical and legal issues than the deputy general counsel allowed.

One of Patton's biographers, Stanley P. Hirshon, credits family opposition as playing a significant role in the artistic success of the film. There is much truth in that observation. As McCarthy admitted, the involvement of the Pattons would have required concessions about the general's personality and actions. These compromises would have dulled some of the more controversial elements of the man's life. Family resistance also delayed the formation of the writing–acting–directing team that made the movie. It is highly unlikely that McCarthy could have assembled a team in the 1950s that was as good as the one he put together in the late 1960s.[50]

Patton family opposition and stalling clearly ended up producing a better writing team. The same press release that announced McCarthy as the producer also declared that Robert Allen was writing a treatment. McCarthy agreed to this assignment with profound reservations. Allen seemed to have the right background to write on this subject. He was an accomplished journalist. He and Drew Pearson had written the "Washington Merry-Go-Round" syndicated column on national politics. He had also served on Patton's staff and written a book on the general: *Lucky Forward: The History of Patton's Third U.S. Army* (1947). Despite this background, McCarthy feared that Allen had no background in dramatic storytelling and would revert to a fact-driven military history. Whatever the producer's concerns, Allen had enthusiasm for the project. He told McCarthy he found the task exciting. Given his background in newspapers, Allen had plenty of experience writing on deadline. He turned in a 174-page profile. "Robert S. Allen has done a fine job of research for us," McCarthy told Baruch, "particularly in the field of anecdote, although it has no dramatic form whatever." Only later did McCarthy learn that Allen had cannibalized his book.[51]

McCarthy also began looking for an actor and director. He contacted Burt Lancaster immediately, sending him a copy of Allen's treatment through the actor's agent. While McCarthy had serious reservations about the treatment, Lancaster found it interesting. On January 8, 1962, McCarthy and Lancaster had a two-and-a-half-hour meeting. "I was able to answer all of his questions and to comment on his several reservations, which were not only well taken, but very astute," McCarthy reported. "We wound up talking the same language and endorsing the same approach to the material."[52]

Both men were interested in having Richard Brooks write and direct the film. Brooks was a particularly hot property in Hollywood at the time, having just won an Oscar for his script for *Elmer Gantry*. Lancaster had also won the Oscar for best actor for his performance in that film. Later that year, another Brooks film, *Sweet Bird of Youth* (1962), would garner more critical acclaim and collect three Oscar nominations: best actor, best actress, and best supporting actress. McCarthy found that Brooks was interested in teaming up with Lancaster again on the Patton project. The busy travel schedules of Lancaster, Brooks, and their agents delayed the signing of contracts.[53]

Then this tentative agreement and the entire Patton project fell apart because of Elizabeth Taylor. Twentieth Century-Fox had not had a major blockbuster film since Zanuck had left for France. The studio needed a hit, and Skouras decided to invest significant resources in *Cleopatra* (1963). First, the studio bought out the contract of Joan Collins, who was set to play the lead role, and then offered Taylor a million dollars ($7,330,401 in 2010) to play the part. She agreed. Walter Wanger, the producer of this film, decided to do the principal shooting in England at Pinewood Studios. Only after building an outside set and planting palm trees did the crew discover that English skies maintained an even gray color. The heavy, dreary rain and fog did not produce the proper lighting for a story set on the Nile. The director, Rouben Mamoulian, was too busy test shooting with Peter Finch, the actor set to play Gaius Julius Caesar, to notice these problems. Shooting moved to Italy and along the way the studio replaced Wanger, Mamoulian, and Finch. Joseph L. Mankiewicz finished the film as writer/producer/director. With the approval of Skouras, he began shooting to make two Cleopatra films: one about her life with Caesar, and another about her relationship with Marc Antony. Then Taylor's health problems—she ended up in the emergency room while in London—halted filming. The studio was bleeding money. Executives were canceling projects, releasing actors from contracts, and selling assets far below market value to get desperately needed cash.[54]

Zanuck observed this disaster unfolding from France, where he was making *The Longest Day* (1962), a film about the D-Day invasion, a project that was close to his heart. Because the studio was in a financial meltdown, it would have less money to devote to other projects, like marketing for his nearly finished film. With Skouras clearly on his way out, Zanuck decided to protect his economic interests. He still owned 280,000 shares of stock in the studio, which was the major source of his income. At a meeting of the board of directors, Zanuck initiated the removal of Skouras and then got himself elected president by an 8-to-3 vote.[55]

Zanuck immediately decided to shut down the studio. Twentieth Century-Fox would only complete films that were already underway or to which it was legally committed to making. He made his son, Richard, head of production. The younger Zanuck then had to fire and lay off scores of people, many of whom he had known since he had been a small boy.[56]

McCarthy and the Patton project were victims of this corporate downsizing. McCarthy knew what was coming. In August, he wrote a two-page memo for Richard Zanuck. He quickly summarized the work that had been done on the film. The Allen profile was intended to serve as a lure for an actor and director. It had performed this function with Lancaster and Brooks. Neither had signed a contract, but both were personally willing to make it their next project. In an effort to save himself and the film, McCarthy told Zanuck that his father wanted John Wayne to play the lead, and after seeing The Longest Day, he agreed. Wayne would be better than Lancaster in the part.[57]

Financial realities dictated the actions of the two Zanucks. When McCarthy's contract with the studio ended in October, the studio allowed it to expire. He was never fired or laid off. He wrote a short note to Lancaster telling him what had happened. The priority that the Department of Defense had granted would stay with Fox. He hoped that the studio would begin shooting again in the future and wanted to be involved with that effort, but for now his involvement was over.[58]

McCarthy was still determined to make this film. That sentiment became clear in a letter he wrote Patton's daughter, Ruth Ellen Totten. "No matter where I may be working, my interest in the Patton project will remain alive," he told her. He suggested that she see The Longest Day, because if it was financially successful, he suspected Zanuck would want to make a film on Patton next.[59]

McCarthy's suspicions were correct. Zanuck's determination to make the movie is also why McCarthy eventually returned to the studio. But first the studio had to survive Cleopatra. That was anything but certain.

3. The Screenwriter

The near-total collapse and bankruptcy of Twentieth Century-Fox had undone eleven years of McCarthy's work in trying to produce a Patton film. He, however, was a determined man, and continued to work at making the motion picture. In 1965, this drive paid off.

When McCarthy's contract with the studio expired, he quickly ended up at Universal as a staff producer. Although Fox had the priority with the Department of Defense and owned the rights to several Patton biographies, there was nothing to prevent another studio from shooting a Patton film of their own. "I have tried hard to interest Universal in the project, but the potential cost of $4,000,000 [$28,169,290 in 2010] is too rich for their blood," McCarthy told an army colleague.[1]

Despite Universal's lack of interest, he still continued to work on making the film. "During all that time, and for many years before, it was the project foremost in my mind," McCarthy explained. He knew that any studio, including Fox, could shoot a film without him, but he used his expertise and contacts in both Hollywood and the army to his advantage. Hearing that John Wayne might be interested in a Patton film, McCarthy was now willing to work with the actor. He wrote Wayne's son, who produced his father's films, explaining what he had previously done on this project and adding that he was still a brigadier general in the reserves and the deputy chief of information for the U.S. Army. "The picture would be big and expensive, but it could be the finest film to come out of World War II. It has everything that *The Longest Day* had, in addition it has the most successful, the most flamboyant, and certainly the most misunderstood combat commander as its leading character." John Wayne, though, had different ideas. He told McCarthy that the lead character was "too tough, too difficult to lick" for him to play the part.[2]

McCarthy also wrote the new army chief of information and asked him to let him know if any producers contacted the information office seeking Defense Department assistance. Since his reserve assignment was to serve in that same office, he said it was in the army's interest to have him involved in the project, and that he could contractually leave Universal when he wanted.[3]

Like McCarthy, Darryl Zanuck had never lost interest in Patton, and as his studio recovered financially, he once again initiated work on this project. In 1964, the historian Ladislas Farago's biography of the general, *Patton: Ordeal and Triumph*, appeared on bookstore shelves. Twentieth Century-Fox bought the film rights to the book, and Zanuck had David Brown, his son's producing partner, begin work on developing the film. He told Brown that the Patton family had thwarted McCarthy's earlier efforts, but Zanuck thought they could make the film cheaply because there was a good deal of Signal Corps stock footage of Patton and his armies. "I would like more information on the project and particularly how far the family would let us go not only on the slapping incident but on the development of his 'wild' character. Since I had many meetings with him personally and saw him in several of his 'rages' I believe this is the fascinating, as well as the controversial angle of any screenplay." Building on McCarthy's previous work, he had a few names to suggest for the part: "Patton could be played by Burt Lancaster or Barry Goldwater whom I understand is available."[4]

Two weeks later, Brown reported back to Zanuck. The feelings of the Patton family were irrelevant. Patton was a public figure, and both he and his wife were dead. He had even checked the laws of various European countries where the film might be released and believed that the studio was in the clear. He also informed Zanuck that Fox Movietone had 5,000 feet of documentary footage of Patton. The studio's representative in Washington had warned him, though, that they would need the permission of the Department of Defense to use film that the U.S. Army Signal Corps had provided. Brown was fairly sure that the studio would need some type of support from the Pentagon but was uncertain about the attitudes in the army. He planned to go to Washington to meet with the chief of information to learn his view about a Patton film.[5]

McCarthy acted before Brown had a chance to make that trip. When the studio announced that it had bought the film rights from Farago, he wrote a letter directly to Darryl Zanuck. He congratulated Zanuck on this move and then gave a quick overview of the efforts he had made to get the film made. The key was getting U.S. Army cooperation, and McCarthy reminded him that he had played an important role getting that support. He told Zanuck: "Quinn told me he did this because he was convinced of the good intent and good will of the producer" (which is to say McCarthy). Now the commanding general of the Seventh Army—Patton's old command—Quinn had a military reservation in his area of responsibility that would be perfect for the shooting of tank battle scenes that was better than anyplace available in the United States. The subtle message of the letter was that if Twentieth Century-Fox wanted to make the film, they needed him. McCarthy was too polite to be that blunt, but he made it known he would like to be part of the project. "If you have a requirement for my services in some appropriate capacity, I should like to work on the Patton project because of my long dedication to it."[6]

The Zanucks understood McCarthy's implications, and a few days later, Richard Zanuck called him and said they wanted to start up again. In March 1965, the studio announced that McCarthy had returned to the studio to make a Patton film. McCarthy was fairly clear about what he wanted to do with this film: "I am sincere in saying that what I want to make is an inspirational film which will bring only credit to General Patton, the Army, and the United States."[7]

The producer needed to put together a script for the movie, and to do that, he required the services of a writer. His choice was Calder Willingham. After having a long talk with the writer, McCarthy told Richard Zanuck that Willingham was "excellent," but he was also honest and admitted that he was only the "best writer available."[8]

There was reason for this ambiguity. The forty-two-year-old Willingham was primarily known as a novelist. He had six books to his name, and had done some screenplay work with uncredited revisions on *Paths of Glory* (1957) and *The Bridge on the River Kwai* (1957). Despite the military nature of these two films, the writer knew little about the army and World War II. This lack of experience was no barrier to having a definite take on his subject: "George S. Patton, Jr. was not only a great fighting General of World War II, perhaps the greatest fighting General of that war, a fantastic and colorful man of larger-than-life size dimensions, he was also one of the most pitiful victims of World War II, a figure worthy of comparison to the mythic heroes of ancient Greek tragedy." Burt Lancaster liked Willingham's previous work and thought he would bring a new perspective and an imaginative approach. Since McCarthy still wanted Lancaster in the lead, he agreed to give the assignment to the novelist.[9]

The studio quickly worked out an arrangement with Willingham. The writer would spend ten weeks writing a script treatment. For this effort, he would receive $40,000 ($272,221 in 2010). If the studio liked the end product, it could exercise an option and commission him to write a full-fledged screenplay. He would receive another $60,000 for another ten weeks of work and another $500 ($415,832 and $3,465 in 2010) a week to cover his living expenses in Los Angeles. (Willingham lived in New Hampshire.[10])

Willingham began work on the treatment in late April. McCarthy gave him copies of the Farago book as well as several other Patton biographies, and had him watch three Patton documentaries and *The Longest Day, Elmer Gantry*, and *The Desert Fox* (1951). "Willingham has taken to the project very well, is highly enthusiastic about it, and is showing what I consider the right kind of curiosity for delving into all the facts and all the points of view," McCarthy informed the younger Zanuck.[11]

McCarthy also had a research assistant, Mike Lambert, creating a card index file documenting Patton's life. This tedious project was necessary to ensure that the studio used facts only from books that the studio owned the film rights to, or that were in the public domain. McCarthy wanted to avoid infringing on the copyrights of other authors and facing the lawsuits that would follow. "Mike will be able to keep us legally straight on these things," the producer observed. A month later, McCarthy and Willingham met with Burt Lancaster and explained the direction in which they planned to take the screenplay. Lancaster seemed to like Willingham's notes and thought the film was going in an interesting direction.[12]

While the studio and Willingham negotiated a contract, McCarthy's next move was to renew the priority that Fox had with the Department of Defense, which was granted after an unusual delay. This might have been an otherwise routine matter had not the Patton family once again requested that the army not cooperate with any production. Major General George V. Underwood, the army chief of information, told McCarthy about the family's attitudes only after the matter was resolved. Richard Zanuck was confused about the army's delay: "Since they gave it to us once, what excuse could they have now if they were to with[h]old it? I think we should do everything possible to get cooperation but not in any way change our script or present 'attack' on the material to accommodate it." This attitude was inconsequential at the time, but it would serve the production well in the years to come.[13]

The third thing McCarthy had to do was find an actor to play the part. His first choice—in fact, his only choice at the time—was Burt Lancaster. The actor remained interested in the part, but was unwilling to make any promises. He had a strong interest in the part and was willing to make a commitment based only on a reading of the treatment.[14]

McCarthy's desire to have Lancaster play the lead gave the actor a good deal of influence over the production and the producer's next task: selecting a director. Lancaster wanted John Frankenheimer to direct, an idea McCarthy and Richard Zanuck liked. Frankenheimer had directed Lancaster in *The Young Savages* (1961), *Birdman of Alcatraz* (1962), *Seven Days in May* (1964), and *The Train* (1964). Despite this work, Frankenheimer was best known at the time for a Frank Sinatra movie, *The Manchurian Candidate* (1962). McCarthy met with the director and found him interested. Frankenheimer, however, was already legally committed to other projects and was not sure he would be available during the time frame McCarthy had in mind. He wanted to work on the project and reached an informal agreement with the producer not to take on any other new projects, just in case. "This is wonderful," Richard Zanuck observed. "If we want him and he is available so much to the good. If not, we have at least scored some points with Burt."[15]

Everything seemed to be moving forward until Robert Allen reentered the picture. Allen believed that Farago had plagiarized from *Lucky Forward* and decided to take legal action. His lawyer contacted the studio's legal team and informed them of Allen's lawsuit. Fox executives quickly commissioned B. Duncan Boss to study the two books. Three months later, Boss reported that there were indeed instances that might constitute plagiarism. From his analysis, it seems that Boss was not entirely clear about what constituted unauthorized usage or fair use under copyright law. Although Farago did not use footnotes to document his study, he employed quotation marks and a bibliography to indicate where he had gotten his information. When he used exact words, they appeared in quotation marks and fell within the boundaries of fair use. He did not try to pass off the words or ideas of others as his own. More importantly, Boss explained that Allen had a legal problem of his own. Allen may or may not have grounds to sue Farago, but he had no grounds to go after the studio. Fox owned outright the copyright to his treatment, and Allen had cannibalized his book to put together that study. The studio had basically "inherited" the rights to *Lucky Forward*. This position was the one the studio took with Allen's lawyers. "Clearly, Mr. Allen has divested himself . . . of any motion picture rights he previously may have had in his book." That approach killed the legal threat to the production.[16]

Much of the movement forward on the production depended on Willingham's treatment. His focus was on developing the personality of the
lead character: "What I have been most concerned about has been to establish a strong dramatic narrative, and also to breathe life into Patton,
make a sympathetic human being of him, an appealing and dramatic and
exciting hero."[17]

The work of writing a dramatic but generally accurate screenplay appears to have exceeded Willingham's abilities. He had, as he admitted at
the time, problems getting started. "It is always hard to break into a new
work, whether it be a novel, a play, a screenplay or whatever. One must
overcome inertia, get going, etc." He told McCarthy that writing the treatment was "a long and brutal haul." He also admitted that the assignment
was taxing his abilities. "The truth is that I've worked as hard as I know
how, and I must say it has been a hell of a job. You know, I thought I had a
real good deal with the studio, but this damn thing is the equal of three
screenplays, I swear to Gawd."[18]

Showing a real lack of understanding and even hostility toward history,
as well as limited creativity, Willingham basically told McCarthy he did not
let technical military matters or the facts get in the way of telling a good
story. In a memo he titled "Truth or Fiction?—A Problem of Screen Biography," Willingham argued that although academic history should be accurate, "the primary point about dramatized biography is that it's
emotionally accurate, or, if you like, poetically accurate." After what he called
"six weeks of back-breaking research," he decided that the actual Battle of
El Guettar "was a rather dull conflict." To compensate for what he saw as a
lack of drama, he invented maneuvers and elements that he thought were
more entertaining. "In my belief, my 'Battle of El Guettar' is closer to the
emotional or poetic truth about Patton than the real battle. I believe that—
and I know that my battle would make an infinitely more exciting and dramatic sequence in a motion picture." If McCarthy wanted something more
accurate, Willingham said he would need another year to do the research
and even then the result would be a "wooden and lifeless 'historical' figure" and the resulting film would lose money.[19]

The difficulties Willingham faced with the subject were readily evident
when he missed his contractual deadline of June 30. This was not too significant in and of itself. He gave McCarthy a draft of the first act on June 30, but
McCarthy quickly realized that Willingham needed help. From his reading
of the first act, the producer suggested to Zanuck that they get an outside

consultant with good knowledge of the period. His candidate was General Paul Harkins. A retired four-star general, Harkins had served on Patton's staff during World War II. Zanuck loved the suggestion. "This sounds like an excellent idea," he scribbled on McCarthy's memo.[20] Harkins promised to read the treatment and to meet with Willingham. The studio agreed to pay him $1,000 ($6,930 in 2010) for roughly ten hours of work.

Willingham was not pleased about meeting with Harkins. "You are really and truly putting the cart ahead of the horse, Frank. It would be impossibly hampering to me to have General Harkins sitting on my shoulder while I am trying to write this first draft." He explained several times what he really needed to do: "Let me repeat the *important* problems of this picture have to do with *human values*, not with technical impediments. Once we have a real script, any competent military man can help us make our script air-tight militarily."[21]

It took Willingham another two weeks to finish, but on July 12, he turned in a 130-page treatment for *Patton!* He also included a four-page memo in which he explained his approach:

> I have tried, in this treatment, to create a story and a character out of the huge and amorphous, chaotic mass of material on Patton. In a sense, this is lengthy outline for *an original screenplay.* Believe me, Farago's book is only a convenient research depot, that is all. There is no story in Farago's book and there are not any dramatic scenes in it; I have had to construct, invent and create the equivalent of an original screenplay. It has been even harder than an original screenplay, because I have had to respect and be bounded by over-all historical accuracy. The job has been an absolute BACK-BREAKER and I shudder to think what a regular screenwriter would have done with this thing. I must say Dave Brown's idea of putting a novelist on it was an inspiration of the first order; believe me, I have had to use all of my resources as a creative writer on this job. In all humility, I think I am giving you something here you could never get in a million years from a screen technician. The truth is that the studio is paying Farago for a very high-class research job; there is no "property" in this book, and there is no picture in it—you have only the raw materials of a property and a picture. But there is a property and a picture in my treatment, if I have succeeded in my basic aim of creating a *story* and a living *character* out of this mass of incoherent history.[22]

Willingham was hanging himself with his own words. McCarthy, according to his notes, found that Willingham's Patton "speaks in platitudes" and there was "too much cornball" dialogue. "Military actions too many + inaccurate, but can handle." McCarthy thought the treatment was a beginning, but only a beginning. He wanted to meet with his writer and have him refine and improve certain parts of the treatment. The novelist had no interest in having those meetings. He was determined to return to New Hampshire on July 22 with his wife and five children.[23]

McCarthy reluctantly forwarded the document to the younger Zanuck, explaining his reservations: "I am generally disappointed in the treatment." He recommended that the studio executive read Willingham's cover memo, which spoke volumes about the problems the novelist was having in writing historical fiction. In was clear that Willingham had written the treatment "rapidly and carelessly." Far more significantly, Willingham had failed to develop a strong lead character. "Patton is present in his many moods, but they are not harmonized or adjusted in such a way that the character jells and comes off as a whole man." The writer's lack of expertise in military affairs also showed: "Willingham always takes Patton's point of view, with a resultant loss of genuine conflict and controversy."[24]

As the producer, McCarthy planned to make the screenplay the foundation of the film, and he wanted to meet with his writer on a regular basis and shape the direction that the script developed. In an era before overnight delivery services, fax machines, e-mail, and other communication technologies, this contact would not have been possible if his writer lived on the other side of the country. "If Willingham had written an inspired treatment—and if, as he originally agreed, he had listened to a technical advisor and rewritten the initial treatment in accurate form—I should have been willing to have him go off and try the screenplay alone," McCarthy told Zanuck. "Such was not the case, however; you know how I feel about the treatment. It represents a good step forward, but there is nothing in it which leads me to think that Willingham can write anything approaching a satisfactory first draft in isolation in New Hampshire."[25]

McCarthy decided to look for another screenwriter. He found him in the person of Francis Ford Coppola. "He arrived with a full beard," McCarthy recalled. "I wouldn't say exactly a hippie. He had more of a Bolshevik look than anything else."[26]

Born in Detroit, Michigan, to a first-generation Italian American family, Coppola was twenty-six years old in 1965. His father, Carmine, had studied flute at Juilliard and played with the Detroit Symphony Orchestra before taking the family to New York to play with the NBC Symphony Orchestra. One of the most life-changing events for the younger Coppola came when he was nine and contracted polio. "I think any tough time you go through, any real crisis where you break down, then survive, leaves you in a far different place from where you were," he reflected about his childhood trauma. Unable to leave his bed, Coppola developed his imagination to keep himself entertained and created puppet shows that he performed for friends and family after he got better. "I am sure that from those shows came the idea of my studio—a place where we could work together like children, with music, puppets, scenery, lights, dramatic action, whatever we wanted to do." He attended Hofstra University, where he decided to study film after watching *October: Ten Days that Shook the World* (1928). "On Monday, I was in the theater. On Tuesday I wanted to be a filmmaker." He thrived at Hofstra, becoming the president of the drama and the musical comedy clubs.[27]

After graduating from Hofstra in 1960, Coppola went to film school at the University of California, Los Angeles but was disappointed with UCLA. "There was none of the camaraderie I had imagined while I was in college," he confessed. "All they know was how to criticize the lazy ways of Hollywood film producers, implying that only they could be capable of directing great films." Although primarily known as a director, Coppola first made a name for himself as a writer when he won the Samuel Goldwyn Writing Award, a prize that the Samuel Goldwyn Foundation gives to a student at any of the University of California campuses. Suddenly, several studios were interested in hiring him to write screenplays. He accepted an offer from Seven Arts Productions, where he wrote a number of scripts, but none was ever developed into an actual film. "The position of the screenwriter is an absurd, ridiculous one," he later reflected. "He earns a great deal of money but has no say whatsoever about the film, unless he is one of the more famous screenwriters. This is particularly true for young authors." His first major credit came when Seven Arts sent him to France to do on-set revisions of the script for *Is Paris Burning?* (1966). Unhappy with this experience, and bitter that Seven Arts would not allow him to direct, he quit or was fired—depending on which account one believes—after he returned to the United States.[28]

Although Coppola had disliked his time in France, McCarthy thought that his work on *Is Paris Burning?* gave him a solid background to work on a

Patton film. He arranged a meeting with the budding filmmaker and liked what he saw. Coppola "is the most impressive young writer I have met in years," McCarthy declared. "He is standing on the edge of a great screen-writing career." He saw real talent in the UCLA graduate: "Of all the writers with whom I have discussed PATTON, he impresses me as having the best potential." After Coppola met with him and Lancaster, and after the actor read some of Coppola's previous screenplays, McCarthy offered him a contract to write a screenplay for $50,000 ($346,526 in 2010). The unemployed writer quickly said yes.[29]

With a new screenwriter signed, McCarthy informed Willingham that the studio would not be picking up his option and that Coppola would be replacing him. McCarthy made it clear that the main issue was Willingham's insistence on writing the script in New Hampshire. The novelist replied a day later, thanking McCarthy for his honesty and integrity, but he reminded him that he had always been clear of his intention to write the script in New England. "I am conscious of your desire to maintain control of and contact with the Patton project, aware as I am of the importance of this picture to you both personally and professionally. It is perfectly understandable you would feel as you do—and when we come to grip with emotions, prior agreements mean nothing!"[30]

As Coppola wrote the screenplay, McCarthy mentored him. He gave the writer a bibliography of books and articles on Patton and had him do much of the same research that Willingham had just done. The two met regularly. "We had history lessons every day," McCarthy later said. Coppola would then write after their conversations. McCarthy played a major role in shaping the themes that appeared in the film. In an article that appeared in the *Atlantic*, Major General James Gavin, who had pioneered airborne assault operations during World War II, observed: "In dealing with two strong-willed characters such as Patton and Montgomery, Eisenhower seemed unwilling to suppress either totally, and thus neither was given all the resources available, while both sought to advance the attack in their own sectors." McCarthy gave Coppola the article and noted: "Francis—Let's discuss—this is the general idea, I feel." Omar Bradley emerged as a major hero of the film, and that development was no accident. McCarthy sent Coppola a copy of a *New York Times Magazine* article on Bradley with a note: "It is a fact that Bradley originally conceived and ordered a number of the projects which Patton executed so brilliantly. Let's credit Gen. B. wherever + whenever we can in the interest of fairness and accuracy." Next to a passage about Bradley developing the ideas for a breakout from St. Lo a month after the D-Day landings, McCarthy wrote: "Can we credit him with conceiving Patton's dash across France?"[31]

McCarthy also had a good ear for dialogue. In the *New York Times Magazine* article, Patton is quoted as saying, "Between my screwy ideas and your brains, we certainly come up with some wonderful plans. Dammit, Brad, you and I make a wonderful team." McCarthy wrote at the bottom: "Good line." In Gavin's *Atlantic* article, he quotes Patton as saying: "Now, I want you to remember that no son of a bitch ever won a war by dying for his country. He won it by making the other poor dumb son of a bitch die for his country." McCarthy sent Coppola the article with the notation: "Francis—Let's discuss."[32]

The producer also wanted humor in the film. When someone mentioned Patton's dog, Willie, to McCarthy, he figured the cowardly canine would make for good comic relief. "Francis—Don't fail to give Willie careful consideration," he suggested. "Willie was ferocious looking—which was why GSP bought him—but he was a sissie as GSP soon discovered."[33]

Coppola enjoyed the process. He worked daily at an office that the studio provided. "It was a real privilege to go to work at Fox in that period." He had a huge bulletin board/chalkboard. He posted index cards and notes from McCarthy on the board. McCarthy was impressed with Coppola's organization and liked showing the board to visitors. Coppola found McCarthy a good boss to work for because the producer was a "genial, kind man." There were also small perks to the job. He often visited the set of the Fox television series *Voyage to the Bottom of the Sea* (1964–1968) and got to eat his lunch on set while playing with the props.[34]

Although McCarthy had a good deal of influence in the writing process, the script that Coppola produced was his and his alone. "I said, 'Wait a minute, this guy was obviously nuts,'" he explained later. "If they want to make a film glorifying him as a great American hero, it will be laughed at. And if I write a film that condemns him, it won't be made at all." Coppola's decision was to present the general as a quixotic character. He drew heavily from Farago and from Omar Bradley's memoir, *A Soldier's Story*. He wrote most of the memorable scenes in the movie, including the opening monologue, the best one-liners, the conclusion, and the creation of the fictional character of Steiger, a German staff officer, who serves as a dramatic device to provide background information on Patton and make observations on the general's character. Steiger often advances the view of Patton as a warrior with pretentious and impracticable romantic streaks. Coppola even managed to insert references to other films in his screenplay. The shooting of the two mules and the dumping of their bodies over the side of the bridge was a reference to Sergei Eisenstein's *October: Ten Days that Shook the World.*[35]

Coppola delivered a finished screenplay to McCarthy on November 10. The studio quickly decided to exercise its option without using the reading time it was contractually allotted. Coppola would revise the script, ensuring the writer got paid the full $50,000. McCarthy made no effort to exaggerate his influence in the development of the script. "Now, I don't claim one iota of credit for the script, of course. However, I'm glad that I got a man who was malleable and whom I could guide in certain well selected channels."[36]

Coppola knew that film is a collaborative medium, even the writing of a screenplay. He gave McCarthy early pages from the screenplay before he had even finished writing. Between November 10 and December 27, when he turned in the next version of the script, Coppola cut for length and combined scenes. At the same time, McCarthy wrote a series of memos, ranging in length from three pages to nineteen, suggesting possible script changes. Many of McCarthy's comments concerned stage direction, but he also suggested eliminating scenes because of production costs. McCarthy's main concerns at the time were the use of foul language ("police, on profanity"), historical creditability (the early draft is littered with citations to pages of books that he wanted Coppola to consult to make the presentation more accurate), and the various markets for the film ("Germn mkt—use Nazi throughout when being derisive. Otherwise German"). He did fine-tune the section in the opening monologue when Patton explains that it is better for a soldier to get his enemy to die for their country than it is for the soldier to die for his, changing the phrasing for the better.[37]

McCarthy had three major concerns with Coppola's work. First, he wanted to develop Patton's personality more. To that end, he wanted to delete the mule-shooting incident. "It doesn't seem fair to Patton to introduce the subject of shooting the mules unless you indicate the circumstances." He also directed Coppola's attention to a quote from Eisenhower's memoirs that discussed Patton's "emotional tenseness." He told Coppola that passage "explains, more accurately than anything else I have read. That is why Marshall, Bradley, Eisenhower—and even Stimson and Roosevelt—put up with all Patton's derelictions." He wanted him to incorporate that observation in the script in some manner.[38]

McCarthy was also extremely worried about gender issues, and for good reason. There were no women characters in the script, and the female audience was huge and influenced the male audience. Would women buy tickets to see this production on their own? Would they even be willing to see the film with their boyfriends and/or husbands, or would they insist on seeing other pictures? "We need to introduce Mrs. P. in a better way, perhaps earlier, perhaps through Steiger," he advised Coppola. "Her influence should be more constantly and strongly felt. We must do some-thing for the ladies in this film. The Pattons' relationship was unusual + something should be made of it, although Mrs. P. never appears."[39]

The third matter that worried the producer was the slapping incident. In actuality, Patton struck two soldiers in two different army field hospitals. The film only used one, which was what McCarthy wanted. "To begin with, I should like to suggest that you use one slapping scene or the other, but not both. I also suggest taking the more violent and the rougher of the two, but don't try to combine them." Coppola had originally used both, but McCarthy knew one worked better dramatically, and he was also afraid of legal issues. In case there should be complications, he wanted to be in a position to say it was an accurate depiction of what had actually happened. He also wanted the scene in the hospital to be emotional in and of itself: "Build up for real tear-jerking effect." The script called for the hospital floors and sheets to be stained with blood. The producer liked these features. "Dwell on this a bit—have him speak to one or two + be deeply affected. Also audience should be moved." The idea was that when Patton slaps the cowardly soldier crying about his nerves, the incident would be all the more shocking. Yet McCarthy wanted to strike a balance: "Can't this scene be written in such a way that without condoning his action, audience will feel it might have done some [good]—at least men."[40]

One of the things that did not concern McCarthy or others at the time was the opening monologue. "I wrote the first scene by combining several of Patton's speeches," Coppola recalled. As a result, it was far more bloodthirsty than what actually made it on to screen. "At first, some of the executives at Fox thought the script was too 'strange,' and they objected to that opening among other things." The speech does much to establish the personality of the lead character, but it is a bit surreal. Coppola had Patton in full dress uniform wearing the four stars of a general, but when the film starts after the credits, the character is wearing the two-star rank of a major general. Coppola was right; the opening scene would indeed be the subject of contention, but those battles would take place later. At the time, the speech was not a matter in dispute.[41]

Every major figure involved in the production realized that Coppola had produced an impressive screenplay. "He wrote a very imaginative script. He really wrote a wonderful script," McCarthy stated. Richard Zanuck believed the script was something special. "My feelings regarding the second half of the Coppola script are identical with the way I felt about the first half, i.e., long, sprawling, at times confusing, but it is nevertheless very promising."[42]

McCarthy showed early pages of the November screenplay to Burt Lancaster. After having a phone conversation with the actor, McCarthy reported, "Burt said specifically that he likes the construction of the story and the direction in which it is moving. This represents a step forward, I feel, because he has always been concerned in the past about whether we could create a satisfactory dramatic structure for the property." Lancaster worried about some dialogue. While he thought the bombast of the opening scene made sense, he wondered whether it worked in other places. He also questioned the role of the Omar Bradley character. "In my opinion, Burt's comment is just about what one would expect from an actor," McCarthy observed. "Satisfied with story and structure, but eager to improve the character he is going to play. All this seems normal and healthy to me." Richard Zanuck agreed. "You're right, this is just about what was to be expected. I'm not at all disheartened by his attitude at this stage—as a matter of fact, I think it's very healthy." (Coppola, in his DVD commentary, thought that Lancaster hated his script.)[43]

Even Darryl Zanuck thought the script was excellent. "Have completed reading Patton and believe it is a remarkable first draft," he informed his son. "It is terribly overlength and contains many extraneous episodes that can easily be eliminated without destroying the basic line." He also believed that the film would be extremely expensive to shoot and that they should get Bradley to take a look at the script because he was basically a second lead. He closed by repeating his sentiment about the screenplay: "Coppola should be congratulated on a rough but outstanding first draft that has captured the spirit of Patton."[44]

McCarthy traveled to Paris, where the elder Zanuck was living, to get his input on the major revisions. The shadow head of the studio suggested that they use a narrator to reduce the script and provide a general narrative thrust. Both McCarthy and Zanuck thought that Bradley should be the narrator. This dramatic device would allow the Patton character to be as controversial as required while allowing the more rational views of Eisenhower and Bradley to emerge. The use of a narrator would also mute Patton's harsh statements about U.S. allies and other key figures. McCarthy suggested that the studio compensate Bradley by buying the film rights to his book. He figured Bradley's association with the production would bring about automatic cooperation from the Department of Defense. Zanuck also suggested a series of brief scenes in either Eisenhower's or Bradley's headquarters as messages about Patton's advance steadily arrive. These short shots were crucial because they would show that the man was a military genius. He wanted to use graphics, maps, and scenes in German headquarters to make the film more coherent; he also wanted to have the Germans speak in German with English subtitles. He liked the idea of using the general's actual poetry and thought that they should include more efforts like that to show the multifaceted personality of Patton. "Of course, we can compromise and make an obvious heroic Seventh Cavalry film with Duke Wayne and Hathaway[45] and probably do the kind of business they are doing on 'Battle of the Bulge,' but this is not good enough; we do not want an art house picture or anything resembling it, but I think that if we try hard enough, we can have a phenomenal box-office production as well as an art house triumph."[46]

Despite the enthusiasm that the studio executives had for Coppola's work, the screenwriter left the project in February 1966. He was eager to continue work on the Patton film, and the studio was in talks with John Huston about being the director now that Frankenheimer was no longer available. Huston wanted to write the screenplay. There was a real possibility that Coppola and Huston would share credit as the screenwriters, which would have been a big boost to the younger man's career. At the same time, Coppola had received an offer to direct You're a Big Boy Now, another screenplay that he had written. While McCarthy wanted to keep his writer, he sensed that Huston wanted to work with other writers. McCarthy also worried that if the studio kept Coppola under contract and cost him a chance to direct his first film, he might not have the same excitement for the Patton project that he had now. The producer wanted to wait until they had a firm deal with Huston, but he knew that Coppola's passion was in directing, and he did not want to stand in his way. "So I reluctantly recommend that we release him tomorrow," he told Richard Zanuck. "I agree," Zanuck noted on the margin of McCarthy's memo. The studio still wanted Coppola and worked out an agreement with his representation that the screenwriter/director would make himself available to Twentieth Century-Fox as a writer immediately after the completion of *You're a Big Boy Now* for possible revision work on the script. Before Coppola left the studio, McCarthy screened a film with him and arranged for him to meet Richard Zanuck.[47] The parting was on good terms and reflected well on the managerial style of both McCarthy and Zanuck.

In later years, Coppola has distorted the facts, claiming he was fired. "I was let go sort of in failure, and specifically I was let go because of the opening sequence," he stated later. "They told me they found the script very odd and this opening sequence which just begins with Patton in front of a big flag talking to the audience was totally strange." He cast his departure from the film as an issue of artistic integrity:

> Now, all you young people bear note that the things that you are fired for are often the things in later life that you are celebrated and given life-time achievements for. So, don't worry when you, you find that your are ideas are, are put down, it's just because they are new or they're, they're against the grain. And indeed, I was fired from *Patton* for the opening scene of the picture, which you all know and which has become a famous scene. So, a word to the wise.[48]

None of this distortion of the historical record changes the fact that Coppola's involvement in the project was crucial to the development of the film. When McCarthy rejoined Twentieth Century-Fox, he picked up right where he had left off. Despite the false start with Willingham, McCarthy had a screenplay that would ultimately prove to be crucial in the film's development, even if he did not know it yet. Coppola's departure was a harbinger of things to come. While 1965 had been good to him, McCarthy would find 1966 far more challenging, and the Coppola script would prove to be an important asset in surviving that rough year.

4. The Director

While the production of any motion picture is a group endeavor, it is no democracy. Frank McCarthy was clearly the driving force behind the project. He had kept it alive for years and he was far more influential in its making than any other individual associated with the final product. Despite that influence, he needed others to turn his dream into reality. His efforts to find a director nearly killed the project. The thing about film is that creating one is a group effort, and others stepped in and saved the Patton project.

In early 1965, Twentieth Century-Fox was talking to John Huston about coming on board as the director. "DZ feels, as I do," McCarthy informed the younger Zanuck, "that the most important single and immediate item is to get John to direct the picture." Huston was in the middle of his long and prestigious film career. An Oscar-winning director, he also wrote and did a good deal of acting, mainly in supporting roles. Twentieth Century-Fox was willing to offer him half a million dollars and the incorporation of his name into the title along the lines of *John Huston's The Life of Patton*. Darryl Zanuck met with Huston to discuss the film. "This is basically the story of a man named 'Patton,'" the studio executive later reported about the meeting. "It is not fundamentally the story of a War." As a result, the film would primarily be a character study. "We do not want to give the impression that we intend to avoid battles," Zanuck explained, "but our emphasis, particularly in the first half of the Patton story, is going to be based almost exclusively on this remarkable character who was probably the most unorthodox individual that ever wore a uniform."[1]

Zanuck and Huston thought about using some unconventional techniques in their narrative, including flashback scenes. "We do not intend to follow in chronological order the life or the career of Patton. We intend to be as unorthodox in telling the story as Patton himself was unorthodox."[2] Zanuck thought they could make a unique piece of art with this approach. "This is not the story of a conquering hero. This is the story of a strange man who did very heroic things and whose personal behaviour at times was utterly impossible. If we can capture this on the screen we will have emerged with something that is both fascinating, entertaining and unique. It will get away from the old cliché treatment of biographies."[3]

Zanuck also wanted an actor other than Burt Lancaster in the lead. He told McCarthy that Lancaster had lost his box office drawing power. He pushed two others for the part: John Wayne and/or George C. Scott. He wanted the two actors for different reasons. "There is no doubt but what Lancaster is the better actor but at the same time I believe the idea of Wayne is real boxoffice," he told his son. Scott, on the other hand, "is the exact age and physical resemblance to Patton and when you see him in The Bible you will see one of the great all time performances. In real life he is just as unpredictable as Patton was and yet he is capable of the most sympathetic scenes then can change in one second to savagery and wildness."[4]

Huston had worked with both actors on previous films. Neither experience had been a happy one. While shooting The Bible (1966), Scott had started an extramarital affair with his costar, Ava Gardner. When the relationship went sour, Scott had physically beaten Gardner. Another confrontation between the two occurred in a bar that the cast of the film frequented. In an effort to keep Gardner from getting hurt again, Huston intervened and grabbed Scott from behind, wrapping his arms around the actor's head. An enraged Scott grappled with his director, who was riding on his back, bouncing against the walls and furniture. It is a testament to Huston's interest in the project that he was even willing to consider working with the actor again. "When I suggested Scott to Huston," Zanuck reported, "he said that if he was available to do the picture he would get on his knees and plea for Scott." The director was willing to do so only for artistic reasons. "I have little use for Scott as a private person," he explained, "but my admiration for him as an actor is unbounded."[5]

John Wayne was a different matter. Huston made it clear that Wayne was unacceptable. He had directed the actor in The Barbarian and the Geisha (1958) and despised the man. The feeling was mutual. Wayne and Huston had clashed over politics—Huston was as liberal as Wayne was conservative—and filmmaking. The actor preferred structure, and Huston believed in extemporaneous adjustments. Huston made it clear he would never work with Wayne again.[6]

McCarthy had little problem with the director's objections. Wayne was Zanuck's idea, not his. He also thought Wayne was wrong for the role. In notes he wrote:

Lanc.

Controversy—[dual nature/violence-charm]—Elmer Gantry. Chance at great film complete differences.

On the next line he wrote:

Wayne—typical General—flatten out—leaving parts x [out]—hero impression. Good John Wayne film.[7]

Huston was also no fan of Coppola's work and wanted extensive revisions or an entirely new script. Zanuck had no problems with this requirement. Huston, however, soon left the film—only a month after Coppola. He had committed to doing two other films, and those took priority over the Patton project. As it turned out, one of those projects died and the other, *Waterloo* (1970), was made without him. In the end, Huston made no real contribution to the Patton production.[8]

Even as Zanuck was talking to Huston about the film, McCarthy was considering other directors as backups. One name he suggested in a meeting with Darryl Zanuck was William Wyler. "DZ looked quizzical and questioning but said 'Don't by any means write him off.'"[9]

Unlike Huston, Wyler had a significant impact on the Patton film. He nearly derailed the entire project. An Austrian immigrant to the United States, Wyler was one of the leading directors in Hollywood from the 1930s to the 1960s. He had won three Academy Awards for *Mrs. Miniver* (1942), *The Best Years of Our Lives* (1946), and *Ben-Hur* (1959). By 1966, he was nearing the end of his illustrious career. McCarthy knew Wyler was looking for another project to direct and thought he had found a topic that might be of interest to him. He met with the director to let him know about the property. According to McCarthy's account, Wyler raised the issue of *Patton*, and the two discussed the project for about half an hour. McCarthy said he avoided trying to sell Wyler on the film—the studio was still talking to Huston at this point—but as the director stated toward the end of their talk, "That is a picture I would certainly be interested in doing."[10]

Two weeks later, as it became clear that Huston was unlikely to take on the film, McCarthy approached Wyler again. A Hollywood veteran, Wyler knew how the business worked and that Huston was the studio's first choice, but he expressed interest a second time in the project. When Huston left, Wyler was offered the job and accepted it. The new director was, to use McCarthy's word, "dissatisfied" with the Coppola script. He requested a new screenplay, and McCarthy agreed. He described Coppola's script as "a serviceable but not brilliant first draft." Finding a new writer proved tougher than one might expect. McCarthy and Wyler went through a long list of names, including Truman Capote, James Clavell, Blake Edwards, Harlan Ellison, Nunnally Johnson, Stanley Kubrick, Norman Lear, Arthur Miller, Edmund North, Carl Reiner, Cornelius Ryan, Rod Serling, Aaron Spelling, and Gore Vidal. McCarthy ruled out some and found most of the others either previously committed or simply not interested.[11]

In the end, Wyler got James R. Webb to take on the writing duties. On paper—which is where writers live—Webb seemed like an excellent choice. He had a proven track record in the film industry and had written scripts for military pictures like *Pork Chop Hill* (1959). He also had won an Academy Award for his work on *How the West Was Won* (1963). Webb had also served in the U.S. Army in World War II and had actually met Patton.[12]

Webb decided to make the script his own. Although it appears that McCarthy wanted him to revise the Coppola script, the screenwriter decided to start anew. "There are very few scenes which can be called bad," he observed, but it was clear that its author had never served in the military. In the end, it seemed rather "dull" because there was "little or no suspense or buildup to a forceful climax." He wanted to put the triangular relationship of Bradley, Montgomery, and Patton at the film's forefront, casting Bradley as the man in the middle. Using the opening speech as the beginning of the film was wrong, but Webb thought he would probably keep it somewhere in the film. He also liked the scene where Patton complained about his lack of fighter cover, only to have a German air attack break up the meeting. He also intended to retain other scenes that Coppola wrote that showed the dichotomy of Patton's personality. One example was the general's frequent use of profanity but his deeply religious nature.[13]

In reality, though, Webb was the wrong man for the job. In 1942, he had been an aide to Major General Lloyd R. Fredendall, the commanding general of II Corps. In an incident that briefly made it into the final version of the film, Patton replaced Fredendall after the Germans defeated II Corps at the battle of Kasserine Pass. Webb went with Fredendall and spent the rest of the war running training units back in the United States; thereafter, he was something of an advocate for the general. In an understandable but unfair reaction, Webb blamed Patton for destroying his patron as well as his own military career. "I have had a little difficulty talking Webb out of his prejudice, but I think he will be the most objective man we could get, and fortunately he knows the language," McCarthy told a friend. He was also the only writer the studio could find who was interested in the project. Webb took the job reluctantly after Wyler recruited and personally lobbied him and after Twentieth Century-Fox offered him $200,000 ($1,346,777 in 2010).[14]

Webb's conflicted feelings were evident. He took much longer than ex-pected to produce his script, roughly a year. At 186 pages, it was also too long. He used flashbacks—much as Darryl Zanuck wanted—to develop Patton's character. He also made Patton's wife, Bea, and Pershing major figures in his account, and he included scenes set during the Mexican Ex-pedition of 1916 and World War I. Webb insisted on writing about inci-dents he had personally witnessed, made Fredendall a significant figure in the film, and even included himself as a character in one scene. Repeating gossip that had started back in North Africa, he blamed the death of Pat-ton's aide, Dick Jensen, on the general's order that helmets should always be worn with the chin strap fastened. He also ended the film with a mon-tage of episodes from the general's life.[15]

People at the studio were not exactly sure what to make of Webb's script. McCarthy and Wyler met to discuss the screenplay. According to McCarthy's notes, the director thought that the construction was solid and that the sequence of events built to a climax. The film, however, was episodic, which was the very thing the producer had found wanting in Coppola's draft. Wyler also thought the script was too long and would translate into a seven-and-a-half-hour film. Of these observations, Mc-Carthy wrote: "accurate." He personally thought the Coppola version was "lighter, more airy" and had more humor. Webb knew the military well but had gotten lost in the technical details of combat operations.[16]

Studio executives generally agreed with these views. Byron Sage wrote in a lengthy script evaluation, "It seems to me that this is a fine, practical script with solid basic construction." He noted that Webb had used a lot of Coppola's material and had done so with great skill. The problem was that Webb was a good storyteller, but Coppola was a better writer. "Some of the Coppola material, at times, came through with more vitality, especially in certain bits of dialogue." He thought that Webb should add more from Coppola's draft instead of using his own "rather heavy-handed" words. He also recommended cutting the Fredendall scenes and rethinking the use of the flashbacks—at least those that came early in the picture—because they tended to be confusing. Darryl Zanuck basically agreed with this assessment. "I find this Webb script far superior to Coppola script in conception and continuity. Some of Coppola[']s dialogue may be better and perhaps we can save some of it but Webb should certainly do the final job."[17]

In Hollywood, such ambiguity is usually deadly. In an action that spoke volumes, McCarthy wrote a sixty-nine-page analysis of the Webb script—roughly a third the length of the screenplay. Years later, after the film had been shot, McCarthy observed in an interview that Webb "delivered a script that did not—in our opinion—that is, the Zanucks' and mine—compare with the Coppola script." He told Webb to cut the Fredendall scenes, the material about interclass feuds of West Point graduates, and the flash-backs. McCarthy also encouraged Webb to use the dramatic Coppola opening and to inject more humor into the screenplay. He also warned Webb off from bashing the British. "Not only should we be fair to them, but we should bear in mind that Great Britain and the Commonwealth still constitute by far our largest audience outside the United States." Throughout the memo, he kept urging Webb to use more of Coppola's language.[18]

As McCarthy wrestled with the script, he lost Burt Lancaster. George C. Scott was now the first choice of Darryl Zanuck, but the studio head thought that there was little chance that Wyler would agree to this casting because of issues the two had on the set of *How to Steal a Million* (1966). Zanuck thought Lancaster was an acceptable choice as a backup. McCarthy talked to Lancaster and learned that he was still interested in the project and "enthusiastic over the idea of doing it with Willy." The agreement between the two had always been informal, and during the long script revision process, Lancaster's interest waned. When the revisions of the screenplay pushed shooting into 1968, Lancaster had finally had enough; he backed out of the project. It is hard to blame him. He had been patient, having expressed a steady interest in a Patton biographical film for seven years, a stance that suggests that his biographer, Kate Buford, was wrong when she wrote that *Patton* "was not his kind of project."[19]

The film needed a new star. McCarthy sounded out a number of actors, and all of them turned him down. In a moment of frustration, the producer wrote on a note pad:

These people turned down the Patton project:
Actors
Burt Lancaster
Lee Marvin

Rod Serling

John Wayne[20]

McCarthy wrote Rod Serling, but he meant the actor Rod Steiger. Serling was a screenwriter best known for his work on the television show The Twilight Zone. Steiger, the actor, later regretted passing up on the Patton role. "I'm not happy I didn't play Patton. I had a childish ego," he told a British newspaper. "I said I'm not going to glorify war. Maybe if I had done Patton just as well as Mr. Scott I might have got to play 'The Godfather.'" McCarthy's list was hardly inclusive. He had also considered Robert Mitchum, but he believed that the actor was too fat to play the role. McCarthy appears to have never considered one actor who badly wanted the role: Ronald Reagan. As an actor, Regan did not have the reputation to merit the role, and the timing was wrong anyway. He was moving seriously into politics, and as long as he succeeded in this arena, there was no chance of doing any more screen work.[21]

Wyler and Scott had worked together briefly on How to Steal a Million. At first the two had gotten along well, but then the actor failed to show for his first day of filming. He had been out drinking the night before and was still intoxicated. Wyler adjusted his shooting schedule, and when Scott finally showed up, the director asked him to wait until the takes for that day were done so they could discuss what had happened. Scott said he would wait in his dressing room, but when Wyler had finished filming for the day, the actor was gone. That was enough for the director. He quickly informed Twentieth Century-Fox that they needed to recast the role. "Willy told me instantly what happened," his wife explained. "He said, 'Once George's face is on the screen and we've got a week in the can, then what happens when he doesn't show up? Who are they going to replace, me or him?' So he stuck to his guns. He said, 'That's that.'" Scott was immediately fired.[22]

Three years later, though, Wyler was willing to consider working with Scott again. "Willy thought he was right for the role," Robert Swink, Wyler's longtime film editor, recalled. "In a sense, he cast Scott. He wanted him. Scott was Patton. He was better than Patton." With George C. Scott acceptable to Wyler, the studio approached the actor about taking the part. He expressed an appropriate amount of interest and asked to see the script.[23] Scott liked the Coppola draft but was less than thrilled with Webb's screenplay. He decided to pass on the project. "Scott was halfway on the hook on that script, but when he realized they wanted to do the second script, he said count me out," McCarthy explained later. "Suddenly I found myself with Wyler, the second script and without an actor."[24]

While Scott was considering the screenplay, Wyler was reconsidering his involvement with the film. His health was starting to fade, and he was less certain that he wanted to make a picture that would be as physically demanding as Patton, with its many outdoor scenes in temperatures that would range from the freezing cold to the boiling heat. Because most of the film was going to be shot in Spain, his wife was opposed to the idea. She was worried because Spanish food had made Wyler sick during a previous visit, and he was suffering from ulcers. The climate, the food, and the stress of working with Scott were too much for him to handle. "My wife absolutely refused to spend eight months in Spain. Maybe if I had been younger. The physical work, aside from the intellectual work, just was not worth it." He also had second thoughts about working with Scott.[25] "Now I had no actor and no director," McCarthy remarked.[26]

There is no way around the fact that Wyler did a good deal of damage to the development of a film about the life of Patton. He had mandated a new screenplay that the producer and most of the studio executives had strong reservations about. This delay cost the studio a year as well as two lead actors.[27]

The Patton project was close to dead. McCarthy diverted his attentions to producing the Walter Matthau comedy A Guide for the Married Man (1967). The Patton project might have died after the Wyler debacle had Richard Zanuck not intervened. He suggested that the studio give the directing job to Franklin J. Schaffner.[28]

In 1968, Schaffner was just reaching the peak of his career. He had just directed a monster blockbuster for Twentieth Century-Fox, Planet of the Apes (1968). "He wasn't the obvious at the time, ah, to do it, but I was convinced he would [bring] scope as well as significance to this project," Zanuck said in explaining his reasons for recommending Schaffner. "Having seen his work on Planet of the Apes, was tremendously impressed, and he brought that same talent to another very difficult piece, which was Patton."[29]

Schaffner had taken an odd path into the film business. Fred J. Koenekamp, who would work with the director on several films, said the most striking thing about him was his politeness. Schaffner was born in Tokyo in 1920 to missionary parents, but his father died six years later. "I scarcely remember him," the director told an interviewer. "I remember two or three incidents out of my childhood which are indelible, but he is an elusive figure in my life."[30]

His mother settled the family in Lancaster, Pennsylvania, a small city located in the southeastern corner of the state. After high school, Schaffner stayed in Lancaster, becoming the third generation of his family to attend Franklin & Marshall College. After graduating in 1942, he joined the U.S. Navy and was an officer on an amphibious ship. After the war, he moved to New York and began looking for almost any kind of job. He eventually found work as a fund-raiser for a nonprofit world peace organization, where he met his future wife. He also wrote the script for a radio show series titled *World Security Workshop*. This minor professional success convinced him that his future lay in radio, but he was unemployed for six months afterward. Eventually he found a job as an assistant director for *The March of Time* newsreel series. The problem with this job was that the day of the newsreel was coming to an end, and in 1948, Schaffner took a job with the CBS television network.[31]

At CBS, Schaffner found his niche. At first he did such a bad job covering a Brooklyn Dodgers game that the producer relieved him of his duties before the last out. Instead of directing sports programming, he ended up working on a number of news shows. After a year, he left the news division and began directing dramatic productions for a live CBS television program, *Studio One*. His first show aired in 1949 and was a disaster when an actor forgot his lines. Despite this poor beginning, the moving camera that would be a distinctive feature in his films was readily apparent. *Studio One* also marked the first time he worked with Charlton Heston. Schaffner directed television programs well into the 1960s, winning several Emmy Awards, but his best-known television project took him back into news.[32]

In 1962, Schaffner directed *A Tour of the White House with Mrs. John F. Kennedy*, which aired on all three of the networks then in existence. "It's always an interesting problem when you're fitting a radio mike to the first lady of the land," he wryly observed. The program consisted of Jacqueline Kennedy taking CBS correspondent Charles Collingwood on a tour of the White House that the average visitor to the executive mansion would experience. "What turned out to be about 45 minutes of tape that should have taken a minimum [of] three days to shoot, I think we did in one day," the director recalled with evident pride. The first lady spent seven hours on the set. President John F. Kennedy appeared in the special, but after viewing the film shot that first day, the president decided he wanted to do his segment over again. Schaffner was in the White House shooting various rooms from different angles to supplement the first lady's narration when he received a phone call informing him that the president wanted to do another take in forty-five minutes. "One never stops to consider in that circumstance. Ready or not you say, 'Yes, we'll be ready.'" The crew had to scramble to reposition lights and cables, and they had to figure out how to incorporate the president in the program because the first lady was not available for another take. "It worked, but it was the fastest 45 minutes of my life."[33]

The program featured long tracking shots that gave the viewer a sense of the building's size and physical layout. The program won an Emmy and a Peabody Award. Schaffner also won a Directorial Achievement Award from the Director's Guild of America for this program.[34]

The Kennedys and the White House staff were so impressed with Schaffner and the final product that they asked him to do other work for them. "As a result of that tour of the White House, they simply called me and said, 'Hey can you do this?'" The "this" Schaffner was referring to were televised speeches from the White House, including one on the state of the economy and another on October 22, 1962, in which the president revealed the presence of Soviet missiles in Cuba and announced that the United States would impose a naval blockade around the island to force their removal. "The principal function was trying to make him look effective and relaxed on camera," Schaffner recalled, "which had to do with the way he sat, if he sat, how he was lit, how he would move." The president was less than cooperative at times. "He would never wear make-up, but we'd always get the make-up on him at the last minute."[35]

Given this success, a move into film, where there was far more money than what Schaffner could make in television, only made sense. "It wasn't a pressing kind of 'Gee, I've got to do a film now!'" he explained. "It would just lay there in your mind but eventually you were going to have to make the transition, and the question was: 'Yeah, but when.'"[36]

For the third time, his initial directing work in a new medium went poorly. His first theatrical production was The Stripper (1963) for Twentieth Century-Fox. The film starred Joanne Woodward, the Academy Award–winning actress, and was based on William Inge's play A Loss of Roses. Those who saw the director's cut were impressed with Schaffner's work. "It was his vision, and they took it away from him. It was a good film," director George Roy Hill remarked. "He did a very good job on it." Schaffner was finishing the film just as Darryl Zanuck retook control of the studio. Zanuck had problems with cutting the part of an actress who the studio had under contract. What was her $30,000 ($217,727 in 2010) salary buying? The studio executive decided to edit the film himself. He "just lifted entire scenes," Schaffner explained, "which cut out what was in many ways the most appealing part of the picture—which was non-plot line, just color and character and that kind of thing." Zanuck reduced the amount of screen time that Woodward received, emphasized flesh in her striptease acts, and removed a scene in which her character attempted suicide. Richard Zanuck realized Schaffner's version was better than his father's. The elder Zanuck, however, was determined to make his mark on the film, and his version held. Critics abused the film in review after review.[37]

The next film Schaffner directed was The Best Man (1964), which was based on a Gore Vidal screenplay. Henry Fonda and Cliff Robertson play two presidential candidates with very different personal histories: one had a messy private life but was ethically clean in his public life, while the other was the reverse. "I've always said that out of all my films I am most fond of The Best Man, because it probably met up to about 80% of what my expectations for the film were going in," the director explained.[38]

Schaffner returned to television as he was wrapping up work on The Best Man, a move he made mainly for financial reasons. He directed a dramatic anthology series, the genre in which he had first made his name. The DuPont Show of the Week lasted only one season because situation comedies were earning better ratings than dramas. Schaffner was bitter at this outcome. "Television has failed miserably to keep pace with the modern complexities of our 20th century and will, if it does not soon recognize this problem, eventually be as passé as the nickelodeon." Before returning to film, he directed a live television special, John F. Kennedy, May 29, 1964. Televised on what would have been the president's forty-seventh birthday, the special featured interviews with his brother and wife as well as comments from a number of foreign leaders.[39]

His next film, The War Lord (1965), reunited Schaffner with Charlton Heston. The film was a historical epic. Heston had done well in this genre, starring in The Buccaneer (1958), winning an Oscar for best actor in Ben-Hur (1959), and playing the lead role in El Cid (1961), 55 Days at Peking (1963), and The Agony and the Ecstasy (1965). The magic ended with The War Lord. It was box office loser—the first for Heston in this genre, but the third film in a row for Schaffner.[40]

Schaffner then directed a spy thriller for Warner Bros. staring Yul Brynner, *The Double Man* (1968). The director also appeared in the film, making his only on-camera appearance in any of his movies. The film received strange praise from studio head Jack Warner. "Is this a one, two, or three piss picture," he asked the director during an advance screening. Warner explained when Schaffner said he had no idea about what he had been asked: "Well, if I get up and piss once, it's okay. If I go to piss twice, I'm losing interest." More would be a disaster. "If you see me piss three times, the picture's no good." Warner stayed in his seat throughout the screening. "See? Didn't piss once. Pretty good picture." It took Warner Bros. thirteen months to release the film. It was another flop.[41]

That result did not matter because it came out after *Planet of the Apes* (1968). This motion picture teamed Schaffner with Heston again. A monster commercial success, the film had taken years to produce. The biggest hang-up had been prosthetics. It took John Chambers, a makeup artist working at the studio, a year and a half to develop masks that looked real but allowed the actors to move their faces so they could act. In the end, 20 percent of the budget went to makeup. Even then, another question worried the studio: would the audiences take the presentation seriously, or would it seem absurd to watch an ape deliver lines in English? Richard Zanuck arranged for Schaffner to direct a screen test, but Heston was an established star in Hollywood with an Academy Award and thought screen testing was beneath him. In the end, both he and Edward G. Robinson agreed to do the test. The board of directors of the studio saw the short film, but approval came only after the commercial success of another science fiction production, *Fantastic Voyage* (1966). There were a number of unexpected problems; most revolved around the makeup. Robinson was having health problems that his ape wear only made worse. He left the production and was replaced by Maurice Evans, a British actor best known for his recurring role as Samantha's father on the television series *Bewitched*. In addition, certain camera angles exposed both the fake ape teeth and the human teeth underneath. The masks affected sound recordings and often looked fake when not in motion. At the end of shooting, Schaffner was $800,000 over his $5 million ($5,015,586 and $31,347,413 in 2010) budget. Studio executives looked at this motion picture with concern and confusion; was the film going to be a blockbuster or an enormous financial flop? "They were of the same nature as myself," the director explained. "They didn't know what they had, nor did I."[42]

Schaffner had many offers coming to him after the commercial success of *Planet of the Apes*, and he decided to go with the Patton project. "I found the whole fact of history being recorded through Patton's eyes honestly stimulating," he explained. The screenplay also stressed a theme that was present in most of Schaffner's work. "My interest has always been looking at guys who are out of place in their time and I do believe that Patton was out of place in his time with the exception of this two or three quarter year period." Such an individual, in the director's opinion, demanded examination: "Now somehow or another he stands out—at least in American folklore—above and beyond the rest of these chaps and that is what fascinates me in story telling, the why of that."[43]

He also saw the production as something of a challenge. "I wanted to see if a biography could be done objectively," he explained. "Hollywood's reputation with biographical films is not a very good one. Most of them were heavily romanticized (and often falsified) and featured a famous star playing the role tailored to his personality and not to the personality of the subject of the biography."[44] Such an approach was folly. "If you try to tilt with history—as so many Hollywood pictures have—you are going to come out with something that is unreal and unacceptable," he told a reporter in Texas. "I'll argue with anyone who says this is a war picture. This guy could have been a newspaper mogul or a banker, or a politician. The fact is he was a general who found his one just war."[45]

It was 1968. Seventeen years into the project, McCarthy had a director and two flawed scripts. He now needed to find an actor that could play the role and figure out what to do with the screenplays. He would solve both problems in a matter of days.

5. The Actor

While McCarthy and Twentieth Century-Fox finally had a director, they still needed a lead actor. The casting decision on the lead of any motion picture has an enormous impact on the artistic quality and themes of the film as well as with audience expectations given the reputation of the actor. With a biographical picture like *Patton*, where the lead is in almost every scene, that decision was even more crucial. McCarthy had provided the drive and Coppola the foundation, but George C. Scott was fundamental to both the artistic and commercial success of this film. He brought such artistic skill to this role that he, for all practical purposes, replaced George S. Patton Jr. as Patton in the minds of the American public.

In order to understand Scott's role in the film, it is necessary to explain how he became an actor. In 1968, George Campbell Scott was hitting his peak professionally, but the road he had taken to reach the pinnacle of American acting had not been an easy one. He was born in Virginia on October 18, 1927, but grew up in Michigan. His mother died when he was eight years old. Her loss was particularly difficult for Scott. He recalled spending much of his years growing up "being terrified of my father." Others disagree with this claim, leaving accounts suggesting that George Dewey Scott was an exceptionally busy business executive with little free time rather than a remote or uncaring man. Either way, in the end, it was Scott's older sister who played the role of a parent. "With a couple of exceptions," he remarked, "I was completely unloved. I owe much of my being alive to my sister, who more or less raised me. We were abnormally close." This limited type of emotional nurturing was less than ideal, a fact Scott readily admitted. "Since childhood, the whole self-loathing thing was a big part of my makeup."[1]

In high school, he played baseball, but a leg injury he suffered when a car hit him limited his playing potential. He was, however, a fan of the Detroit Tigers. As an adult, he dreamed of buying the team. His father remarried when the younger Scott was in high school and had two additional children, which appears to have alienated him further from his father.[2]

Scott graduated from high school in 1945 and enlisted in the United States Marine Corps. "I was very gung-ho," he stated later. World War II ended by the time he finished basic training. He had mixed feelings about the end of the war. "The greatest disappointment of my life was I was just about to leave Parris Island boot camp, we were on our way to Pendleton on the West Coast to start forming the Seventh Marine Division for the invasion of Japan, when they dropped the Bomb. You've never seen such disappointed people, because we knew we weren't going to get into the war." He spent the rest of his enlistment on burial detail at Arlington National Cemetery. "I count myself lucky that I missed seeing combat although I was terribly chagrined at the time I got out of the Marine Corps in 1949. The Korean War started in 1950 and half of my friends got killed in Korea. I was terribly fortunate. I missed two wars."[3]

He found his work at Arlington extremely depressing. "I was only a boy in my teens and the war had just ended, but the lost dreams and hopes represented by each burial in the cemetery were as real at the end as they had been at the beginning." His decision to handle these intense emotions with alcohol was almost natural. "You can't look at that many widows in veils and hear that many taps without taking to drink," he observed. The bottle eventually came to dominate his life. "I buried a lot of guys in Arlington cemetery and it began to get me down. I haunted sleazy bars in Washington. It was another ten years before I got to be a violent drunk, but I was drinking pretty good even then for a kid of eighteen."[4]

Unlike many problem drinkers, Scott admitted he had a problem. "I'm a drunk," he told a group of reporters in 1970 as he finished a beer and started on a martini. Controlling his problem was the real issue. "It used to be a major problem, but not any more," he explained. "I don't know why I started. Frustration with getting nowhere, I guess. And then, later, after things were breaking for me, finally after I was a success, well, ah, I had the problem then." The damage at this point had been done. "And once you got it, ah, you don't need any reason to continue. I quit completely once for two years. I had gotten to the point where it was ruining my life. When it gets to that stage, you know you have to quit. I've hit that situation only twice in the 12 years since I was in Alcoholics Anonymous."[5]

Despite the personal turmoil that he attributed to his service in the Marine Corps, Scott said he had no hesitation and would serve again if asked. "I think everyone owes a debt of service to his country," he explained.[6]

After leaving the corps, he enrolled at the University of Missouri and majored in journalism. He slowly discovered he had no inclination for life as a reporter. "I studied journalism very hard, and for me, very devotedly, and the more I got it, the more I realized I had no talent for it whatsoever." He found acting accidentally instead when he saw an announcement for auditions for the play *The Winslow Boy* on a bulletin board. He won the lead role. "I stole it. I stole it from great American movie actors," Scott said in trying to explain his immediate success. He believed he had simply absorbed acting talent from watching movies growing up in Michigan. "It was like tumblers falling in a lock. I knew what a good safe-cracker felt like. From then on, I never doubted my ability for a moment." He believed that acting was a natural talent. "Acting is unteachable. Some people have it and some people don't."[7]

Scott became a staff actor at the Stephens College Playhouse in Columbia, Missouri, while he continued his studies. His personal life was going well at least. He got married and had a child. He was honing his skills, and he appeared in 135 plays. Then things changed. He struck up a romance with Karen Truesdell, a Stephens College student, causing a scandal at the small school when they had a child out of wedlock. His marriage, unsurprisingly, fell apart, and he dropped out of Missouri, just a few units shy of graduating.[8]

Scott continued to pursue acting, performing in the traveling theatrical productions that transited the Midwest. Such work was infrequent and paid poorly. He lived with his father and stepmother for a time after his divorce. He drank constantly, briefly flirted with the film industry, and then gave up on acting altogether. He was homeless for a time, but then moved to Washington, D.C., where he lived with his sister and her husband and worked in his brother-in-law's construction business. He returned to acting with some evening work in community theater.[9]

In 1955, he remarried, and moved to New York to pursue a serious acting career on Broadway. It took Scott two years' worth of auditions before he began to work regularly as an actor. He paid his bills with a job at a Wall Street bank. The constant rejections at audition after audition drove him deeper into the bottle. Still, he tried to improve his skills. "During the depressing periods of most actors' lives, they sleep a lot," he observed. "I went to the movies. Movies kept me off the street and taught me everything I know."[10]

Eventually in late 1957, Scott landed the lead role in the New York Shakespeare Festival's production of *Richard III*. From that point to the end of his life, he would always be a working actor. Despite this success, his personal life was once again a disaster. His second marriage was breaking up, and he was drinking heavily. "The more successful I got, the worse the drinking became. I'd suffer blackouts and loss of memory. Life became a sort of crazy charade."[11]

A year after he landed the role of Richard III, he hit a significant low. While at a party, he got into a fistfight at the gathering and awoke the next day in jail, facing assault charges with no memory of the party, the fight, or his arrest. "I got scared," he remarked. "I was active in Alcoholics Anonymous for about two years. Drinking was not so much a craving for me as it was a habit. You begin to rely so much on a habit that it becomes a rhythm. If you get out of that rhythm, you're no longer helpless. But it's a lonely struggle."[12]

While fighting to control his drinking urges and staying sober, he married actress Colleen Dewhurst. They had met and started dating when both were married to others. Neither was a celebrity at the time, but their friends—and more importantly their spouses—knew about the affair. "Within that circle—and rightly so—George and I were looked upon by many as being not only scandalous, but in some ways reprehensible," Dewhurst reflected toward the end of her life. The two were conflicted about their romace. "We both bore guilt about the pain that we were certainly causing our spouses," she added. These qualms carried little weight in the end, and they started living together, even though their previous marriages had not yet ended. She helped him in his efforts to stay clear of the bottle. "Colleen was wonderful because she never pushed me," he observed. When both were free of their previous marriages—an issue complicated by the fact that Scott's wife was pregnant—they married.[13]

Despite this turmoil, the former marine was becoming an accomplished actor on the stage. He was never certain about how to approach his characters. "I'm an extremely cold actor," he reflected. "I don't feel that there's any necessity to have any kind of affinity for any part that you play except perhaps an intellectual affinity." Another time, he remarked, "It's never been difficult to subjugate myself to a part because I don't like myself too well. Acting was in every sense my means of survival." In a news interview, he explained that he never let himself think he was becoming the character. "Absolutely fatal," he stated with a scowl. "You would be torn in a thousand pieces. I believe in *acting* the part. Good acting is the illusion of being."[14]

The basics of creating that imaginary figment were quite simple to Scott. "Look, acting is just a matter of observation, imitation and communication," he told one reporter. "That's what it is all about." Good acting required skill. "Technique is making what is absolutely false appear to be totally true in a manner that is not recognizable. The moment you can see how it's being done, it's no good." He feared that the cult of celebrity that often accompanies those in the acting profession worked against this skill. "The great danger for most actors is that the more successful they become, the less risk they will take with their careers. They forget why they became actors in the first place. They become successful personalities instead."[15]

Scott's first love was the stage. His relationship with the film industry was an ambivalent one. "Film is not an actor's medium," he explained. "You shoot scenes in order of convenience, not the way they come in the script and that's detrimental to a fully developed performance. There's the terrible tedium and boredom involved in waiting around for the camera to be set up, and then you have to turn on and off when they do the scene over again. When you see the rushes is the first time you begin to judge your performance. If you get 50% of what you hoped for you're lucky." Why, then, did he make any films at all? "I make movies for financial reasons, and this allows me the luxury of acting on Broadway."[16]

His first role in a motion picture came in *The Hanging Tree* (1959), but this was a small supporting role, and audiences largely ignored his performance. He found the stop-and-start nature of filming incredibly frustrating and difficult to act in. While making his second picture, Jimmy Stewart taught him a new acting technique. Stewart would stay in character and read lines to other actors when he was off camera so that his colleagues would have a cue to respond to while they were delivering their lines. Scott was impressed and adopted this courtesy to his fellow actors in his subsequent films.[17]

By the time Scott began talking to McCarthy about the role of George S. Patton Jr., he had just become a major player in the film industry. He received an Academy Award nomination for best supporting actor for his work in *Anatomy of a Murder* (1959). The Academy, however, chose to give the Oscar to Hugh Griffith (Ben-Hur), a defeat that wounded Scott deeply. That same year, he was nominated for a Tony Award for his role in the Broadway play Comes a Day. He lost that prize as well. Two years later, he received another Oscar nomination for his role in The Hustler (1961). He tried to decline, but the Academy paid him no heed. He disliked the marketing and publicity campaigns, believing they cheapened the honor. He lost again, this time to George Chakiris, who won for his role in West Side Story (1961), but Project Hope (1961), a documentary that George D. Scott's corporation had sponsored, won. In a telegram, the actor told his father, "IF ONE OF US HAD TO WIN I'M GLAD IT WAS YOU."[18]

Scott followed with a series of plays, then delivered one of his signature roles that lives on in U.S. Air Force ready rooms around the county, General "Buck" Turgidson in director Stanley Kubrick's Dr. Strangelove (1964). Scott based the role not on General Curtis E. LeMay, as so many people believe, but on a work associate of his father's back in Detroit. He delivered some memorable lines: "I'm not saying we won't get our hair mussed. I'm saying ten to twenty million people killed—tops—depending on the breaks." The film was a success, and Scott's performance kept him from being typecast as a villain.[19]

To Scott, the difference between a good film and a bad film was the director. With that point made, he believed there were significant limits to the input the director could make. "The important thing about directing . . . is creating an atmosphere in which people work well together. That's what it's all about." A good director often makes an actor better. "By knowing the actor's personality and gauging his strengths and weaknesses, a director can help him to overcome specific problems and realize his potential. But I think this aspect of directing is generally overemphasized."[20]

Directors who were familiar with both stage and screen found that Scott had an intensity about him. "It's a concentrated fury, a sense of inner rage, a kind of controlled madness," José Ferrar, the actor/director, explained. Richard Lester said Scott was "intelligent, constructive, decent, professional. If there was a difference of opinion between us, we worked it out in five or ten minutes."[21]

His relationship with Stanley Kubrick was different. The director preferred performances that were unnatural and hysterical; he had Scott deliver in this manner on Dr. Strangelove by making the actor repeat his performances again and again. What made it into the final version of the film were the most manic moments in a series of takes. Kubrick kept Scott in check off camera with a regular chess game the two played. The director had at one time been a New York chess hustler, and he quickly assessed his actor as a weak player who thought he was better than he really was. He beat Scott regularly. "This gave me a certain edge with him on everything else," the director later told a writer. "If you fancy yourself a good chess player, you have an inordinate respect for people who can beat you." After the film's release, the actor was less than pleased with what he saw. Kubrick recorded several rehearsals that Scott thought were nothing more than acting exercises, which did not reflect well on him. He vowed never to work with the director again. And he never did.[22]

Despite his intense talent, the insecurity and frustration that fueled his rage and drinking damaged others. Before he died, he had been married five times to four women, and he admitted that he had cheated on all of them. In one notorious episode, he had an affair with Ava Gardner during the filming of The Bible (1962). "That was a bad, bad relationship," a friend of Gardner's stated. "He was not good for her. And she was bad for him."[23]

"So what was the problem?" Gardner wrote in her memoirs. "The problem, honey, was booze."[24]

Gardner was starting to drink heavily herself, which lit the spark for what would follow. "She got him drinking again," a friend of hers remarked. The two were in a passionate affair and were inseparable both on and off the set. Then, in a hotel in Avezzano, Spain, where they were filming some scenes, the two lovers got into an intense, alcohol-fueled argument. Gardner decided to leave. "When George got drunk he could go berserk in a way that was quite terrifying," she stated. Scott was having none of it, and he charged at her as she tried to leave. He then punched her in the side of the head, sending her down into a spiral onto the floor. Scott pinned Gardner down and hit her again and again. The beating ended only when he left the room. The bruising to her face required extra work on the part of the makeup department to hide her injuries. Word of what happened quickly spread throughout the crew. Director John Huston was disgusted, but he was too far into shooting to replace Scott and had to tolerate this behavior. Huston later called Scott a "shitheel." When asked in a 1985 interview—long after his brief flirtation with Patton was over—if he would ever consider working with Scott again, Huston's reply was direct: "No."[25]

Wyler was even less tolerant of Scott's behavior. When the actor arrived on the set of *How to Steal a Million* five hours late because he was sleeping off a drinking binge, Wyler had the studio fire him.[26] Despite this baggage—and the fact that Twentieth Century-Fox had fired him once before—the Zanucks and McCarthy were willing to have him involved with *Patton.* "I—never considered anyone except Lancaster until Darryl Zanuck—I went to an early screening of *The Bible* in which Scott played Abraham—turned to me and said, 'There's your Patton,'" McCarthy recalled. After Lancaster left the project, the producer contacted Scott, gave him a copy of the Webb script, and offered him the part. Scott turned McCarthy down. After talking to a number of other actors, including Steiger, the producer learned that Scott had read Coppola's screenplay and would play the part if the studio used that script.[27]

McCarthy agreed. Scott was a major star, and the studio agreed to pay him $600,000 ($3,761,689 in 2010) for the film. "I think to have gone with anybody else would have been madness," Schaffner stated. His reasons for making that observation: "Scott, I think, particularly is—uh—has brilliance coming off the screen." He went into detail in supporting this view: "George Scott precisely right for it; the interest, one, in the character; an overwhelming interest in the character; the resourcefulness to play the character; the energy to make the character live; the fanaticism to make the character acceptable and unacceptable; the talent that he has for vulnerability in a character as Patton was; and uh, I think the grace and the humor—all of these combinations made him absolutely perfect casting for it." The studio signed Schaffner and Scott on the same day.[28]

Why was Scott interested in Patton? There were many reasons. "He was a professional," the actor explained, "and I admire professionalism." There was more to it than that, though. Hitting on a major theme of the film, he explained, "But foremost, about Patton, I believe this was an individual in the deepest sense of the word. And the beauty of the individual soul and the individual personality is the message, isn't it." After shooting ended, he told a reporter that what he liked about his character was "the uniqueness of him possibly more than anything else."[29]

Because of Scott's preference for the Coppola screenplay, McCarthy went looking for another writer yet again. "Coppola's script was effulgent, imaginative, airy, really awful good, but in needed some restructuring. We lined up Ed North, who is a very good writer and craftsman. He took the Coppola script and worked it to the point where it had more cohesion and hung together better, and had a much more workable dramatic structure."[30]

The Ed North that McCarthy was referring to was Edmund H. North, a well-respected screenwriter. North had started in Hollywood in the 1930s, writing musicals and romantic comedies. His second film was *One Night of Love* (1934), which received several Oscar nominations, including best picture, best director, and best actress. He worked steadily in film until World War II. He served in the U.S. Army Signal Corps, obtaining the rank of major. It took him a while to reestablish himself in the film industry, but in the early 1950s, a number of his scripts became notable films, including *Young Man with a Horn* (1950) starring Kirk Douglas, and the science fiction classic, *The Day the Earth Stood Still* (1951). His career began to slow down again in the later part of the decade until he wrote the screenplay for *Sink the Bismarck!* (1960). The success of this film boosted his career, and he acquired the reputation as a writer of war films. Another of his better-known films was *Damn the Defiant* (1962). His career began to slow down yet again in the mid-1960s, and he wrote some scripts for television programs set in World War II. He was active in the Writers Guild of America, West, and served as president of that union's screen branch.[31]

North's assignment was not to write a screenplay but to revise Coppola's existing work, and that is exactly what he did. "What the script needed was structure and direction. That's really what I was brought in to do. What we tried to do was keep the best of the Coppola material and take off from that and construct a story," he stated. He respected Coppola's work. His "contribution was as large as it was obvious, and we made every effort to retain the many brilliant things in his script. In addition, his basic approach to the material was the correct one—and that is no mean contribution."[32]

Even though Coppola and North were listed as coauthors of the screenplay, the two never met. In his DVD commentary, Coppola called him "Mr. Edmund North" as a sign of both respect and distance. "I never worked with him. I never had the pleasure of really collaborating with him," Coppola explained. North turned in a revised version of the screenplay in July 1968. He removed a story line about the attempted rescue of Patton's son-in-law from a German prisoner of war camp. Coppola noted that North did most of the historical research and made the film accurate. "He focused really working with the director on really making some of the history related to the actual battle scenes and perhaps some of the historical situations more accurate."[33]

Scott had made his participation in the production conditional on the script. As a result, he needed to be consulted. There was no stipulation in his contract for such approval, but it was a commonsense move on McCarthy's part. According to Schaffner, he and McCarthy met with Scott three times. These conferences amounted to the two listening to the actor's concerns about developing his character and wanting to transpose certain scenes. The meetings ranged from two and a half hours to four. "That was the extent of our script conferences with Scott. That was it."[34]

During the fall of 1968, McCarthy, North, David Brown, and the Zanucks held a series of conferences to work out the final version of the screenplay. Most of the changes from Coppola's screenplay to the shooting script occurred during these meetings. Some of the changes were, as Coppola suggested, designed to make the picture more historically accurate. For example, North changed the type of planes that appeared on screen, based on the machines that the studio found available for rent. He also had to do some more pruning. He eliminated all references to Patton's son-in-law, John K. Waters. North also pared down the time the Captain Steiger character appeared on screen. In addition to being a commentator on Patton, Steiger had a significant story line as a leader of the July 20, 1944, plot to kill Hitler and a suspected Jew who must prove himself and ends up dying in combat. North eliminated this part of the script. Coppola originally had Steiger working out of a futuristic, highly electronic map room. Much of *Sink the Bismarck!*, an earlier North film, took place in a control center, and he changed the setting to a far more mundane one, with paper charts and physical displays.[35]

Coppola invented the device of having a moving ticker at the bottom of the screen report on German casualties, much as one sees on cable news programs or at Times Square in New York. Since these figures had little to do with the scenes that were taking place above, the filmmakers changed this to a series of quick cuts to the German map room, which got the same information across. North had every historical character introduced with subtitles that listed his name, rank, and position. He also ended the first half of the movie with the general saying of the soldier he slapped, "I wish I had kissed the sonuvabitch."[36]

North was no ghostwriter, though. There was more to his job than simply refining his Coppola's script, even if it was his foundation. He added material about the Buchenwald death camp that never made it into the film. He wrote two other scenes that made it into the film's final cut: the scene in Morocco, and the one showing Patton's confrontations with the Soviets after the end of the war. He also created the lighthearted moment when both Montgomery and Rommel say "damn" when they are informed that Patton has reached Palermo. (In an early version of the script, it was Colonel General Alfred Jodl, not Rommel, who makes the remark.) He also gave Patton the line, "Rommel, you stupid bastard, I read your book." In the film, the word "magnificent" replaced "stupid."[37]

McCarthy was a little wary of the fifth scribe he had work on the film. He called North "a very good, straight forward writer." He got the impression, though, that North was trying to rewrite enough of the screenplay so that he could claim sole authorship of the script according to the formula that the writers' union had negotiated with the studios. "That was a constant point with North," McCarthy told a seminar at the American Film Institute several years later.[38]

A bigger problem arose with Darryl Zanuck. He had been McCarthy's biggest asset in making the film. About this time, Zanuck inserted himself into the creative process in a counterproductive manner. In meetings in France, he insisted on making a series of changes that made no sense. He wanted the death of Patton's aide, Richard Jensen, removed, but he also insisted that his funeral remain in the film. A funeral without an explanation would have been rather confusing. McCarthy agreed to all Zanuck's suggestions at the time, but then later refused to make them. The studio executive responded by canceling the film. A confrontation quickly developed between the Zanucks, and the father backed down.[39] The elder Zanuck might have lost the *Patton* battle, but his grievances with his son continued to fester. The ramifications would become significant in a few years.

During this time, McCarthy even consulted General of the Army Omar N. Bradley. The producer changed some of the dialogue at the general's request. This consultation was the beginning of Bradley's association with the production, which would become more significant in a few months.

One of the major battles fought in a series of script conferences held throughout the second half of 1968 was over the opening monologue. A major effort in the revision process, given Scott's admiration for the original script, was to add as much of Coppola's dialogue as possible; but almost everyone involved in the film—McCarthy, Schaffner, North, Bradley, and even Scott—wanted to move away from the Coppola introduction. There were a number of reasons for wanting to make this change. Scott respected Coppola's work, but he was not sure he could equal the perform-ance: he thought that the film would start off on too strong of an emo-tional high. Others worried about timing. Bradley was worried that several lines would damage U.S. standing in the world. The only person who liked the opening dialogue was Darryl Zanuck. In this battle, the results were different. He carried the day.[40]

McCarthy wanted to make a motion picture that was historically accu-rate, and although by the standards of the film industry he was a World War II expert, he wanted a set of fresh eyes. He turned to Paul Harkins again and had him take a look at the screenplay. The general was eager to provide this service. He made several comments. When the screenplay de-scribed the Pasha of Marrakech as a "chubby" man, Harkins observed: "He was tall & lean." At this point in the production, Harkins was to have been a character in the film. "I did not go to Tunisia with him," he ex-plained. He also caught factual errors about which units performed which actions. Not all of the four-star general's commentary was the type that McCarthy wanted to hear. When Harkins read the opening scene and saw that Patton would appear in his dress uniform, he noted, "He never ap-peared in public in this uniform." He also added: "3 stars never 4 on pis-tols." When Patton admits he is a prima donna and the difference between himself and Montgomery is that he is willing to make that admission, Harkins observed, "I don't think Gen. P would say this either." He also picked up on the Don Quixote theme that Coppola had injected into the screenplay three years earlier. "No relation between Don Q + Patton."[41]

The third revised screenplay was dated December 10, 1968, and Mc-Carthy again consulted with Scott. These remarks coming at the begin-ning and end of the process gave his input the nature of advice and confirmation. His comments, preserved in McCarthy's handwritten mar-ginal notes, show that the actor was more concerned about tinkering with dialogue—adding even more of the original Coppola—than making sub-stantive changes to major themes of the film. There were, however, some scenes that the actor wanted to add. McCarthy sent the younger Zanuck a memo about the changes Scott wanted. One of these was deleting the opening monologue. Zanuck's response was blunt: "NO." Although he agreed to some of the requested changes, few of them ended up in the fi-nal version of the film. The reason was fairly simple: at 155 pages, the script projected into a film over three and a half hours in length. Zanuck explained the problem with changing the script at this point: "The only way we can add these things is by subtracting others."[42] Scott got more Coppola dialogue but changed few of the scenes.

George C. Scott played a crucial role in the making of *Patton*, but primarily as an actor. His input into the script was significant but limited. He was the primary force responsible for bringing Francis Ford Coppola's script back into use. He had little voice in the detailed wordsmithing that dominated the second half of 1968, but this effort never would have happened without Scott and his small but important contribution. Coppola's script was the foundation for the success of the film. McCarthy was on the verge of having a script, a director, and an actor lined up and ready to start shooting, but fate intervened one more time. This time it came in the person of Omar N. Bradley.

6. The Field Marshal

General of the Army Omar N. Bradley emerges as a hero in *Patton*, and that is no accident. His participation demonstrated the ties of the military-industrial complex in areas that one might not imagine. The results were also unexpected because it was Bradley, rather than the studio, who got manipulated.

During World War II, Bradley developed the reputation as the "GI general," a brilliant general who was a plain, soft-spoken, down-to-earth, humble man, lacking the ego so manifest in others like George S. Patton Jr. He dressed like, and sympathized with, the common soldier. This reputation was largely the work of syndicated newspaper columnist Ernie Pyle, who coined the phrase "G. I. general." Pyle wrote, "The outstanding figure on this western front is Lt. Gen. Omar Nelson Bradley. He is so modest and sincere that he probably will not get his proper credit, except in military textbooks. But he has proved himself a great general in every sense of the word." Pyle also added, "Having him in command has been a blessed good fortune for America."[1]

It is a great reputation, but one that is largely undeserved. "The GI's were not impressed with him," the military historian S. L. A. Marshall, a general himself, declared. "They scarcely knew him. He's not a flamboyant figure and he didn't get out much to the troops. And the idea that he was idolized by the average soldier is just rot."[2]

Omar Nelson Bradley grew up in Missouri and started his military career when he attended the United States Military Academy. "The four years I spent at West Point were among the most rewarding of my life. I loved every minute of it," he remembered. He was a member of the class of 1915, which became known as "The Class the Stars Fell On" because roughly a third of them became generals. He earned varsity letters in baseball and football. He was part of the 1914 team that went undefeated but hurt his knee during the season. The injury plagued him for the rest of his life. Dwight D. Eisenhower and Bradley had been classmates and were even in the same cadet company, but they were not particularly close then and did not keep in contact with one another over the course of their military careers. They occasionally saw each other at class reunions, but their wives disliked one another, and that limited the chances of them building a friendship.[3]

Like Eisenhower, Bradley encountered much frustration in his early military career. He saw no combat duty in World War I. He was an instructor of one sort or another for thirteen of his first twenty-one years in the army, including a return to West Point and another teaching ROTC at what is now known as South Dakota State University. During his time at West Point, he began studying military history and the biographies of generals who emphasized maneuver.[4] He was never a master of this type of warfare, but this course of study helped prepare him for what would come later in his career.

The key to his later advance came not through his West Point connections, but from the four years he spent at Fort Benning. From 1929 to 1933, he was an instructor at the Infantry School, where the assistant commandant in charge of academics, Lieutenant Colonel George C. Marshall, was implementing profound morale and intellectual changes in the school and, indirectly, the U.S. Army. "My association with Marshall began during this tour at Fort Benning and, with brief gaps, continued for more than two decades. No man had a greater influence on me personally or professionally."[5] Frank McCarthy could easily have said the same thing.

In 1941, lightning struck. Marshall, now chief of staff of the U.S. Army, made Lieutenant Colonel Omar Bradley commandant of the Infantry School. Bradley jumped at the opportunity because the position was normally the job of a brigadier general. When Bradley and his family arrived back at Fort Benning, a telegram was waiting announcing that the U.S. Senate had approved his promotion to that rank. He had skipped over the rank of colonel and was the first member of his West Point class to become a general officer. "I had half suspected the honor, but the reality of it floored me." Six months later, Marshall gave him command of the 82nd Division. The news caught his breath because it included another promotion, this time to the rank of major general.[6]

World War II was a better war for Bradley than World War I, although his first deployment in North Africa was rather undefined. His job was to act as Eisenhower's "eyes and ears." It was odd duty. Eisenhower initially had another general doing the same work, but Marshall wanted Eisenhower to give the job to Bradley. "I was not overjoyed at my assignment," he conceded in his memoirs. Bradley doubted he would have much influence and would be bitterly resented. It was during this posting that he renewed his acquaintance with George S. Patton Jr. Never fond of Patton, he came to see his former neighbor as an able commander, but one with a questionable approach to leadership. Patton, for his part, did not want a spy in his command and had Bradley assigned to II Corps as his deputy commander.[7]

Bradley was ambitious in his own right and wanted command of II Corps for himself—a point he made in his first set of memoirs. Bradley did not like it when Patton biographers picked up on this rivalry because it ran counter to his reputation as the down-to-earth GI general that he had earned in the war. "Nothing could be further from the truth," he wrote in his second set of memoirs. "The fact of the matter is that not in Tunisia, nor ever did I feel a 'professional rivalry' with George Patton, or any sort of jealousy."[8]

While on this assignment, Bradley was nearly killed twice. He was only fifteen feet away when Patton's aide, Dick Jensen, was killed by a Luftwaffe strike on a forward command post. (This incident is depicted accurately in *Patton*.) Bradley took over from Patton as II Corps commander and led this unit in the Tunisian and Sicilian campaigns. "I gave my division commanders broad objectives but usually left the details of achieving these objectives up to them," he stated. He also regularly visited the front lines. "I visited each division commander at his CP and usually went up to the front with him to study the terrain and enemy positions firsthand, and to show the GI's that their commander was no rear-echelon tent hog." During one of these trips, he was nearly killed a third time, this time by enemy artillery fire.[9]

As a professional officer, Bradley acknowledged that the U.S. Army had much to learn about fighting. The British had forced operations in North Africa on the United States. In his memoirs, Bradley acknowledged, "On reflection, I came to the conclusion that it was fortunate that the British view prevailed, that the U.S. Army first met the enemy on the periphery, in Africa rather than on the beaches of France. In Africa we learned to crawl, to walk—then run. Had that learning process been launched in France, it would surely have—as Alan Brooke argued—resulted in unthinkable disaster." While he admitted that the Americans had much to learn, the British were not going to be of much use in the learning process. "The

British had fought a long, hard, costly battle across North Africa, and I admired their courage and battlefield expertise. But I was not convinced that they were infallible or as good as their press notices." In particular, he noted that Montgomery's efforts against Rommel "'lacked vigor and imagination'; it was more akin to moving trench warfare than the fast, open maneuvering of Sherman or to the German blitzkrieg personified by Rommel himself in his better days." He confessed that he had grown on the job and gotten better. He nonetheless harbored profound reservations about Eisenhower. "Ike was too weak, much too prone to knuckle under to the British, often." He decided he would have to be more forceful in advancing American interests when it came to differences in deciding which strategy the coalition should pursue. Still, something had to be done about the morale of the U.S. Army. American soldiers showed an "unwillingness or reluctance to reconnoiter, maintain contact with and aggressively close the enemy." By the time the allies had taken Sicily, he thought the U.S. Army had become a much better fighting force. "We had learned a great deal more about fighting a war."[10]

While in Sicily, he received command of the First U.S. Army, making him the ground commander for the D-Day invasion. Eisenhower told him of his assignment in person. "I could not have been more stunned or elated. It was going to grow into the most important combat job in the U.S. Army in World War II. No soldier could have wished for more." This position would have been Patton's had it not been for the slapping incidents. American soldiers, however, might have been better off with Patton in command on D-Day. The United States took heavy casualties, and the Germans came close to breaking the assault on the beach code-named Omaha. At one point, Bradley considered evacuating from the beachhead. In the 1970s, he wrote, "Even now it brings pain to recall what happened there on June 6, 1944." In *A Soldier's Story*, Bradley revealed, "I was shaken to find that we had gone against Omaha with so thin a margin of safety." Late in his life, Bradley publicly admitted that his allies had done a better job. "The combined sea and air attacks in the British sector were far more effective than those in the American sector."[11]

How did this happen? The blunt answer is that Bradley was timid during the planning process. He tried to combine two conflicting military amphibious doctrines: one that used the cover of darkness without much firepower, and one that used heavy firepower during a daylight assault. The British had used the first in the Mediterranean, and the U.S. Navy and

Marine Corps had used the latter in the Pacific. American troops were going to take on fortified positions in daylight without significant airpower or naval artillery. Bradley was reluctant to challenge his superiors and advance reservations and concerns up the chain of command. He had no hesitation, however, in relieving his subordinates from command, particularly if they were new to their positions and units. Patton, for his part, had profound reservations about this approach. "Bradley and [VII Corps commander Major General Lawton] Collins are too prone to cut off heads. This will make division commanders lose their confidence. A man should not be damned for an initial failure with a new division."[12] Patton was basically right. Bradley's approach made many commanders averse to taking risks and unimaginative.[13]

In an ironic twist, Bradley was not one to take risks himself, and this conservatism caused him to miss opportunities. Patton noticed this trait. After a dinner Eisenhower had with several of his generals before D-Day, Patton noted, "As usual, Bradley said nothing. He does all the getting along and does it to his advantage."[14]

As this comment indicates, Patton and Bradley were not particularly close. In France, even though he was senior, Bradley still called Patton "sir." Nor was there much of a bond with Eisenhower. Montgomery, on the other hand, was a bitter rival. Bradley disliked him even before the British field marshal publicly denigrated his command ability in a press conference after the Battle of the Bulge. "There was no 'chemistry'; our personalities simply did not mesh," Bradley declared. "He left me with the feeling that I was a poor country cousin whom he had to tolerate."[15]

Bradley's career advanced even after the fighting ended when President Harry S. Truman asked him to serve as the administrator of veterans affairs. When he first learned of this assignment, he was devastated because he considered the job meaningless. The general accepted this position, but only after Truman personally assured him that he would not lose his rank or pay as a four-star general, and a promise that he would be named the next chief of staff of the U.S. Army. The president made the announcement personally. "On hearing the news, the reporters were as stunned as I had been. The official transcript of the press conference notes 'low whistles and exclamations,'" Bradley observed after the war. Truman, as good as his word, named Bradley to this position in late 1947. He assumed office early in the new year.[16]

Serving as the chief of staff of the U.S. Army with the four stars of a general should have been the culmination of Bradley's military career. After only a year and a half—the normal tenure for a chief of staff is four years—Truman selected Bradley to become the first chairman of the Joint Chiefs of Staff. (Fleet Admiral William D. Leahy had held this position in World War II, but on a temporary basis. Congress passed legislation making the position permanent in 1949.) With the outbreak of the Korean War in 1950, Truman decided to give Bradley a fifth star, promoting him to the rank of general of the army. Congress passed the required legislation authorizing this new rank, and on September 22, 1950, the president of the United States personally pinned the new rank on Bradley's epaulets. Bradley had become the last American "field marshal."[17]

The quality of Bradley's leadership in this post is open to much debate. He supported Truman without hesitation in the confrontation with General of the Army Douglas MacArthur. Expanding a war to fight the People's Republic of China would be, as he told Congress, "the wrong war, at the wrong place, at the wrong time, and with the wrong enemy." He had no trouble, however, bending rules and regulations when it suited him. During the Berlin Blockade, he had his son-in-law, a pilot in the U.S. Air Force, assigned to duty in Washington rather than in Germany, where he was stationed at the beginning of the crisis. He also published his wartime memoirs, A Soldier's Story, while he was still on active duty. Both Montgomery and Eisenhower thought this decision was ethically questionable. Eisenhower told Montgomery that Bradley "was a little bit touched in the head."[18]

The U.S. Army adopted many of its traditions from the British Army, and one of them was that five-star officers never officially retire. As a practical matter, however, Bradley's military career ended when he stepped down as chairman of the Joint Chiefs of Staff. In retirement, Bradley moved to Beverly Hills, California, and went to work with the Bulova Watch Company, initially as the head of its research and development division. When Arde Bulova died, the directors elected Bradley chairman of the board. He also served on the board of a half dozen other companies. Almost immediately after his retirement, his son-in-law died in a plane crash. The Bradleys suddenly had their daughter and four grandchildren living with them as they dealt with their loss and sorrow. After Lee Bradley remarried and moved to Washington, D.C., her parents followed in 1957. In the fall of 1965, Bradley's wife became ill. Her doctors diagnosed her with leukemia, and she died before the end of the year. The general was devastated and felt totally alone.[19]

His life changed dramatically a few months later when he met Kitty Buhler. A former newspaper reporter, she had turned to writing for film and television. Buhler had modest success, authoring the screenplay for the film China Doll (1958), and working on several television programs like Dragnet, The Untouchables, and My Three Sons. She bought the film rights to Bradley's book and worked on this project off and on for ten years. She interviewed the general repeatedly, and in 1966, the two married. The second Mrs. Bradley was an intense guardian of her husband's reputation. She was key in creating the Omar N. Bradley Museum at Carlisle Barracks, where his uniforms and medals went on display. After two years of living in Washington, Bradley and his new wife returned to Los Angeles, where they entertained a host of celebrities, including Bob Hope, Elvis Presley, Ronald Reagan, and Jimmy Stewart. The general enjoyed mixing with these stars, and the new Mrs. Bradley enjoyed a social standing in Hollywood that she had never enjoyed before. The new Kitty Bradley, though, was a difficult woman. In later years, she took a class at the UCLA film school and regularly challenged and corrected the instructor—to the displeasure of other students. The various actors and singers who visited the Bradleys were willing to tolerate the wife to meet the famous war hero.[20]

Darryl Zanuck was the first to suggest involving Bradley in the production. This idea made sense since Coppola had drawn heavily on Soldier's Story in the first version of the screenplay. Frank McCarthy instantly saw value in this idea. "Bradley's involvement would mean automatic approval and cooperation from the Pentagon, which otherwise might prove a stumbling block," he told Richard Zanuck. McCarthy informed both Zanucks that the studio would have to offer some form of compensation to the general. All three wanted to get Bradley associated with the production, but showing him a screenplay was unwise because it was uncertain what script the studio would use in the end.[21]

McCarthy met with the general at the Bel Air Hotel. It was less than two months since Bradley's first wife had died, and he had yet to begin his romance with Kitty Buhler, so he had the time to spend chatting. In fact, a lonely Bradley eagerly gave McCarthy two hours. He was gratified that Darryl Zanuck had thought of him. Bradley added that The Longest Day was the best war film he had ever seen. He would love to be associated with the Patton project if it was made with similar integrity. He could provide the studio with unpublished material about Patton and himself, but he was unsure if he had sold the film rights to his book to another production company.[22]

Bradley took three months to get back to McCarthy. When he did, he told the producer that Kitty Buhler was working on a script about him, and that MGM was interested. Bradley wanted that studio to take the first look at her treatment since he was on its board of directors. Buhler's proposed project focused on Operation Cobra, the breakout from Saint-Lo. Nothing happened with the film project. The general did not think that the treatment made for a good film, but he married Buhler nonetheless.[23]

McCarthy renewed contact with Bradley after Webb turned in his finished screenplay. He saw Bradley socially in October 1967—both were members of the George C. Marshall Foundation—and they discussed the progress of the Patton film. Bradley raised several objections to this undertaking. "It is my intention to present you in only the most accurate—and therefore the most favorable—light," McCarthy told him. He wanted to buy the rights to A Soldier's Story and hire the general of the army as a military consultant to the film. In that capacity, he would read various versions of the script and make comments. The two talked about the film at other meetings of the Marshall Foundation, but nothing happened as Wyler left the project and the Zanucks went looking for another director.[24]

The best-laid plans often go awry. In July 1968, as Edmund North was working on the screenplay, an assistant to studio executive David Brown made a routine offer to Bradley to buy his book, but offered no compensation for any other services. The general was put out. Zanuck, worried that a man he considered a friend had been insulted, told his son to fix the problem immediately. McCarthy met with Bradley and his wife for three hours on July 11, 1968. He was pleasantly surprised to discover that they were willing to accept $7,500 ($47,021 in 2010) for the film rights to A Soldier's Story. They both agreed that the studio could get most of the information in the book from other sources in the public domain. "The trick in our situation with the Bradleys is to derive a maximum amount of benefit from them without putting them in a position to interfere and cause us trouble," he informed Richard Zanuck.[25]

As a way of soothing troubled waters, McCarthy arranged for the Bradleys to take a tour of the studio lot, along with the general's grandchildren. He also had a messenger deliver a copy of the screenplay. This gesture actually made the situation worse because the studio sent the general a copy of the Webb script rather than the Coppola–North version.[26]

Bradley quickly decided he wanted nothing to do with the project. McCarthy had another meeting with the Bradleys. The general had a number of objections. He disliked having his character addressing Patton as "Georgie." He and his wife also wanted to make sure the Bradley character got adequate screen time. In the conversation, it became clear to McCarthy that they were not looking for an equal number of minutes, but they wanted more time on screen. Bradley also had an unpublished diary that he would share with the studio, but he wanted errors of fact corrected. Since he had never seen the diary, McCarthy had no way of knowing what specific factual issues the man was discussing. The Bradleys also wanted to vet the script. McCarthy discussed these issues with Schaffner and North and found that both thought that the old general could make contributions that could greatly improve the script. He adopted their enthusiasm. "I am eager," he wrote the Zanucks, "and enthusiastic for Bradley collaboration since it will bring great authenticity prestige and publicity as well as eliminate any possible difficulty with Pentagon[,] Patton family[,] and living characters."[27]

What McCarthy did not expect was that Bradley wanted to make a two-part deal with the studio. In addition to buying the film rights to his book, the general wanted Twentieth Century-Fox to hire him as an advisor to the film. For that effort, the general expected to be paid in a handsome fashion.[28] The stipulation that he be hired as a consultant confused studio executives at first. Bradley, though, was up-front about his reasons for wanting to do the deal in two parts. He had to share profits from the sale of the film rights with the publisher. He also had to share 25 percent of his own proceeds with his ghostwriter, his former aide, Colonel Chet Hansen. He would not have to share any money he was paid as a consultant.[29]

The money did not bother the studio. That was part of business. The fact, however, that the general hired a high-powered agent, Abraham Lastfogel, caught everyone off guard. Lastfogel was no regular talent agent. He was president of the William Morris Agency. His involvement in the negotiation process was unexpected, but Darryl Zanuck was far more upset about the script issues. He and his production team had hammered out a script, and now Bradley seemed to be raising basic issues about its very viability. "I am stunned and disturbed by many of the items," he told McCarthy. "Am completely confused by the recommendation that we balance the characters of Patton and Bradley to make sure contrast is definitely spelled out," he said in the abbreviated language of telegrams. A major concern was that substantial revisions would alienate George C. Scott. He also wanted to know why McCarthy let these small errors get through into the script. The studio executive directed—and that is the right word to use—him to have the matter resolved within a week. Zanuck already had plans to be in New York in nine days, and he instructed McCarthy to be there to explain the situation in person.[30]

McCarthy responded immediately with a letter and telegram. He explained that the Bradleys had seen the Webb script rather than the Coppola–North version—a fact that he had failed to mention in his previous correspondence. He also placed much of the blame on Kitty Bradley, whom he described as a "sharp and show-wise screenwriter" who was "determined to promote his prestige in any possible manner." The factual errors had appeared in the Farago book and were unknown to McCarthy, or they were liberties that he had allowed Coppola to take. Most of the issues were minor, like numbers cited in the film or dialogue that the Bradleys wanted restructured slightly. The general and his wife were not asking for any additional scenes.[31]

The issue was something of a tempest in a teapot. The studio quickly negotiated a deal with Lastfogel that made the general financially secure. According to the terms of the agreement, Bradley would receive $90,000 from Twentieth Century-Fox. Of that amount, $7,500 would be for the film rights to his book. The other $82,500 ($517,232 in 2010), which he would not share, would be paid to him for his service as senior military consultant to the film. He would also get 7½ percent of the movie's profits—a fairly meaningless term, given the creative accounting that studios regularly use. Indeed, even after the film had been out for over a year and a half and had won a slew of awards, the studio reported to Bradley that it still had not made a profit. Payment was made in three installments of $30,000, with the $7,500 coming out of the first.[32]

The elder Zanuck was happy with these developments, and instead of meeting with him, McCarthy spent Monday, July 29—the day the studio head wanted the film producer in New York—meeting with the Bradleys and Lastfogel. Schaffner and North were also present and went over the first twenty pages of the script. The American field marshal wanted the filmmakers to know that he and his staff always traveled in two jeeps, that he always carried a Springfield rifle, and that his subordinates always had a submachine gun and two bazookas. He also did not want his character to use the line that he was a spy for Eisenhower, but he had no problems with the Patton character making that comment. "As you can see," McCarthy wrote to Richard Zanuck, "the level of his questions is low. We are not slavishly doing everything he asks, but we are accepting the suggestions which either help us or do us no harm. Incidentally, he has told us a number of things which are definitely helpful."[33]

Still, the process was slow. According to McCarthy, Bradley was reliving the war, and his wife had a number of ideas that she wanted to express. He raised several objections about factual errors, but Kitty Bradley explained that many of these alterations made for better dramatic structure. Given the amount of time that the Bradleys took on that Monday, McCarthy arranged for Schaffner, North, and himself to meet with the general and his wife from one to six hours every day for the rest of the week. "The exercise is worthwhile, particularly in view of the other advantages which General Bradley will bring us," McCarthy reported to Richard Zanuck. After reading McCarthy's memo, Zanuck wrote on the margin, "This sounds very encouraging."[34]

In August, the Bradleys had officially vetted the script. Schaffner and McCarthy then decided to take a battlefield tour of Europe. They followed Patton's path of progress, going in reverse, starting with the Battle of the Bulge. "I wanted to be educated on the terrain," Schaffner explained. Bradley accompanied them in Belgium. According to the terms of the contract Lastfogel had negotiated with the studio, the general and his wife traveled together and were furnished with first-class accommodations. Although the trip gave the crew ideas, it was not enough in and of itself. Schaffner took three more trips to Europe to scout for appropriate locations. "It took hour upon hour of sitting on your can in an automobile to find these damn places." His associate producer and art director also spent two months looking for the right places to shoot.[35]

After this tour of Europe, McCarthy made an important decision that ended what little influence Bradley had. Although the World War II legend was being paid handsomely, the producer did not want him near the cameras. He had two reasons: "We did not and do not wish [to use] the services of a 75-year-old man, with a contentious and troublesome wife, on the set at all times, and General Bradley is not available for that anyhow." He needed, however, a technical advisor to get tactics and battle operations down correctly—someone who knew the insignia of the various armies and the correct markings of vehicles. His suggestion, for a third time, was Paul D. Harkins. After the two talked, Harkins agreed with the mutual understanding that he would only be an advisor, he would focus on minor details normally expected of a captain or major, and if he did not know the answer to a question or issue, he would find it out. "I have known Paul Harkins since he was a major," McCarthy stated, "and I am confident of his ability and willingness to do all these things, plus giving us the advantage of his intimate knowledge of General Patton."[36]

McCarthy still needed Bradley. "I wanted his name on the picture, frankly. I wanted to be able to say 'this script has been approved by General Bradley.'" He did not need the U.S. Army or the Department of Defense to make the film. Production without official government support was possible and basically what the studio planned to do. Twentieth Century-Fox, however, needed the military to market the film. "The Army can be tremendously helpful in exploiting a picture," McCarthy explained. The service could provide military bands for film openings and allow the film to be shown and advertised on its bases. McCarthy was worried that the script, particularly with Coppola's dialogue, would turn off many public affairs officers in the Pentagon. "But when I could take it in with the approval of Senior Military Advisor Omar N. Bradley, the only five star general we've got, they had to read it through and see what a really fine script it is."[37]

McCarthy's manipulation of Omar N. Bradley's name and reputation showed that although he had a driving artistic and even historical ambition to make *Patton*, he also understood the business issues involved in making a film. Bradley's willingness to sell his name—and, more importantly, the conditions under which he wanted to do so—shows more of the man's true nature than the legend he had acquired during the war. The work involved in getting this film into production had taken an amazing amount of effort, energy, determination, and time—over a decade on the part of Frank McCarthy—and makes the seemingly tumultuous issues on set seem minor in comparison.

Fourth Star. George S. Patton Jr. was promoted to the rank of general by his friend, General Dwight D. Eisenhower. The two generals had been close friends for decades. That relationship fell apart at the end of World War II. (Source: National Archives)

Willie and Patton. Willie the Dog constantly accompanied Patton in 1944 and 1945. The dog was something of a coward, and his depiction in *Patton* is highly accurate. Willie was also smelly—something not in the film. (Source: National Archives)

Peacock. The opening scene of *Patton*, where the general wears all his military decorations and ribbons, was based on a private incident where the real Patton posed for a family photograph. Although he did on occasion give his famous war speech in front of a giant U.S. flag, he never wore all his formal decorations when he addressed his troops. (Source: Photofest)

Boy Genius. Frank McCarthy reached the rank of colonel at the age of thirty-one. After serving at the center of the U.S. military effort in World War II as George C. Marshall's military secretary, McCarthy seemed to have a bright future ahead of him in Washington, D.C. After World War II, he served briefly as an assistant secretary of state before a nervous breakdown forced his resignation. After he regained his health, he used his military contacts to begin a career in the film industry. He retained a commission in the U.S. Army Reserves and eventually was promoted to the rank of brigadier general. He spent nineteen years developing *Patton*. (Source: National Archives)

The Generals. Lieutenant General Omar N. Bradley pins a medal on Patton. Despite the impression given in the film, the two generals were not close. Bradley served as the military advisor to the film, but that was an effort on McCarthy's part to use the legendary general's name and reputation for marketing purposes. Bradley—and more importantly his second wife, a former screenwriter—were kept off the set. They were allowed to vet the script, but McCarthy responded only to small, technical matters, and he never allowed them to make any deep structural changes to the script. (Source: National Archives)

Monty. Field-Marshal Sir Bernard Montgomery emerges as the main villain in Patton. While Patton had a rivalry with Montgomery, the British soldier did not share this view. This depiction of Montgomery, and the fact that Lord Montgomery was still alive when filming started, created legal issues for studio executives. Lawyers in London warned the studio that according to British law, the script libeled the viscount and gave him actionable grounds. (Source: National Archives)

Hollywood Legend. Darryl F. Zanuck was the founder and longtime head of Twentieth Century-Fox. He served in the U.S. Army in both world wars. He hired McCarthy and basically gave him a management trainee program job. He believed that a film about Patton would be both good box office and intrinsically artistic. After McCarthy was nominated for an Academy Award for the first film he produced, Zanuck became a consistent backer of McCarthy's efforts to make Patton. Here Zanuck is on the left meeting with Major General Robert C. Richardson Jr. of the War Department's public relations bureau in 1941. (Source: National Archives)

Legend in the Making. In 1965, after two false starts with other writers, McCarthy hired twenty-six-year-old Francis Ford Coppola to write the screenplay for Patton. The producers and studio executives thought Coppola's work was brilliant, but they let him leave the film when he got an opportunity to direct on his own. The script played an important role in bringing George C. Scott to the picture. (Source: Photofest)

"One of the great pictures of all time in dog circles --
also picture of the week in LIFE -- was General Patton's tack
and luggage being shipped home after his death. In the center
is Willie, his bull terrier. This dog was in the war with him.
One day he and Eisenhower met and Eisenhower had his Scottie.
Eisenhower said his dog could take care of himself and for no
one to worry. No one did -- until they heard a crunching under
the table and Willie had the Scottie. He always addressed him
as "Willie, you son of a bitch -- get out of here." But he
loved him. He was an honorary member of the bull terrier club
whom you met frequently at our house."

Francis - Don't fail
to give Willie careful
consideration

out of character.
Willie was
ferocious looking -
which was why
GSP bought him -
but he was a
sissie as GSP
soon discovered.
First called Wm.
The Conqueror -
later Willie - would
stay away from
Patton when GSP
wasn't smoking

The Creative Process. While Coppola worked on the script, he had an office at the studio next to McCarthy's. The producer often gave his writer news articles and suggestions on things to incorporate into the script. In this note, he discusses the character of Patton's dog, Willie. (Source: author's collection)

The Director. Franklin J. Schaffner was entering the peak of his directing career when he decided to direct *Patton*. He had just made a box office hit for Twentieth Century-Fox with *Planet of the Apes* (1968). A constant theme in his movies was the man out of step with his society, an idea present in both films. (Source: Photofest)

The Actor. Scott appears in almost every English-language scene in the film, but his alcoholism got in the way on several occasions. His binge drinking caused him to be late for the shooting of scenes and on some occasions he missed entire days of filming. This pattern started on the very first day. Since the rest of the cast and crew was present, the studio had to pay them for these lost days. Schaffner and McCarthy calculated they lost eight days in total to Scott's drinking. (Source: Photofest)

History and Legend. Given the supervision that McCarthy provided it is not surprising that Coppola's script is highly accurate historically. Schaffner built on this by filming on location using Roman ruins to play Roman ruins. Coppola, however, relied heavily on Bradley's memoirs and the portrayal of Bradley and Patton that emerges in the film makes Bradley look good at the expense of Patton. Given his own service in the U.S. Marine Corps, Scott doubted the accuracy of several scenes that made no military sense. Unable to figure out how to act these scenes, he wanted on set rewrites. McCarthy refused and this led to several public confrontations. Scott eventually acted these scenes as written. (Source: Photofest)

Tankman. *Patton* depicts Patton as a rebel against the system. The problem with this portrayal is it is misleading and in many instances just plain wrong. Patton was an early pioneer of armored warfare in World War I, but when it was clear that the rest of the U.S. Army saw little future in this weapon system, he understood the internal political realities of his service and returned to the cavalry. He played no role in the development of tank warfare during the interwar period. (Source: Photofest)

The Spanish. Making *Patton* was a major logistical challenge. Reflecting the globalization process, the Spanish crew was a major resource in the making of this American film. The Spanish Army portrayed American and German units in the film. Even though the Battle of the Bulge comes in the last third of the movie, shooting started in Segovia, Spain, during the first month on set. Good weather and the lack of snow put the *Patton* company behind schedule almost immediately. (Source: Photofest)

Boom. The filming of the Battle of El Guettar was a major challenge for the *Patton* company. Schaffner spent weeks planning the scene and had six cameras rolling. The camera work of Fred J. Koenekamp, the director of photography, was crucial, and he earned an Oscar nomination for his work. (Source: Photofest)

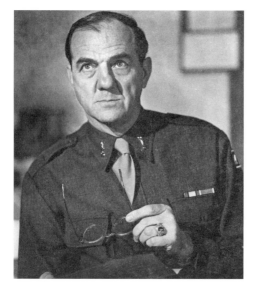

The Craftsman. Karl Malden, who had won an Oscar for his role in A Streetcar Named Desire (1954), played General Omar N. Bradley in Patton. Malden had worked together with Scott once before on The Hanging Tree (1959). In an effort to keep Scott from drinking, McCarthy had members of the cast and crew dine with him without ordering alcoholic drinks. Malden was so disturbed at what the bottle was doing to Scott that he gave up drinking. (Source: Photofest)

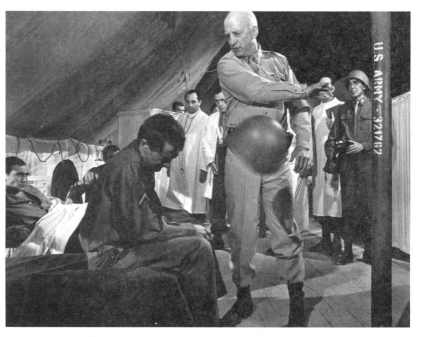

History According to Hollywood. McCarthy and Coppola were serious in their effort to make a historically literate film, but for dramatic reasons they tinkered with the facts. In 1943 General Patton on two different occasions slapped two soldiers which ultimately led to his relief as Commanding General, Seventh U.S. Army. Instead of depicting both incidents, the film offers a fairly accurate account of the second slapping event, but makes no mention of the first. (Source: Photofest)

On the Set. Frank McCarthy spent years obtaining permission from the Department of Defense to shoot a film about Patton. The general's children blocked these efforts for a time with legal threats. Shooting in Spain appeared to negate the need for assistance from the Pentagon. The Spanish, however, were not able to provide equipment for scenes involving amphibious landings. In this case, the permit from the Defense Department proved useful. Although *Patton* is a biographical film about a U.S. Army general, the only official U.S. military assistance to the production came from the U.S. Navy. (Source: Photofest)

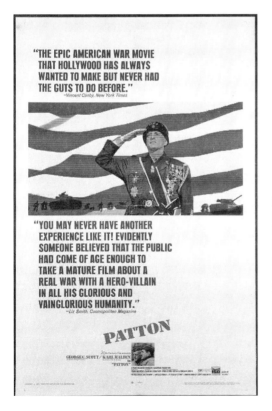

Selling the Picture. Studio executives at Twentieth Century-Fox were very concerned about how to sell *Patton*, a war film, during the height of the anti–Vietnam War movement. The studio decided to sell it as a character study. The strong and positive reaction from critics that often noticed this emphasis in the film was another advantage. This film poster reflects those marketing efforts. (Source: Photofest)

Oscar Time. *Patton* was nominated for ten Academy Awards and won seven. McCarthy accepted Scott's Oscar and the one given to the film as best picture. He is pictured here holding both statuettes while actresses Goldie Hawn and Jeanne Moreau give him a kiss. Standing to the left is Malden, who had accepted the Oscar on behalf of director Franklin J. Schaffner, and to the right is actor Steve McQueen who had presented the Oscar for Best Picture. (Source: Photofest)

The Beginning at the End. Although the introduction to *Patton* is the best known scene in Scott's career, he was worried about being able to deliver a performance in the rest of the film that equaled the emotional intensity of this first scene. As a result, it was one of the last things the *Patton* company shot. (Source: Photofest)

7. The *Patton* Company

The term *globalization* had yet to gain currency when the cast and crew began shooting *Patton*, but it accurately describes the issues the Americans faced as they tried to tell the story of George Patton. Shooting overseas allowed the studio to make the film on a smaller budget than would have been the case in the United States, but complications large and small arose that never would have occurred had they stayed at home and concentrated on selling the movie to a domestic audience. Globalization, though, was not a way of saying Americanization. The internationalization of American culture was not a one-way street. Even the dominant power must adjust to foreign regulation and laws. These were some of the issues McCarthy and the studio faced as they shot the film. There were many others, but the situation involving Field-Marshal Viscount Montgomery of Alamein was the biggest hurdle of them all.

Montgomery emerges as the main villain in the film, with Rommel a distant second, but the real "Monty" was different from the way he was portrayed on the screen. Bernard Law Montgomery was born in London in 1887 and was something of an international man in that he grew up in Australia after his family moved there when he was two. The family returned to England eleven years later, and Montgomery won admission to the Royal Military College at Sandhurst in 1907. An indifferent student, he graduated in the middle of his class eighteen months later.[1]

He excelled as a combat soldier, though, rising to the forefront during World War I.[2] During the interwar period, he alternated between assignments at military schools and commanding various units.[3] Montgomery became a protégé of Alan Brooke during this time. When Lieutenant-General Sir Alan Brooke became the General Officer Commanding of II Corps of the British Expeditionary Force in 1939, he insisted that Major-General Bernard Montgomery be named the commander of the 3rd Division. The battles in northern France went poorly for the British. The Germans outmaneuvered General Lord Gort, VC, the General Officer

Commanding of the BEF. Despite being bested, Gort managed to make the difficult decision to accept defeat and evacuate his force out of the French port of Dunkirk. During the evacuation, Gort lost control of the BEF, but Brooke salvaged the situation, and his most dependable subordinate was Montgomery. "Found he had, as usual, accomplished almost the impossible," Sir Alan recorded in his diary. During the evacuation, Montgomery insisted on eating at regular hours and getting a regular night of sleep. As a result, he handled the stress of the situation well and made sound decisions while the abilities of other generals faded.[4]

Brooke returned to England during the evacuation—he was under orders—and soon thereafter became the Chief of the Imperial General Staff, the title accorded the head of the British Army. As the war moved into North Africa, he insisted that Montgomery, now a lieutenant general, take command of the British Eighth Army. Under its new general, the Eighth Army halted Rommel's advance toward the Nile. Then, at El Alamein, his army forced Rommel back. The training Montgomery had insisted on paid off, as his men knew how to penetrate minefields. He also showed flexibility when the battle did not go according to his plan. The British general might have destroyed the Desert Fox had he been more aggressive, but El Alamein was a victory, and more importantly, it altered the strategic course of the war.[5]

The invasions of Sicily and Italy followed, but Montgomery wanted to put together a cross-channel invasion. During this time, however, he developed a reputation for being a soldier's general, thanks to his regular contact with the units and men under his command. When preparations for the cross-channel invasion began, he made contributions important to that undertaking. He was the individual most responsible for developing the plan actually used on D-Day for a broad assault using five divisions. He blundered with Operation Market Garden in September 1944. This operation was a combined airborne drop and ground assault through the Netherlands designed to take a series of key bridges that would breach the Rhine, making a drive into Germany itself possible. The airborne operation failed for several reasons, but the biggest problem was the flawed premise of the entire campaign. Observers said Market Garden was "a bridge too far."[6]

Montgomery was a problem for the studio. He had a hero status in the United Kingdom along the lines of the Duke of Wellington and Lord Nelson. It is no surprise that his ego matched his status and was extremely sensitive about his place in history.[7] A battle of memoirs started soon after the war ended. He thought Bradley and Eisenhower had drawn first blood with the serialization of their books in American newspapers. Those accounts, as well as American films that glorified the contributions of the United States and slighted those of their allies, particularly the British, angered him to no end. He had some justification in this view, and he intended to rectify matters when he published his memoirs in 1958. In doing so, he managed to insult the Belgian army, Italian soldiers, many British generals and field marshals, and the president of the United States. Eisenhower was so offended at Montgomery's account that he severed all contact with him and never wrote or talked to him again.[8]

The great fear in the studio was that the vain and sensitive field marshal would sue if he disliked his portrayal, which seemed likely. McCarthy changed the names of most officers to avoid similar legal problems. "The one problem remaining is General Montgomery and that's a tremendous problem," he explained. When asked if the studio was legally in the clear, McCarthy's reply was short: "No, we're not."[9]

McCarthy knew he had problems because the studio's lawyers in Britain had warned him. Claude F. Fielding, a solicitor with the London firm of Crawley & de Reya, explained in a four-page memo the legal issues facing the studio. British law did not require consent from living persons as long as they were not defamed. The problem was that the script clearly crossed that legal line. "There is no doubt at all that the script contains a number of defamatory remarks and innuendos concerning Montgomery which are prima facie actionable." It was clear that the film "could result in Montgomery being 'lowered in the estimation of right thinking persons.'" Fielding listed ten scenes that put the studio at risk. "I cannot offer any constructive solution except to submit the script to Montgomery which I do not regard as a particularly satisfactory idea." He doubted that the viscount would cooperate. "On the other hand it is completely impossible to proceed with safety without his authority."[10]

The Montgomery issue hung over the studio for two years. Richard Zanuck decided to proceed with calculated risk. "I strongly recommend against submitting the script to Lord Montgomery because he is a well-known troublemaker and curmudgeon," Zanuck informed several studio executives. He also noted that the viscount was at the time eighty-two years old. At least another year would pass before the film was released, and it would take time for a lawsuit to proceed against the studio. Because the dead cannot be defamed even if legal action was initiated before death, Zanuck figured that nature would solve most of the issues they faced from Montgomery.[11]

In response to a warning from Fielding that the field marshal could get an injunction to prohibit release of the film in Britain and the Commonwealth, McCarthy decided to hedge his bets. He proposed having Schaffner shoot the film so that a different version could be released in the United Kingdom.[12] Zanuck rejected this idea. "I firmly believe that we would be making a mistake to start cutting this film based upon educated guesses," he replied, writing with the distinctively thick felt-tip marker he used to write on memos. "Let's wait until we hear from M and we will know specifically what to do. I also firmly believe it would be a mistake to show the film to M in advance of our opening unless he asked to see it."[13]

As the film neared its release date, the general counsel for the studio, Jerome Edwards, suggested that they reconsider the issue. Zanuck held firm. "I'm willing to take the chance of having the picture as is. Let[']s await the first fire from the enemy before we start making changes—all of which would be guess work at best," he wrote on the margin of the letter Edwards sent him.[14] It was all or nothing.

Another British barrister informed the studio that Montgomery was a bigger hero to Montgomery than the British people. Although not a legal opinion or solution, this observation took the edge of off the issue and also suggested ways that McCarthy and the studio executives could neutralize the problem they faced—at least to a degree. McCarthy contacted Walter Annenberg, the U.S. ambassador to Great Britain, and warned him that the portrayal of Montgomery might be controversial. He added that Patton had complained about many generals, both American and British, and that they were not taking sides. Still, Zanuck ordered test screenings with British audiences to see how they reacted.[15]

Zanuck's decision on the Montgomery issue was a smart move, both in artistic and business terms. The threat of a lawsuit was intimidating to many involved in the production, and having the viscount involved would have compromised the conflict and drama in the film. Any prior contact with him would have almost guaranteed a legal conflict if he were unhappy. Zanuck took a look at the basic legal issues and played the odds. It could have turned out horribly for him and the studio, but trying to play it safe by bringing Montgomery into the process would clearly have been disastrous. Zanuck was a good business leader and manager for many reasons, and this decision was one of them. This decision also shows that globalization is not another way of saying Americanization. McCarthy and Zanuck knew they had to play by someone else's rules.

While the Montgomery issue was never resolved and showcased the problems of internationalization, there were far more benefits to working in an international environment. The movie could never have been shot in the United States for two reasons. First, the film depicts action taking place in North Africa, Sicily, Italy, France, Belgium, and Germany. The geography of these different locales varies significantly, and the studio needed to find locations that could substitute for these battlefields without breaking their budget on travel costs. Much of the geography in Spain was a "dead ringer"—to use McCarthy's term—for areas that the actual Patton visited. The costs of travel from one place to another would not be that high since they were fairly close to one another.[16]

Other locations might have worked, but Spain offered a second advantage that Twentieth Century-Fox needed badly: World War II–era technology. "All the war material was there," McCarthy explained. "The equipment in World War II, the tanks and command cars. They have a very good army, with old equipment. We hired the army. We paid a scale per private and tank. We operated just as if we were operating with Central Casting. It was a tremendous advantage working with a military organization. They loved it, too. It was like an exercise for them and we paid for it."[17]

McCarthy began this process in 1966, when he spent a month in Spain obtaining filming permits and enlisting the support of the Spanish army. "It was not easy because at first they were allergic to the idea of making a military picture that wasn't about them," he recalled several months later. The Spanish also thought the film denigrated military service. This required McCarthy to spend a lot of time talking to individual Spanish officers and getting a careful translation of the revised Coppola script. "Now if I hadn't been able to get their cooperation, we would have had to throw the script away because there was nowhere else we could shoot it." This statement plays fast and loose with the facts because the studio did spend two and a half years developing other scripts. It is also worth noting that by his own admission, McCarthy believed the last version of the Coppola script still needed work, and many of the objections that the Spanish made were ones that, at one time or another, McCarthy himself had made about Coppola's work.[18]

The decision to shoot in Spain reflected a trend in films about World

War II that had started in the 1960s: filming on location. There were two reasons for this development. First, vintage equipment was easier to find in Europe than the United States. Second, the Department of Defense had instituted more stringent regulations governing military assistance. Scripts and revisions had to be vetted by the Defense Department bureaucracy, and that was a slow process. Filmmakers balked at going through this cumbersome review.[19]

Despite these small complications with the Spanish—and they were small—McCarthy's director loved the decision to go on location. *Patton* might have been an American film, but the crew was multinational, and the Spanish shared their techniques. "People aren't making movies in Italy anymore," he told one reporter. "They're going to Spain, because that's where better movies are made. The technicians, the craftsmen, the assistant directors—they're extraordinary."[20] Globalization in this case had been a two-way street.

There were limits to what the Spanish could offer, and McCarthy ultimately needed support from the Department of Defense. The studio needed the assistance of the U.S. Navy to film some scenes with amphibious landing craft, and the service was willing to help. The years McCarthy spent obtaining a priority from the DOD were clearly not wasted.[21]

Before the film started shooting, the studio had to cast all the supporting roles. The cast was international in its composition, which was a crucial decision. "We decided that hopefully we would get the best possible actors we could in these parts who were non-images"—by which he meant, they avoided well-known actors who were recognizable more as movie stars than talented thespians. "I think almost to a man we were successful," Schaffner explained. The decision was also made to search for the actors overseas. English actors would play British army officers, and Germans would play Germans. Ironically, finding an actor to play Montgomery was fairly easy. Schaffner considered only three candidates and quickly decided on Michael Bates: "I think he comes out absolutely perfect on it."[22]

The most important supporting role, though, went to an American. To play the role of Bradley, the studio cast Mladen Sekulovich. McCarthy called him "one of the most professional people I've ever worked with." An experienced and respected actor, Sekulovich, better known by his stage name, Karl Malden, had been nominated twice for an Academy Award as a supporting actor. He won for his role as Mitch in *A Streetcar Named Desire*

(1951). He was nominated a second time for his work as Father Barry in *On the Waterfront* (1954).[23]

Schaffner appreciated the skill Malden brought to the role. "I would like to suggest we had an equal amount of luck in casting Karl Malden as Bradley because I think that he is very superior in a very, very difficult part. You know, it is one thing to play the flamboyant, amusing, angry, insane character. It's quite another thing to play the level-headed dull character and make it a legitimate contrast, make it a motivating character."[24]

The actor knew he had a difficult assignment in playing a living legend. "Here I was playing a person who was still very much alive, someone I had to be accountable to," he observed. "The prospect was a little daunting, if exciting." He also had an advantage in that he could actually talk with Bradley. The two met for a few hours for five days. At one point in the script, Malden decided it was time for his character to lose his temper at Patton. Bradley was noncommittal in his response. A few minutes later, he asked Malden if he really needed to perform the scene in that manner. When he got angry at Patton, he had simply told him what he expected him to do and that he expected compliance. When Malden asked why, Bradley responded that he outranked Patton. "That clinched it," the actor declared. "I played the whole part without ever really blowing my top at Patton."[25]

The set often had a gritty look, thanks to Harkins. "They wanted to film the tanks going into battle just like they came out of the factory," the retired general stated. "But that's not the way it was. They had to camouflage them and the GIs' gear all over them." The director thought the general was worth his weight in gold. "Paul Harkins, bless him, was meticulous in his examinations of these soldiers and their right dress and their right armaments and the right application of them." He often caught mistakes where Spanish soldiers were wearing an American uniform but had on a German helmet. There was also a German technical advisor in the *Patton* company who interacted mostly with the second unit director who filmed most of the German scenes.[26]

On February 3, 1969, seventeen years, three months, and eleven days after McCarthy had first proposed a Patton biographical treatment to Darryl Zanuck, shooting for the film began on location in Spain. For six months, the crew shot some 440,000 feet of film, which equaled 230 to 240 hours of running time. Scenes were shot in five other countries, but the bulk of it was done in Spain. The province of Almería on the southeastern coast served as both North Africa and Sicily, while Pamplona had the right architecture to portray France. Despite all the hard work and phenomenal determination that it had taken to reach this point, McCarthy's only recorded comment at this time was one of bemusement. "Here I am, a one-star general retired, heading a staff that includes one five-star general and one four-star general," he said with a wry smile.[27]

When shooting began, logistics, rather than egos, were the biggest problem facing the cast and crew. Much of this work was in McCarthy's area of responsibility, and he spent most of the time in Spain making sure that Schaffner had what he needed to shoot. "It's like fighting the war all over again. The only difference being that in the real war we didn't have to clean up after the battle," McCarthy explained at the time. He visited the set, but only occasionally.[28]

The logistics demanded much of Schaffner as well. "If I make pictures for the next twenty years of my life, I will never make another picture, I am convinced with as many locations in it," he stated. "It was insanity to have had so many locations—My God! Seventy-two different locations." The director had good reason to feel exhausted. The crew averaged a move for every two pages in the script.[29]

Malden agreed. After his acting career had ended, he was asked what was the most memorable shoot he had on location. His response was direct: "PATTON. Six months in every kind of environment you can think of, *every* kind of weather you can think of."[30]

There were also language issues on set. Schaffner had a minimal understanding of Spanish. Language barriers got worse when the *Patton* company left Spain. When the crew filmed in Morocco, he had his instructions translated from English to French by a Spaniard and then into Arabic by a Moroccan. "When you go through this on three levels you know something is going to go awry somewhere," he said. "It's stunning that we didn't have more problems than those few that arose."[31]

One of the reasons things managed to function was that Schaffner had assembled a talented and capable crew. One of the most important was the sixty-three-year-old production manager, Francisco "Chico" Day, who arrived in Spain six months before shooting began to begin planning the transportation, housing, and feeding of the crew. The fact that Day spoke Spanish was a tremendous advantage. Understanding that he was working with a professional army, he began addressing McCarthy as "general" in front of the Spanish. The Americans in the crew adopted this practice as well. (At one point, McCarthy came to the set dressed in his U.S. Army uniform; Schaffner, for his part, wore a U.S. Navy combination cover with gold braid on the visor—the headgear of an admiral.[32])

Day was also responsible for finding props and animals like camels, vultures, and scorpions that would appear on camera. In addition, he had to negotiate directly with the Spanish army when the crew needed the troops on set longer than originally planned. Schaffner called him an "exquisite human being" and "the best production manger I have ever seen anywhere." McCarthy said the only reason the film came in under budget was because of Day.[33]

There were limits to globalization, as Day regularly discovered. The phone lines in Spain were antiquated. Sometimes it was difficult to hear the party at the other end, or the operator was unable to make a connection. "The telephone service is terrible," he admitted. "You adjust or you go crazy." One way he responded to the environment was to hire a helicopter and have it carry messages back and forth.[34]

Another key member of the crew was the director of photography, Fred J. Koenekamp. He and Schaffner had never worked together before. "I thought the man was English," Koenekamp said of the director. "He had that air about him."[35] Koenekamp was still new to film. His experiences was primarily in television. Schaffner expected *Patton* would be a difficult shoot because logistical demands required a rapid pace. He was, as a result, more concerned about intangibles rather than experience. "I wanted someone durable and alert, and fast but good," he stated. In their first meeting, Koenekamp explained how he worked on set and favored handheld shots. This type of camera work allowed the operator to move quickly around tanks and other vehicles rather than being confined to a dolly or a set location. Schaffner liked this approach. In a calculated gamble, the director hired him. After Koenekamp received an Oscar nomination for best cinematography, Schaffner said, "I think it was a wise selection."[36]

Schaffner also hired Urie McCleary as the art director. A show-business veteran, he led a four-man team on this film. An Oscar winner for his work on *Raintree Country* (1957), McCleary had a reputation for his work in interiors. *Patton* was different because much of it was to be shot in exteriors. As it was, it would be his last film.[37]

The assistant director was José "Pepe" López Rodero. A Spaniard, he had as many as four second assistant directors working for him. Rodero and Schaffner got along well, and they would work together on four other films.[38]

The second unit director was Michael "Mickey" Moore. The second unit generally shoots footage like scenery shoots used to establish context or inserts that are different angles of main scenes. Koenekamp usually had three to four cameras with the first unit, and Moore had two to three. Schaffner was quite detailed in his directions to Moore. "He planned that out more carefully and knew more to be done to meet his standards than any other director I've known," McCarthy told Schaffner's biographer.[39]

Another key element in the making of the film was the director's work ethic. Location shoots often are something like summer camps for adults. The cast and the crew regularly socialize on the set and in the bars and restaurants around their hotels. Not Schaffner. While in Spain, he usually dined at his hotel and spent the evening reading the script and planning the shots for the next day. "Franklin was reserved, but not stodgy," McCarthy said. "There was no buddy-buddy business with him, no hanging around the bar and closing it in the early hours. He conserved his energies for the next day, which usually involved a forty-mile drive back to the location and back." Schaffner was regularly up at 4:30 or 5:00 A.M. He prepared detailed outlines and memos of what he wanted to shoot. "He gave you the time and he wanted you to have the time to go over the script with him personally," Koenekamp recalled. "On Franklin's pictures by the time you are starting to shoot that picture, the communication was minimal between us because we knew, we had already talked about it."[40]

The Battle of El Guettar was an example of the crucial function that detailed planning played in the making of this film. Schaffner combined the first and second units so he could use six cameras. Six weeks before shooting began, Schaffner held a two-day-long meeting of everyone involved with this part of the film. "I had broken it down not according to the script but according to what my choreography of the battle was, scene by scene," he explained. Schaffner then spent a weekend—"an entire weekend"— locked in his hotel room writing out the details of every scene. He had his comments typed up and circulated to the crew as a memo. "Now obviously, in that kind of memorandum you cannot say where every camera position is going to be nor do you care to say but at least everybody knew what the pattern of the battle was to be." Forty-eight hours before the shooting of this combat engagement started, Harkins told him that they had plotted the battle incorrectly. His source was the relevant volume from the *United States Army in World War II* series, the official U.S. Army history. "Well, there was nothing for me to do but rechoreograph this whole thing," the director confessed. Although the plan as it stood was detailed, it was not rigid, and the capable crew adjusted quickly. "You were impressed just to be there," Koenekamp remembered of actually watching the tanks advance on the cameras. "It was exciting. It was totally exciting."[41]

One of the film's major features is the striking photography. Koenekamp and Schaffner shot the film using Dimension 150. *Patton* was the last film shot using this photographic and projection system, which acquired its name from a camera with a 150-degree lens that produces a 120-degree arc on the screen, equaling roughly the peripheral field of human sight. The combination of the camera and projection system produced a good, clean, and well-defined picture that was neither condensed nor diluted from the original image. Koenekamp was proud that they never used anamorphic, blue-screen, or process shots. "It's exciting to work with," he declared. "There is no cheating type shots in the picture. Everything in that picture was shot for real."[42]

His achievements in photography are all the more impressive given the challenges he faced in lighting. About 80 percent of the finished film was shot using natural locations. "These scenes have a very realistic quality and a number of interiors appear to have been filmed solely with existing light. But lights had to be used on all of them!" he exclaimed. "I wish I could walk into a location and say, yes, you can shoot it as it is because it is often so beautiful. But you can't do it. To get up to your film speed, you need light." The problem was the *Patton* company was often shooting interior and exterior scenes in and around historic buildings, and they were prohibited from attaching any fixtures to the walls. The only option he had was to light from the bottom using a bank of Fay lights.[43]

These requirements were another example of constraints that globalization was placing on the shooting of this film, but this same process also offered solutions. Rather than try to use American techniques to solve this problem, Koenekamp turned to the locals. "The Spanish crew was really quite excellent," he explained. "They are truly amazing people. If you tell them you want something and it's not immediately available, they will make it even if it means working all night in some foundry or machine shop."[44]

Koenekamp encountered other problems. He did not have all of the camera lenses that the Dimension 150 process required when shooting started. He was having to learn what his lenses could do as filming progressed. "Because of the tremendously wide screen on that one big lens, you had to think about composition and where you wanted things and where the people are."[45]

A complicating factor in these areas was the weather. It affected lighting, logistics, and the availability of the Spanish army and their equipment. Planning for the exterior shots was difficult. "It isn't easy to know exactly when you're going to have the snow or the leaves or the hot weather in the desert," McCarthy said. Schaffner agreed: "It was a constant juggling."[46]

Since the *Patton* company began shooting in February, they began work on the sections of the film depicting the Battle of the Bulge. This part of the movie was filmed in and around Segovia, a small city in central Spain. The problem was good weather. There was no snow for scenes that were to take place during a winter storm, and almost immediately, the cast and crew were behind schedule.[47]

Even when the climate was right, it produced any number of other problems. "We shot in rain, in snow and slush, and in overcast," Koenekamp explained. "There were many times when we had light changes in the middle of a scene when the sun would either come out or go behind a cloud. I let it stay that way without any changes in the lens. Of course, I had to keep the actors properly lit and looking their best, but that was it!" Schaffner called the filming of the Battle of the Bulge scenes in Segovia "intolerable." The company went from having no snow to having too much when a blizzard blew in. Koenekamp had to winterize the cameras. "We had on every piece of clothing we could get on our bodies but by noon we were all shaking with the cold." It was impossible for the crew to get food up the narrow one-lane road up the hill to the Spanish army. Early in the afternoon, the soldiers had enough of being cold, wet, and hungry. The problem was, Schaffner still had to film two more shots. The sergeant in charge agreed to wait, but after half an hour, his patience wore out. The Spanish began leaving, and in a desperate attempt to get useful footage, the director started running his cameras and setting off explosions as his extras began leaving the set.[48]

The logistical issues, while crucial, were a distinctly secondary concern when compared to the behavior of George C. Scott on set. There were three different sets of concerns with the actor. The first, and the most understandable, was the issue of characterization. Scott was serious about giving a truthful portrayal of George S. Patton Jr. "My sole interest in this picture was to illuminate one man who made a very great impression on his time and who possibly will make an even greater impression in generations to come," he said.[49] The actor respected his character. "I can only say that my relationship with General Patton is one that has not and will not end with simply making a moving picture about him. It is one of admiration for a great individualist. Man of real distinction. A man of really unique personality and talents." He found the task of playing this character a real challenge, one that he enjoyed: "It has been an arduous and at the same time pleasurable experience to be him and my hope is that the work that I have done in the film may in some way clarify some of the misapprehensions, misconceptions about him which were perpetuated upon the general public at the time and have been left over in our generation."[50] That was not the same as making Patton a legend. "As to glorifying him," Scott elaborated, "I don't think that is what we set out to do."[51]

Unlike Malden, Scott could not actually meet the man he would portray. So he did the next best thing. "I must have read 12, 15 books about him. I saw three, four thousand feet of film in my home, daily—documentary film on him. And, uh, just sort of by a process of osmosis soaked it and absorbed it," he revealed during one interview.[52]

Scott also went to considerable lengths to look like Patton. He shaved his head and wore a hairpiece to resemble the general's receding hairline. He had his dentist make caps and veneers to resemble Patton's discolored teeth. He wore putty and makeup on his nose so it would resemble the general's aquiline nose.[53] There were, however, limits to this mimicry. Scott decided to make no effort to reproduce the man's voice. "The more excited he got, the higher it got," the actor explained. "I didn't use that. People are used to my gravel voice and if I tried to use a high little voice it would be silly."[54] There are numerous comments about how authentic people found Scott's portrayal. McCarthy, who knew both men, said, "There were times when I expected him to say: 'This is the way I did it in the war.'"[55]

Having a military background himself, and having spent serious time studying his subject, Scott had concerns about how Patton was being portrayed in the film. He suspected—correctly, as it turns out—that the Coppola–North script was designed to make Bradley look good. Even though the actor had approved the script, he now had second thoughts. The immediate issue was the scene where Patton confronts Major General Lucian Truscott about an amphibious landing designed to take Messina before

Montgomery. Patton comes across as cavalier in his disregard for the lives of those serving under him. As one U.S. Army officer noted, the real Patton was many things, but arrogant with the lives of his men was not one of them.[56]

Scott decided to rewrite the scene to make it more historically accurate. When McCarthy saw these revisions, he rejected them. He had many problems with Scott's writing. First, it made Patton look like a "nicer fellow which of course we don[']t wish to do." Second, they came at the expense of Karl Malden's character. "Bradley approval unlikely if not impossible since we sweated out every line and word with him." He was also worried that Scott might try to revise other scenes. Finally, he found that the writing was not particularly good.[57]

The actor was stunned at McCarthy's blanket refusal to make an adjustment. In meetings that were, according to the producer, "loud," Scott said he had never been on a film in which on-set revisions were prohibited. He thought his changes would help the film realize its larger potential. He said he might have to refuse to play the scenes. "I think Scott underestimated both Franklin and me," McCarthy later disclosed. "Both of us are inclined to be mild-spoken, and I guess Scott thought he could get away with anything. He couldn't."[58]

Scott was livid and went public with his frustration. He told a reporter from the British newspaper, the Sunday Times: "It's an unactable part and I'm not doing too well. It's an inadequate script and it's very difficult for me. Patton was misunderstood contemporaneously and he's misunderstood here—and I'm ashamed of being part of it." He added, "I'm thoroughly disgusted with the entire project."[59]

Wanting to reduce the tension on set, McCarthy canceled shooting the parts of the film that were bothering Scott, hoping that time would allow passions to cool. Schaffner was more generous in seeing Scott's point of view. "I think it's fair to say that George was unhappy playing the part, not because he by any means made the assumption that the script was unfair to the character—he may have made that assumption from time to time— but I have always analyzed his attitude as having been generated out of self-criticism." He admitted he had problems with Scott, but that was the nature of collaborative art. These type of issues stimulated the creative process, "and I would rather have them than not have them."[60]

Scott and Schaffner eventually reached a compromise. The director allowed Scott to hit the map and ad lib. Much later in postproduction, he simply edited around these acting tricks. What ended up on screen was what Schaffner described as "an actor's approach to the playing of these scenes." In another take, Scott decided to play the scenes lying down in his headquarters while he argued with the Truscott and Bradley characters. His reason: the real George S. Patton Jr. never laid down on the job.[61]

This issue bothered Scott for years. In 1975, he made some private comments about his experiences when he was thinking about playing the lead in a movie about the life of Douglas MacArthur:

> Frank Schaffner is a very gifted and wonderful man to work for. Very adept at this kind of film but at the time we made *Patton*, Frank Schaffner did not have the power to argue with the Zanucks—when you could find them—either one of them. Neither apparently did Frank McCarthy and I found myself constantly trying to bolster the Patton character and fighting desperately to keep him from looking like an international buffoon, which is what they seem to lean towards so lovingly. I can say with whatever modesty necessary that the human qualities that were in that film, certainly within the character of Patton, were instilled at my insistence over . . . much blood, sweat and tears[,] believe me.[62]

Even with these confrontations, Scott knew that he was working with a talented director. He described Schaffner as "quiet, very forceful, very hardworking." He added: "It is highly unlikely that I would have been able to—at all—to complete the work on the film without this man."[63]

Still, Scott was frustrated with his portrayal and turned to drink, which became another set of issues that plagued the production. "There were times when I got frightened. Things weren't going right, so I just went out and got smashed. That's me. Something goes wrong, I find a bottle," he told film critic Rex Reed. "But I never vanished for days or held up shooting or quit the picture."[64]

That last statement is not entirely true, as William Wyler could attest. There were also days when Scott was unavailable for filming on *Patton*. In fact, his drinking created problems on the very first day of the shoot. He arrived on the set at lunch but managed to get the scheduled work done before the end of the day. There were other times when he was too drunk to work at all, and entire days were lost. McCarthy and Schaffner calculated that they lost eight days in total to Scott's drinking. Since the rest of the cast and crew were ready to work, the studio had to pay them and available figures—and they are not complete—show that Scott's alcoholism cost the studio $62,356 ($370,700 in 2010).[65]

McCarthy decided to do something about this issue. Less than a week into the shooting, he went to Scott's wife, Colleen Dewhurst, "who is a strong woman and who assures me that even at expense of leaving her four children in Madrid she will remain with subject and can positively prevent further difficulties." While this was for the good, the producer blamed James Edwards, the actor playing Patton's valet, Meeks, for these drinking binges. Scott, like Schaffner, was not one to socialize with the cast and crew much during this shoot. The one exception was Edwards. The supporting actor was also an alcoholic and was instigating and enabling Scott's drinking binges. McCarthy decided they would film key scenes with Edwards quickly, give the rest of his lines to other actors, and then fire him.[66]

Richard Zanuck approved of these measures, although he was "dubious." Getting rid of Edwards was the right move, "but I'm afraid that there will always be another drunk to be found." The executive also had several conversations with Jane Dacey, Scott's agent, and warned her about her client's behavior. "I have gr[e]at respect for Scott as an actor but we will not tolerate any more of this kind of behavior and if it happens again he will be on the next plane back to wherever he wants to go. Since this happened to him before with the same management both he and Jane Dacey should realize that we are not bluffing."[67]

Zanuck's reservations had merit. McCarthy's approaches worked, but only to a degree. Two months into shooting, Scott was drunk when he approached the producer in a restaurant. In the presence of other actors, a press photographer, and a reporter for Esquire, the actor used what McCarthy called "abusive language" and vented about the script. After the interview with the Sunday Times, the producer had canceled all other media appearances with his lead actor. Scott, still angry over this move and claiming that McCarthy was trying to "muzzle" him, told the producer to stay away from his wife when he was not able to work. He continued to drink that evening, and his bender ended in the early morning with him playing Ping-Pong in the lobby of the hotel where many of the cast and crew lived. Needless to say, Scott was unable to work the next day.[68]

A few days later, McCarthy had a less confrontational meeting with Scott. He told the actor to think about what he was doing to others in the

Patton company. They were ten days behind schedule, and four and a half were due to his behavior. Schaffner had lost fifteen pounds from stress. His wife was worried and upset about the impact the film was having on her husband's health. McCarthy had planned to give the crew a three-day Easter weekend, but Scott's drinking and Ping-Pong-playing sprees had ruined that plan. "Every member of the cast and crew knows and understands all these facts," he told Scott. In response, the actor simply said "thank you." The next day, he was on time in the morning.[69]

McCarthy also used the rest of the crew to contain Scott's impulses. As Malden recounts, people were encouraged to dine with Scott and order nonalcoholic drinks. *Patton* was the second film that Malden and Scott had worked on together. They had both been in *The Hanging Tree* (1959), and Malden had done some uncredited directing work on the picture. The Oscar winner enjoyed socializing with the cast and crew and was willing to spend time with his costar. The two were not particularly close, but as Malden tried to keep Scott from drinking, he became disturbed at what the bottle could do to another human being. As a result, Malden decided to give up drinking himself. "From *that* day on," he explained. "Because, maybe I was a *coward*, I was afraid. It could happen to *me*. This kind of . . . he fought *himself*, I think, his inner self."[70]

The real question was how Scott's behavior affected his work and the film. "Okay. He did more than just take a drink, we *know* that," Malden said. "His *reputation* was that he more than took a drink. He could get himself *pissed* and, somehow, he came to work in PATTON, knew his lines. I don't know whether he would have been *better*, if he hadn't or *worse*, if he hadn't. See, I don't *know* that. *Nobody* knows that. I only know he was *damn* good in what he did. I think that is the *best* performance he has every played, barring *none*."[71] Malden is right, but what needs to be noted is that Richard Zanuck, McCarthy, and Schaffner managed a difficult problem effectively. Given the nature of the film, Scott's behavior could easily have destroyed the production.

While Scott was battling the bottle, he was facing some serious health issues, and these became a whole different set of problems that troubled the production and could have easily encouraged his drinking. Three days after his "thank you" meeting with McCarthy, Scott woke up and was unable to open or see out of his right eye. The studio doctor confirmed that he was unfit for work and that it had nothing to do with his drinking. It was possible that he had a detached retina, which had been a problem for him a year earlier. McCarthy agreed to send Scott to Madrid, and Chico Day arranged for the actor's eye doctor, Albert Ackerman, to fly in from the United States.[72]

Scott stayed at Orson Welles's villa in Madrid. The Patton company shot around Scott's medical leave for two weeks, filming many of the battle scenes as well as other scenes with the German actors that did not require his presence. When the doctor arrived in Spain, he found no detachment. The difficulty was neurological in nature, combined with a slight infection. Antibiotics and a little rest cured most of the problem. The next day, Scott found he could open his eye and see. There were still some problems with his vision, but he could and did return to work.[73]

The shooting in Spain ended on May 21, and the last scene was shot in studio on June 11. The Schaffners and McCarthy then took a week and a half off before beginning the postproduction process. The main task during this phase of movie making was editing, scoring the film with background music, incorporating special effects, dubbing (having actors repeat unclear dialogue), and adding Foley work (enhancing or inserting sounds like gunshots, explosions, and footsteps). All told, this process usually takes longer than the actual filming of scenes with actors.[74]

In the case of Patton, Schaffner spent seven months putting the film into its final version. His first rough cut of the film had a running time of four and a half hours. He explained that six months later, he could see how he intended to cut the film, but could often see a different pattern developing. He usually went with what made a better scene. "You look at the footage and you say, 'This is good. This is terrible. This is acceptable,'" he said, describing the process. With the Battle of El Guettar, it was simply what footage he had available. "And you take those pieces and you reestablish your pattern so that the battle makes sense but makes sense in a different way than you intended." He found work on the combat scenes exhausting. "It is a battle that I never thought we'd get past. I was so tired of that battle that I wanted to weep."[75]

The music in Patton was as distinctive as the visual imagery. The composer for the film was Jerry Goldsmith. Under contract to Twentieth Century-Fox, Goldsmith had worked with Schaffner on The Stripper (1963) and Planet of the Apes (1968). "Frank didn't play a musical instrument but he loved the music and understood what music should do in a film and what it should be in a film," the composer recalled.[76]

Goldsmith was scheduled to do the music work for *Beneath the Planet of the Apes*, the sequel to the original, which made him unavailable for *Patton*. His preference was to work with Schaffner again. The director went to his producer, who in turn went to Richard Zanuck. McCarthy stated that the conductor could do both movies, if producer Arthur Jacobs started the new *Apes* movie in December, as originally planned. Zanuck's response was short: "Unless there is a *very* good reason, Jacobs' date will be pushed back as originally agreed."[77]

"Thank *God!*" Goldsmith exclaimed. He called getting to work on *Patton* "the luckiest thing that ever happened to me."[78]

The composer saw three elements to Patton's personality. "So he was a complex personality, and I tried capturing these three levels of his personality in music by the fanfare, which has become sort of well-known, is meant to represent the archaic part of him, the historical, the intellectual part of him; the choral was to represent the religious aspect of him and, of course, the military aspect of him. It was designed contrapuntally so that all three could be played simultaneously or individually or two at a time, whatever."[79]

In a film that was just under three hours long, there were only thirty minutes of scoring. Despite its brevity, the music is well remembered because it is distinctive. McCarthy wanted mood music played during the opening credits, but he was also well aware that this section of the film was also the best place for a military march, which would help the film commercially. Goldsmith gave him both. To emphasize Patton's archaic personality, the composer used echoing trumpets in the music. "I wanted [the note] to be repeated and get softer and softer and softer." Using a echo device, he repeated a single trumpet note, with it fading as it was repeated. It became a popular feature of the film that he often used in concert as a conductor, and it was easy to perform live. Goldsmith also created a score for the slapping scene to create some sympathy for Patton so that the character's violent action would shock the audience. "It *did* create sympathy for Patton; so much sympathy for Patton that you thought he was justified in his act," Goldsmith recalled. "We both agreed it didn't work, it was the wrong thing, but Frank was reluctant to just dispose of the music because he knew I had worked very hard on it and he, he respected the fact that I had put so much effort into it."[80]

The director also knew how to use music in subtle fashion. For the scenes involving the weather prayer, he used no sound effects. Schaffner simply had Scott read the prayer as scenes of battle played out with a soft, low tone chorale that they repeated and repeated.[81]

Working overseas had created its own set of rewards and problems. The cast and crew of this film had been multinational and multilingual, and the American leadership of the *Patton* company had received as well as projected techniques, styles, and cultural values. When Schaffner finished postproduction, the studio was ready to release the film. The thing was, America—not to mention other parts of the world—seemed to many to be a very different place than it had been in 1951, when McCarthy initially proposed the film, or even 1965, when Coppola wrote the screenplay. The marketing and reaction to this film was a major element in the *Patton* project.

8. The Audience

Patton spoke to the American people in profound ways. The complicating thing about that simple statement is that the American public is a diverse group with many different views. What did people see in Patton? The simple answer is that everyone sees what they want to see in art. When Patton made its way to theaters, it became a national Rorschach test. This development was no accident. Coppola had designed the film to appeal to all sides of the body politic. That explanation, however, is frustrating and a bit false. People are free to interpret something as they see fit, but there are limits. After all, they are reacting to something rather than making something new, and the collective reactions to this film tell students of history something interesting about American society in the late 1960s and early 1970s. Patton presented an image about the use of power and the power of the individual, which appealed to fundamental national ideas about self-determination.

Many Americans had distinct ideas on these two themes. Cultural forums are never one-way streets. Different audiences appropriated the film often in ways that Twentieth Century-Fox had to heed. The reactions of many subaudiences to this mass media venue show that while they had different dreams, they were still operating within the same basic parameters. The late 1960s and early 1970s was not a time of radical change but a time when mainstream American values held, and an examination of the public reaction to Patton underscores that point.

By any measure, Patton was a popular film. In 1998, Variety reported that the movie had earned $61.7 million in domestic box office sales, making it the fourth most successful war picture since 1970. Schindler's List (1993), Apocalypse Now (1979), and M*A*S*H (1970) were the only films to top it during the era.[1]

This success begs an obvious question: why? There is an obvious answer: the film was good art. That was the view of Richard M. Nixon. The then president of the United States, like many other Americans, enjoyed going to the movies. He liked *Patton*, and stories about his obsession with the film are legendary. He supposedly watched *Patton* when it came out and loved the film. He saw it again and again and again. He talked about it at meetings. He imitated Scott's physical gestures. The film even shaped policy toward the Vietnam War. Chou En-lai, the foreign minister of the People's Republic of China, said he watched the film twenty-six times in an effort to understand Nixon. Hugh Sidey of Time-Life pushed the story of the president's fascination with the film, and many others in the media picked up on the story. Henry Kissinger encouraged journalists with these stories—and might have been the source of them. Sidey also implied that *Patton* helped initiate the invasion of Cambodia. When Darryl Zanuck saw this article, he stated, "This claim seems to me a little extravagant." For months, editorial cartoonists portrayed Nixon as Scott's Patton.[2]

Nixon was done wrong in these stories. He saw the film more than once, that is true, but White House records indicate that he only saw it a grand total of three times. That number is worth repeating—three times. That is the same number of times he saw *Around the World in 80 Days* (1956), and far less than a whole generation of teenagers who would go to the theaters over and over again to see *Star Wars* (1977).[3] Many of the stories about his obsession were gossip passing as journalism. Sidey and others told fun stories, but they were hearsay that they could not corroborate as fact.

David Frost was different. He got the opportunity to get Nixon to put his views about the film on the record during his famous 1977 interviews with the former president. In their discussions on Vietnam and Cambodia, Frost asked Nixon if *Patton* influenced his decision to invade Cambodia, noting that Nixon had watched it twice before he ordered the operation. "Well, I've seen the *Sound of Music* twice, and it hasn't made me a writer, either," Nixon said with a hand gesture toward Frost.

Afraid that Nixon was about to wander off on a tangent, Frost whispered, "*Patton*."

Nixon responded instantly. In fact, if not for Frost, it would not have appeared that he had ever wandered off topic. Leaning to his left and resting his chin on the back of his hand, he looked deep in thought as he said, "*Patton* is an interesting movie. I recommend it curiously enough, not so much for what it tells about Patton, but in a sense it is like Tolstoy's *War and Peace* or any Tolstoyian novel, *War and Peace*, *Anna Karenina*." While he was talking, he shifted his body weight again, sitting straight up and gesturing with his hands to give his words more emphasis. "The *war* part of the *Patton* movie didn't particularly interest me, the character sketch was fascinating," he said, saying "war" louder than the rest of the sentence. "And as far as that was concerned, it had no effect whatever on my decisions," he said as he chuckled the last few words, then shifted his body weight away from Frost. He did not take seriously the suggestion that *Patton* had been a major influence on his foreign policy.[4]

What did Nixon see in this film? The moving picture probably spoke strongly to the president in unique ways. He too was a man apart, out of step with his own society. The enormous power and responsibilities of his office in and of themselves could not help but separate him from others. He also understood the torment that the Patton character experienced. The unseen Dwight D. Eisenhower had been Patton's close friend, and Patton thought Ike had betrayed him. When Nixon had been vice president, he had suffered when he received the sometimes ambiguous support from the very same Dwight D. Eisenhower. He could relate to Patton's experiences in powerful and personal ways. McCarthy always figured that the Eisenhower association was key to Nixon.[5] There is another explanation. In the film, Nixon saw Patton exerting the same strength of character and leadership that he wanted to offer to the nation.

The diary of Nixon's chief of staff, H. R. "Bob" Haldeman, makes this point clear; it shows that the stories about Nixon and *Patton* are exaggerated. Nixon was fascinated with Patton, not *Patton*. In 1969, the president was reading the general's memoirs. Nixon talked about Patton's approach to leadership and was trying to adopt it as his own. Much has been made about Haldeman's entry on April 7, 1970, about the film. The White House chief of staff wrote after meeting with Nixon: "A lot of talk about enthusiasm, in the Administration and especially in White House staff. No one takes the offensive, all just lie down. . . . Don't radiate enthusiasm, because don't feel it. Said I should see movie *Patton*. He inspired people, charged them up, chief of staff has to do this. Pointed!" This entry assumes a different context when one reads the other entries about the general. On May 18, 1969, before the film was even finished shooting, Haldeman noted: "P is reading Patton's book and quoted point that a successful commander has to have leadership and be a superb mechanic, but most important be ruthless in analyzing his staff and throwing out the people that are not up to it. Another quote, that there are more tired division commanders than there are tired divisions, and all tired men are pessimists."[6]

Nixon liked the film as good art, and there were a number of indications within the industry even before it was released that McCarthy, Schaffner, and Scott had made something special. In an advanced screening for studio salesmen, the individuals who persuade theaters to show films, the group broke into spontaneous applause on four occasions. "I have never witnessed in a projection room a screening that equaled this one," the elder Zanuck remarked.[7] It would seem that salesmen craved strong national leadership.

One could dismiss these superlatives as the exaggerations that are commonplace in the film industry, but there are other indications—from people who did not have to keep either of the Zanucks happy—that the film was one of exceptional quality. Charlton Heston wrote Richard Zanuck after watching the film at a special studio screening: "I want you to know I think it's possibly the best war picture I've ever seen in my life."[8] S. Lee Pogostin, a television script writer who had worked with Schaffner during his *Studio One* days, gave the director uninhibited praise: "It's a fucking masterpiece." He compared Schaffner's directing work to Sergei Eisenstein's classic *The Battleship Potemkin* (1925). "What I am saying, Franklin Schaffner, ex–'STUDIO ONE' director, is that your achievement is one of authentic beauty and I am proud that an American did it. (I'm not particularly proud of America today, so that it is twice as important to be proud of an American director.)"[9]

The biggest of these issues boiled down to one word: Vietnam. This issue was one that McCarthy saw early on. "People told me when I was producing 'Patton' the time for war pictures was past. But this was the story of a man in World War II. It didn't relate to Vietnam," McCarthy told one reporter. He had no intention of getting into contemporary politics. "Neither support on right politically or condemn on left—no *political* tinge on either side," he recorded in undated notes. Vietnam and World War II were two separate conflicts. "The Vietnam war is a particularly unpopular war. World War II was not. It was characterized by great exuberance on the part of everybody."[10]

Studio executives worried about this attitude—that the public would interpret a World War II film as a subtle statement about Vietnam. To determine where the film stood with the general public, Fox commissioned a research firm to test the film. The use of focus groups was not as sophisticated as it would become in later years, but there are a total of 442 legible polling cards from audience members. These individuals were asked to

Table 8.1. Polling results of 442 polling cards for the film *Patton*

Rating	Overall	Men	Women
Excellent	414 (94%)	228 (91%)	186 (96%)
Good	23 (5%)	18 (7%)	5 (3%)
Fair	5 (1%)	4 (2%)	1 (1%)

rate the film as excellent, good, or fair (Table 8.1). The results were lopsided. These numbers were actually better than the mistake-filled report that McCarthy gave to the younger Zanuck. The audience members were also asked to self-identify their age and gender. Breaking the results into these categories produces some interesting results, as Table 8.1 indicates. What is important to note about these figures is that there would be no gender gap with this film. Women actually liked the film slightly better than men.

The written comments of the test audience members are also highly instructive. When correlating age and gender together, it becomes clear that the group that objected the most—and even then it was a fairly small group—were men between the ages of eighteen and thirty. These individuals were those that were most likely to go or have gone to Vietnam. The objections that these individuals made to the film was its focus on the glorification of war. "Too much bloodshed," one person wrote on a comment card. Another added, "I am glad I saw, but disliked the violence and mass deaths [sic]."

Far more of the questionnaires contained comments about the acting. "SCOTT—FANTASTIC!" one participant scrawled across the form. In the section where audience members were asked if they would recommend the film to others, a woman between the ages of thirty-one and forty-five scribbled, "You better believe it."[11]

Studio executives were optimistic. These findings confirmed the basic marketing approach Fox planned to take. "The preview didn't tell us much that we didn't already know," McCarthy observed.[12] The studio emphasized four reoccurring themes in its publicity efforts. The first was that the film was not a war film at all, but a character study. A studio campaign strategy makes this point clear: "While 'Patton' is obviously a war picture, a film in which World War II and its battles play an important part, the selling of the film on the promotional, advertising and public levels should primarily concentrate on the *personal* story of Patton, the man; the colorful, non-conformist soldier; the brilliant but controversial leader."[13]

McCarthy had no problem in advocating his line because it was what he had been trying to do with this film. "We are really telling the true story of one of the most fabulous and interesting *characters* that I have ever observed in action. I think that General Patton could have been a banker and we might be making a picture about him, or he could have, he could have been uh, uh a jockey and we might be doing his story. Our story is primarily a character study."[14]

His director agreed. "The intent here was simply to study the character of an enormously controversial, enormously anti-establishment, enormously provocative, enormously skillful, professional—whether he might have been a movie mogul, head of the newspaper empire, communications empire, grocery chain, or simply sat it out as the head of 'do-good' fund is unimportant to me." There, however, was no gainsaying that Patton had been a soldier. "In context he lived the life of a professional soldier. In context he believed in being a soldier." With these points made, Schaffner could not help but put his own spin on the film: "But opposed to all the other contemporaries of his time he was entirely separate from them. Didn't believe as they did. Had utterly different ambitions and aims than they had."[15]

Closely related to the character study theme was another: Patton as the antiestablishment man. To underscore this interpretation, the studio planned to use the subtitle *Salute to a Rebel*. Studio executives expected that this portion of the title would help attract younger viewers, and early promotional material was sent out with this subtitle. Jonas Rosenfield Jr., the director of marketing for the studio, told McCarthy, "It is definitely our intention to expose the picture to opinion makers among young people to clearly create the anti-establishment image of this picture."[16]

Schaffner opposed the subtitle. "Perhaps that was my most significant contribution to the film," he told a reporter with the *San Francisco Examiner*. His opposition had nothing to do with the theme itself. He agreed with the concept but found the marketing manipulative. "I didn't like the word 'rebel.' It seemed to me to be a calculated and dishonest attempt to get young people into the theater for all the wrong reasons. But I objected even more strongly to the 'salute' implication." He thought Patton was antiestablishment, but he was not trying to honor him; he had simply offered a study of the man's character. Nothing more. It is also important to note that Schaffner had also objected to using *Blood and Guts* as a subtitle.[17] Schaffner made a deal with the studio. If it got rid of the subtitle, he would agree to go on a tour of college campuses promoting the film. They agreed, and he did.[18]

A third theme was that *Patton* was actually an antiwar film. Schaffner was one of the biggest proponents of this view. "It's an anti-war film," he said while he was promoting the film in Philadelphia. "Otherwise I wouldn't have gotten involved." He never backed away from this view, but he did offer more explanation on other occasions. "Now nobody is fool enough . . . to make a pro-war picture. Human beings are anti-war." *Patton* had nothing to do with contemporary issues. "I did not set out to make a political tract, but my own feeling is that the movie is a strong indictment of war. Perhaps, some audiences won't agree, but that's how it seems to me." [19]

North agreed. In later years, he said the "strongest comment the picture makes is that war is the kind of business that requires 'this' kind of man. I think this is a commentary of the institutions of war itself, condemnatory of its brutality, mindless glory-seeking, and insensitivity to the value of human life." He did concede that others might see things differently: "I see other interpretations possible." One does not have to look far for a dissenting view. When asked if he had made an antiwar film, McCarthy bluntly replied: "No. I don't say that at all." That statement should be taken at face value. In 1961, he made it clear that he was determined to "to make a film which will reflect great credit upon the Army." David Brown, the studio executive, thought they had succeeded in this effort. He saw the film "as an appeal for patriotism and a tribute to a wrongly maligned military leader."[20]

A fourth theme was that *Patton* was a period piece. "World War II has become a period war. It doesn't relate to Korea, doesn't relate to Vietnam," McCarthy explained. To that end, the studio sold the film as both history and nostalgia. The studio held advanced screenings for key individuals, hoping word of mouth would encourage ticket sales.[21]

More significantly, *Patton* was the last film released in a road-show format until *Dreamgirls* (2006). The showing of films in the United States was beginning to change in 1970. By the end of the 1960s, television had marginalized the movie industry. In the decade to follow, multiscreen theaters that were often part of shopping malls would become the way most Americans would watch a theatrical release. The filmgoing audience had grown old, and exhibitors were trying to attract new viewers. This effort was difficult. The youth market had grown up on television and was less than likely to spend their disposable income on films when television was free.[22]

In the road-show format, a film would be released on a limited basis in a small number of theaters in select cities. The idea was to build interest in the movie and let word of mouth have its impact. Theaters required reservations and charged higher-than-usual prices for these limited seats— sometimes as much as four times that of a regular ticket. As a result, only those with significant disposable income were likely to see the film early on. The people with this type of money were older individuals—that is to say people over the age of forty. Twenty-five years after the end of World War II, these audience members would have strong memories of that conflict and had a built-in interest in the subject. Road shows had intermissions and programs to go along with the screening, reproducing the feel of a stage production. These similarities to plays often resulted in multiple reviews in local newspapers, which helped generate interest in the film. When it came to *Patton*, this approach worked. "I can't recall a film which inspired as much varied advance interest as 'Patton' did," Chicago film critic Mary Knoblauch stated. The number of phone calls she was getting about the film was ten times higher than normal. "People I hardly KNEW called me up on one pretext or another to see what I thought about 'Patton.'"[23]

The film had a ready market among those over forty, but the studio also worked to build interest among younger Americans. To that end, they created a study guide that schoolteachers could use in the classroom. Twentieth Century-Fox hired Louis L. Snyder, a historian of Germany, to write the teaching manual. A prolific scholar who wrote primarily for the general public, Snyder taught at the City College of New York. He produced an eight-page document primarily for use in kindergarten through twelfth-grade classrooms.[24]

The guide had three major themes. The first is that war is bad. "The film depicts with great authority the utter brutality and horror of war on a mass scale—in this sense may be said to project the strongest of anti-war feelings." The second was the historical accuracy of *Patton*. Photos of the real Montgomery, Patton, and Bradley are intermixed with those of Bates, Scott, and Malden. Snyder often treated the film as an actual historical source. "1. What did the German intelligence officer mean when he described Patton as a 'pure warrior'—'an anachronism?'" The third theme was the brilliant acting of Scott and Malden. One question asks students, "3. Point out elements in George C. Scott's remarkable portrayal of Patton that reflect an actor's research and study in preparing for such a part." [25]

The guide is a poor teaching tool. It often assumes expert knowledge about issues not covered in the film or discussed in the guide. "4. How was Eisenhower able to get British and American commanders to work together for the common good?" Snyder also discussed events not depicted in the film. A good example is the defense of Bastogne by the 101st Airborne Division under the command of Brigadier General Anthony C. McAuliffe. Patton's successful efforts to relieve the division are a major element in the film, but there is nothing in it about the defense. Snyder nonetheless devotes one of the ten sections in this guide to the defense of Bastogne. Other questions reflect education school methodologies and approaches to teaching. It asks students to explore the differences between a documentary and *Patton*. Another question is: "5. Why is this film valuable for a student of history?"[26]

Although the primary audience for *Patton* was domestic, selling it to foreign audiences was a major concern of the studio. Twentieth Century-Fox executives had some powerful concerns. Was the United States all that popular overseas? They were not sure they knew the answer to that question. Antiwar sentiment was strong in many countries, and with the film being a war picture and with the United States fighting in Vietnam, the two could easily combine to work against ticket sales. Was the portrayal of Montgomery too negative for the moviegoing audiences in the United Kingdom and the British Commonwealth? George C. Scott was not well known in Europe. Could he be of any use as a marketing tool? If so, where should he go? It was simply impossible to have him attend every foreign premiere. A final concern was that there were no female characters in the film and that women were not particularly fond of war pictures.[27]

The basic plan was to sell the film as a character study. A marketing campaign that focused on this aspect of the film would draw in women and the youth market, which the studio defined as those born after 1945. "This is a picture that simply cannot be sold by advertising alone," a studio document declared. The basic idea was to generate public interest in the general by encouraging local media outlets to do stories about Patton that emphasized his personality.[28]

With that general theme in mind, the advertising team planned to have a slightly different emphasis in various countries. In Germany, the stress would be on the respect that Rommel and Patton had for one another. The studio would also emphasize the work of the German supporting actors. In Italy, the advertising campaign would stress that Patton was religious, could read Latin, and was convinced that he was a reincarnated Roman soldier. In Spain, they would emphasize that most of the film was shot in that country. In South Africa, publicity efforts stressed that the film was a character study, but because war films had done well there, they held a number of advance screenings for senior military officers. "And one should not shy away from controversy, because that—and its outspoken honesty—is precisely what will fascinate millions of people about 'Patton,' whether former service-men or youngsters," one studio executive declared.[29]

Since Scott was the only major star in the film and his publicity value was suspect, the studio wanted to market to the military in ways that did not require the lead actor. They wanted to hold special advance screenings for foreign veterans who had served under Patton. These efforts would also help minimize any Montgomery backlash in commonwealth nations. They wanted to have veterans' groups sponsor premiers, particularly in cities that Patton had liberated, and take out ads in the paper lauding the general's accomplishments. Publicity kits would be sent to the film critics at local newspapers, defense correspondents, and editors of veterans' organizations newsletters.[30]

In the United States, many of the themes that the studio wanted stressed in its marketing campaigns appeared in the critical reviews of the film, but an examination of the reaction among film critics is important because it shows that *Patton* was an artistic, historical, and political venue all at the same time. Writers making a living as film critics fell into three categories. The first worked for the various trade publications like *Variety* and the *Hollywood Reporter*. Their commentary was focused on artistic and technical issues. In both areas, the reviewers were extremely positive. "The film grabs attention in the gut and won't let go," the reporter for *Variety* observed. This journalist continued, "It is 100% American, in every way: sometimes ennobling, sometimes disgusting, always vital." The writer for *Boxoffice* agreed, calling this film biography "the best of the genre." George C. Scott drew a good deal of attention, all of it strong and positive. The anonymous reviewer for *Variety* called the performance "a high-water mark in his career." Other elements of the film received praise. The *Independent Film Journal* called the Dimension 150 film process one that "renders everything with absolute clarity." The *Hollywood Reporter* described Goldsmith's score as "expert," noting that he used trumpets and piano chords with "fine" and "dramatic" effect. The only exception to this unrestrained professional praise focused on the performance of Karl Malden. Critics remained divided on his contributions, some seeing it as a brilliant counterpart to Scott's theatrical Patton and others thinking Malden was playing his stock-in-trade average humble guy.[31]

The second group of critics wrote for major media outlets like the *New York Times* or *Life* magazine. Many of these individuals—Gene Shalit, Judith Crist, and Liz Smith—were celebrities in their own right. All of them saw *Patton* as quality art and focused on the lead actor's performance. Many of these journalists were women and drew attention to their gender and to the absence of female characters in the movie. Yet they still liked the film. As a group, they described it as a character study. "All the glory emanates from Scott, who dominates the large screen as no single actor has, in my memory, making us party to the very depths of the soldier's soul," Crist observed. "To say that *Patton* is about war is like saying *The Merchant of Venice* is about moneylending," Shalit observed.[32]

In Chicago, the film received positive reviews from Gene Siskel and Roger Ebert. At the time, the two were still rivals writing for competing newspapers in Chicago and not yet paired up on *Sneak Peaks*, the television show that would make them nationally famous. Both were, however, already influential in the country's third largest city, and they saw the film as basically a character study rather than a war picture. Siskel focused on filmmaking issues, calling the opening scene "a thing of beauty." His review, while positive, was mixed. He saw much he did not like (the directing and the screenplay), but what he liked (Scott's acting and specific scenes) was far more significant. "In sum, the movie is a step forward in film biography."[33]

Ebert's review was less critical and took more note of social issues, explaining that the film appealed to strong nationalistic feelings. He observed, "We have all of these buried inside of us, waiting for a movie like 'Patton' to release them. The reflex patriotism of World War II is still there, we discover; Vietnam has soured us on war, but not on the war." With that point made, the movie was neither antiwar or warlike. "It is not about war but about Patton at war, and it is one of the best screen biographies ever made." He also praised the screenplay, giving most of the credit to Coppola and Schaffner's directing. In 2002, Ebert hit the same notes in another review of the film, but he noted that Scott was much like his character. When the actor, like the general, was doing his job, he was in his element, but once the war or the acting project came to an end, both were without purpose.[34]

One of the most important reviews was that of the *New York Times*. During this period, the *Times* was the flagship of American journalism and had the resources to achieve its goal of being the newspaper of record. While the individual journalists at smaller papers were often better than their counterparts in New York, the *Times* on average delivered a better product to its readers. As a result, it often set trends in the profession as others took their professional cues from what was generally perceived to be the first tier of journalism. Studio executives, needless to say, awaited the review of *Patton* in the *Times* with extra interest. Vincent Canby, the chief film critic, wrote a long essay that appeared in the paper on February 8, 1970: "'Patton: A Salute to a Rebel' looks and sounds like the epic American war movie that the Hollywood establishment has always wanted to make but never had the guts to do before." He also said the film was "an incredible gas" for being a personal look at Patton's professional life. Canby appreciated the production values in the film, noting the depth, clarity, and focus of the image on the screen. Battle scenes were more spectacular than bloody. Normally Canby was not interested in seeing big-budget films, but "'Patton' is the first $12-million movie ever made that I could imagine seeing twice." What he found interesting was that it was a literate movie with ideas. "The fact that a supposedly sympathetic character, in a superspectacular such as this, will admit to loving war is, in a negative way, a refreshing change from the sort of conventional big-budget movie claptrap that keeps saying that war is hell, while simultaneously showing how much fun it really is."[35]

This review was one that cast, crew, and studio executives could find gratifying. Four months later, though, the *Times* published another essay, this one from Peter Schjeldahl, entitled "Is 'Patton' a Lie?" A staff writer in the paper's arts and leisure section, Schjeldahl had a book of poetry to his name at the time, and he criticized the film less as a work of art but rather as a work of social and political commentary. He praised the film, calling it "one of the most tightly conceived and rigorously executed historical movies ever made." He also observed that Scott was "simply terrific." Despite these positive traits, he had profound reservations about *Patton* because it damaged the historical record. "In order to get away with its bald exploitation of historical fact, the film must continually scramble to evade the pointed moral questions upon which it is always verging." He did note that it was bad criticism to fault a production for what it fails to do, but did it anyway: "But a movie like 'Patton,' which bears so directly on some ambivalence in our national character and on the agony of our current history, deserves to be viewed in a harsher light." He thought calling Patton a man out of his time, a modern-day Don Quixote, was a dodge. Patton was responsible for the deaths of thousands. "What is fraudulent in 'Patton' is the intimation that George Patton, a uniquely American hero, was not like other Americans."[36]

This commentary struck at one of the biggest concerns that McCarthy, Brown, and the Zanucks had when the film was released: Would it be seen as a political statement about Vietnam, the U.S. military, or U.S. foreign policy? Given the importance of the *New York Times* and the sensitivity of this concern, Darryl Zanuck himself decided to respond. In a letter to Sy Peck, the editor of the arts and leisure section of the *Times*, Zanuck defended his property and attacked the essay directly: "While the question made a challenging headline, the answers given were, to say the least, quite puzzling and less than illuminating." *Patton* was getting praise for its honesty, which cut across the political divide. He found Schjeldahl's criticism of Scott's "terrific" performance infuriating. "Demeaning a film by virtue of a great performance is indeed a new wrinkle in criticism and I wonder how many people who have seen PATTON would agree with his accusation." Schjeldahl's last point—that the American people were just like Patton in his love of war—was too much for the studio executive. "To me this is arrant nonsense and the conceit of a critic indulging in an exercise." Zanuck was more than a little frustrated with the assessment of his product and his feelings poured out of his pen. He added that the *Times* essay was "cloying, arrogant, pompous, irritating," and "contradictory."[37]

Peck responded with a letter of his own, defending Schjeldahl. He replied that the political observations in the original essay had merit: "If one feels sympathetic toward this 'adorable' man, one then goes further and endorses war—a notion that is difficult for many Americans today." There may or may not have been a point in equating certain political views to an audience's assessment of a fictional character, but the point that Peck was making was slightly different than the one Schjeldahl made in his original essay.[38]

Zanuck answered with a three-page letter. He questioned Schjeldahl's credentials, noting that the man did not regularly review films for the paper. He also questioned the political positions that the men at the *Times* were taking. "It is very difficult for me to believe that a general is in favor or 'endorses war' just because he is a great General who has a record comparable only to Stonewall Jackson and Ulysses S. Grant." He then spent a page defending Patton, drawing on his own experiences in World War II. He added that generals do not have the power to start wars; that authority was political in nature and in the American system, one reserved for the Congress and the president. In the last of his letter, he returned to what he knew: film. "My basic quarrel with Mr. Schjeldahl's article is that he implies the film endorses war—and that this is a notion that is difficult for many Americans today." He let his feelings get in the way again, calling the critic an "arch-pacifist." He added, "Here in New York City and throughout the nation, city by city, our film is breaking box office records and this must be an indication of 'something.'" He continued with the observation that "it took a lot of guts to make the picture" in the first place. They had worried about public reaction, but they had believed that if they made a good piece of cinematic art, then the public would respond—and that was exactly what was happening.[39]

This debate seems silly in retrospect for two reasons. First, the journalists were comically absurd in their condescension and arrogance. Second, Zanuck's attempts to use fiction to make political and historical arguments was sophomoric: "The authenticity of the film cannot be challenged by Mr. Schjeldahl as it is authentic in every detail."[40]

The third group of critics were those spread out across the United States in smaller media markets. Small does not mean bad. In fact, the criticism was often better written and more insightful than what readers in major media markets—like New York—might receive; but when it was bad, it was far worse than what appeared in the *Times*.[41] Put another way, the major critics produced on average the better reviews, but not always, and it was pretty certain that the most ill-informed reviews would come in smaller cities.

Much of this artistic commentary focused on issues similar to those that the major critics had discussed. The bulk of these reviewers realized that the film was a character study. "'Patton' is undoubtedly one of the finest biographical movies ever filmed," Abe Weiner of the *Denver Post* observed.[42] Several noticed the Don Quixote theme. One called *Patton* "the most arresting and literate of all war films."[43] Closely related to this commentary was the praise for the ability of the lead. "Scott's performance is one long lesson in great acting," a reviewer for the Newark *Evening News* declared.[44] Another element of the film that drew noticeable praise was Schaffner's directing work.[45] Because critics are writers, a number of them noticed the quality of the script and appreciated the effort: "The screenplay by Francis Ford Cuppola [*sic*] and Edmund H. North is exceptionally competent and intelligent. It makes us accept a man who was a poet and a fool."[46]

A major difference between the reviewers in the smaller media outlets and those in the larger ones was that many in the smaller markets focused on the language in the film. "There are more cuss words per minute than in the average lecture to new recruits by a Marine drill instructor," one reviewer observed. A writer for the *Salt Lake Tribune* added that Patton was "one helluva motion picture, and if that language startles you don't bother to see the show."[47]

Many journalists got lost and ended up writing about history, confusing or substituting *Patton* for the real thing. Others used their reviews as opportunities to vent on U.S. foreign policy, the war in Vietnam, or social and political matters.[48] A writer for the *Indianapolis News* stated in the very first line, "'Patton' is guaranteed to unstring the beads of the flower-power generation." On the other hand, a critic writing for *Entertainment World* commented,

> Curiously, the screenplay (frequently a cotton candy version of a great man's life), treats Patton even more ruthlessly than Ladislas Farago's 800 page *Patton: Ordeal and Triumph*, one of the sources of the script, and General Omar N. Bradley's *A Soldier's Story*. The honesty of the movie script is refreshing and praiseworthy as it offers the tragedy of a man so trapped by his own celebrations and spirit in the past, that he was unable to cope with the present. It is a tribute to the artisans at 20th that *Patton* is a chiseled-in-granite, lasting monument to a repulsive old fossil of a general.[49]

There were some odd reactions among the critics in markets both large and small. The *Detroit Free Press* sent six reviewers to watch the film and published all six assessments on the same page. Don Morrison of the *Minneapolis Star* used two of his columns to write about Patton. The first was a review of the film. The second was an essay on the actual general. *Stars and Stripes*, which rarely carried film reviews, published one on its front page.[50]

The *Honolulu Advertiser* published two reviews three days apart. One critic's assessment was positive, and the other used the forum as an opportunity to express antiwar feelings.[51]

In a few instances, the film initiated political commentary. An editorial that appeared on the opinion page of the *Daily Advance* of Lynchburg, Virginia, declared that the film should receive a XXXX rating from the Motion Picture Association of America just for its language. (In the rating system in place at the time, the X rating was for adult-only films, and the pornography industry had taken to using multiple Xs to market their productions.) After the paper's film critic reviewed the movie, the editors of the New York *Daily News* observed, "With all his faults, Patton was a fine American who loved his country deeply and considered service to its cause the highest and noblest of callings. The nation could stand a healthy infusion of that spirit today."[52]

Some reviews were negative. A critic for the Cleveland *Plain Dealer* objected to what they saw as manufactured history, notably the shooting of the mule on the bridge and the harsh treatment of the British. A handful of critics, while appreciating that it was a biographical account, believed that the film fell short in that effort.[53] Karl Malden's performance drew decidedly mixed commentary. Some thought his work quite good, but others agreed with one critic who called his acting "remarkably colorless."[54] Scattered about otherwise positive reviewers were complaints that the film was episodic and slow.[55] Taken as a whole, these were minor blemishes to an otherwise strong and positive reaction to the film among the critics in smaller media outlets.

The youth market was another element of the segment of society that Twentieth Century-Fox wanted to reach. The baby boomers—the children produced during the post–World War II demographic bubble—was a growing part of the consumer market, and as is so often the case with the young, they were spending money rather than saving. The problem this generation posed for film studios is that they had grown up on television, and film audiences had grown old. Movies were starting to lose money as a corporate product. One response from the industry was the blockbuster, which Twentieth Century-Fox had pioneered with *Cleopatra*. That film also showed the danger in that approach: it could easily break a studio financially.[56]

The importance of the youth market would fade in the decades to follow as the boomers aged, but in the early 1970s, they were an important target audience. College newspapers offer a small window into sentiment on various campuses. The reviews were often more sophisticated than what one found in medium-sized media outlets: they understood the symbolic references to Don Quixote and the dramatic reasons for the opening speech. The reviewers also praised Scott's acting as a real strength in the film. With these points made, some clear trends emerged among the collegiate journalists; they gagged on both the history in the film and war itself. The papers at the University of Southern California and the University of California, Los Angeles, home of the nation's two leading film schools, offered highly sophisticated critiques. The *Daily Trojan* reviewer said the film would have been nothing other than an objectionable war film if not for Scott's acting. The reviewer for the *Daily Bruin* went further, adding that the film was the type open to many political interpretations. Those issues were probably of more interest to older audiences. College students, the reviewer noted, should appreciate more the fact that the film was a character study rather than a war film.[57]

The anecdotal evidence also shows that the film was extremely popular on college campuses. At a special advance showing arranged for college students from several California campuses, the audience reacted strongly. "When I screened the film for 6,000 college-age students in San Francisco they were the single most enthusiastic audience the film has had," Schaffner said.[58]

The international reaction to the film is important as well; it provides a view of American society from a different angle. It is also permits an analysis of how American culture was received and/or rejected in foreign cultures. Studio executives were particularly concerned about the reaction in the United Kingdom, where the film was called *Patton: Lust for Glory.* The biggest concern was the reaction of Lord Montgomery. Although he was unhappy with his portrayal in the film, the field marshal apparently never seriously considered any legal action to prevent the distribution of the film. There might have been a reason: the reviewers loved the film. In the *Daily Express,* film critic Ian Christie wrote, "Michael Bates plays Field Marshal Montgomery with devastating accuracy."[59] He and other British critics tended to focus on the fact that the film was a character study.[60] "It is an engrossing study of a man who believed in his own destiny, but could not control it," a critic for the *Daily Mirror* observed.[61] A second major theme was the quality of Scott's acting. Another critic in the *Observer* said the actor delivered a "brilliant performance."[62]

Not every critic in the United Kingdom was happy. Dilys Powell in the *Sunday Times* complained about the nationalism of the film. The film presented all the Americans as competent military professionals, but the British were made to look inept, be it Montgomery or Conningham, to enhance that image.[63]

After looking at these reviews, people at the studio breathed a sigh of relief. "In view critical viewpoint it is well that you prohibited changes since minimal lumps we received were based upon general characterization rather than specific scenes," McCarthy told Richard Zanuck in the clipped language of a telegram. For his part, Zanuck was happy with the reviews.[64]

The reviews in Canada gave him less to enjoy. In the Great White North, the reviewers were at best ambivalent about the film, but several were critical, even hostile. A reviewer for the Toronto *Telegram* noted, "*Patton* . . . is purposely ambiguous about its central character, presenting him as both hero and devil." That was one of the most positive reviews that appeared in British North America. "We are offered nothing of the man and everything of the myth and the implication is that maybe Patton wasn't much of a human being but he was one hell of a guy to win wars," a reviewer in the *Montreal Star* commented. In the *Montreal Gazette*, one critic closed his review with the words, "Seldom has the truth been less moving on such a grand scale."[65]

In Ireland, the critic for the *Irish Times* argued that the film raised troubling issues, but "it slides around its subject and never indicates a point of view." He also added that the real hero of the film was Omar Bradley.[66]

The critics in France loved the film, but for reasons that were often quite different than those found in the United States. Many Frenchmen saw it as a real work of art. Scott received praise in review after review. One critic observed: "Brutal, power-crazy Patton becomes a sort of Borgia to which George C. Scott adds the breadth of a Shakespearean character." French film director Alexandre Astruc, writing in *Paris Match*, praised the film. What had started out as a piece of propaganda for the U.S. Army had exceeded the original intentions of the studio. He attributed this achievement to Schaffner's direction and to Scott, who gave a "near perfect performance." Film critic Robert Chazal agreed, calling the lead's performance "unforgettable" but added that Karl Malden's "sobriety brings out even more Patton's excessiveness." Others appreciated the film politically and socially. As a reviewer in the satirical *Le Canard Enchaine* observed, "Once again the Americans teach us a lesson. Who in our country would dare paint such a candid picture of one of our national figures?" Didier Raguenet, the consul general of France in Los Angeles, thanked McCarthy for making such a sensitive film: "I was moved by your tact and the emotive eloquence with which you have illustrated the pages of the Liberation of France by the American Army, the Free French Forces and the French Resistance. Too often have we seen these moving events, which have left all Frenchmen sensitized even after 25 years, treated in a flippant manner which is offensive to our country."[67]

The film also received excellent reviews in Denmark. Most Danes took little interest in the politics that the film seemed to represent. Their reviews showed more interest in its artistic merits. In a review, novelist Anders Bodelsen asserted: "George C. Scott simply is the picture." Bent Grasten, the writer of many film scripts, observed: "Probably the first war-picture to accept a very human situation which I most certainly won't keep secret— the fighting instinct." Another novelist, Rolf Bagger, added that Scott "never allows his spectators a moments rest." He did notice that there was a good deal of nationalism in the film; it portrayed any people other than Americans as fools. This emphasis hurt the integrity of the picture.[68]

The film even spoke to foreign heads of state. Prince Rainer III of Monaco, who was married to American film actress Grace Kelly, detected a nice American irony in the film. "I was so impressed by the end of the film, and I sort of felt guilty, that this great 'guy' and chief . . . had to be beaten, and put away by those lousy politicians (there is a great similitude between Patton, and MacArthur . . . in the fact that politics struck them down, and put them away!)."[69]

Reaction to the film overseas shows that there were things in American culture that foreign audiences were willing to accept and other elements they were willing to reject. The most important of these was an openness in evaluating the character of national heroes. What many saw as the excessive nationalism of both Patton and *Patton* was something that many foreigners rejected. That negative, however, was less important than the positives.

Patton also spoke to various different segments of the American public about powerful legends about the nation itself. There was considerable concern among studio executives, the producer, and the director about public sentiment in the United States. The Vietnam War was starting to roil society in a way not seen since Reconstruction, and *Patton* was a war film—at least at first glance. What would happen when the film was released? Would people see it, would politics keep an audience from developing, or would friends and family encourage others to see the film? These questions worried many at the studio. Reactions among the public revealed fundamental issues about the character of American society. Results varied significantly, but most audiences generally viewed the film through the lens of how the United States of America did or did not live up to its own high ideals. This issue transcended gender, which explains why women went to see the film, despite the lack of female characters.

Why did *Patton* provide this forum, as opposed to *The Dirty Dozen* (1967), *The Planet of the Apes*, or some other production? While most people understood that *Patton* was a work of fiction, it was much closer to nonfiction than most theatrical films, and it touched on timely, relevant social issues more than most Hollywood productions. Given that the Vietnam War had become a partisan, even divisive, social issue, combined with the harsh language of the Patton character's war speech at the beginning of the film, many people accordingly interpreted the film as a patriotic statement on behalf of the military. "COUNT ME AMONG YOUR MANY ADMIRERS," Nixon told McCarthy in a telegram.[70]

Ronald Reagan was thinking along the same lines. Retired from acting and now the governor of California, he wrote McCarthy at length and admitted that Scott was a better choice to play the lead than himself. After telling him it was a good picture, Reagan added, "It says some things that very much needed saying today. I have been greatly disturbed for sometime over the pernicious and constant degrading of the military. This picture restored a great deal of balance." He often forgot while watching the film that it was a fictional story. "It was so real." He also added that while he thought there was too much profanity in films, this film got it right. "I've never believed that I was a total square and have never been opposed to the use of anything absolutely essential to the telling of the story. It did not offend me in the slightest that you had Patton talking as Patton talked."[71]

Not everyone in the entertainment industry agreed with this view. Playwright Jerome Lawerence told McCarthy: "What impresses me most is what a fantastic *anti-war* document it is. I think this is especially significant coming from a General!" Carole Kass, the film critic for the *Richmond Times-Dispatch* and a friend of McCarthy's, agreed. She wrote him a long letter on the film, touching on issues she did not mention in print. One of those was the political sentiment in the film. "Perhaps you will receive an adverse reaction from those who believe that Gen. Patton was a monster or those who have deified him. But those, who like me are anti-war, will find much supportive substance, and the hawks will be happy too." Another acquaintance of the producer wrote McCarthy to discuss his experiences watching the film. "This being a super-conservative area, you would have been amused at the amount of applause during certain portions of the film."[72]

It is easy to see why some people interpreted *Patton* that way. Schaffner believed he was making a statement opposed to war. During a press conference just after shooting stopped, he called Patton a "necessary evil."[73]

Many interest groups reacted to the film from their specific perspectives, believing that they had a vested interest in this film. One of the more obvious groups were veterans of World War II. McCarthy received numerous letters from alumni of the war, passing their own judgments on the movie. General Mark W. Clark told McCarthy: "With regards your picture, I could never tell you how much I have enjoyed it and of my feeling that it was a timely production to help get the military out of the dog house. You did a supreme job and I congratulate you." Others thought the same way. Colonel Russell "Red" Reeder, a former head baseball coach at West Point, liked the film. "What I like best: the film does not glamorize war. I wish G.C.M. had lived to see it." Reeder knew of what he wrote. He was awarded the Distinguished Service Cross for his actions on D-day, and his sister helped Master Sergeant Martin Maher write the book *Bringing Up the Brass*, which later became the movie *The Long Gray Line* (1955). Major General Charles E. Johnson also wrote McCarthy: "You 'told it like it was'— and I was there, and believe me George Scott is George Patton."[74]

British veterans had similar possessive views about history, and Bradley became their point of contact. "I rather regretted that the film caricatured Monty quite so much," Colonel Thomas S. Bigland told Bradley. "There was enough success to share, and the theories of both sides were not always right." He was not the only one thinking that way. Major-General Sir Francis de Guingand, Montgomery's wartime chief of staff, wrote Bradley and told him he was "very impressed" with *Patton*. "One was left with the impression that the viewer was meant to get a pretty poor picture of Monty. I don't say he did not deserve some of the 'diggs' that he received, but I have always felt that he did a good job." He also raised several questions about historical facts about the picture's depiction of the past.[75]

A Montgomery issue seemed to be developing, but not in the manner that the studio executives had feared. Bradley turned out to be a useful tool for McCarthy in this matter. Without Montgomery raising the issue through the courts, Bradley's status was influential in neutralizing British nationalist sentiment. The five-star general responded to each of de Guingand's questions about the history. He admitted that Sir Francis was right about distortions in the film, but condensing four years of history—it was actually two and a half—into three hours was difficult. "Dramatic license had to be taken to capsule time," he explained. These alterations took nothing away from what the British had done. "The courage of the people of England and their valiant stand against the Germans prepared the way for an Allied victory. It was never the intent of the film to take away the pride of the British in one of their great fighting leaders."[76]

Historians of this era were another group that saw Patton, but also Patton, as their own. This reaction is both understandable and reasonable. Who, if not historians, have a vested interest in history? "I hope the movie portrays Patton as he really was," John Eisenhower, the son of the World War II legend and a published historian of this conflict, told McCarthy in 1968. "The pearl-handled pistols and fancy uniforms covered up a great amount of professional skill and knowledge." Two years later, Eisenhower wrote from the embassy in Brussels, where he was the U.S. ambassador, and told the producer that he was impressed. "It was a great emotional experience—partly from the nostalgia, I suppose, but also because of the way the thing was handled and because of the outstanding performance of George Scott."[77]

While Ambassador Eisenhower liked Patton, he saw some distortions. The film never discussed Patton's humility and his sense of humor. It was also clear that Bradley let his hatred of Montgomery color his account. The British field marshal had made crucial contributions to the advance into Germany, including the seizure of Antwerp, and these never got their due. He also thought McCarthy had stretched history by making claims on the central importance Patton played in rapidly ending the war. On a personal note, he thought removing his father from the story was a bad decision. It certainly altered the nature of the Verdun conference during the Battle of the Bulge. "As a result, the meeting of 19 December, 1944 lost the impact of the exchange between Patton and DDE. I shouldn't be so sensitive about this, but I think that the Verdun meeting was one of my Dad's finest hours."[78]

On the other hand, Patton's biographer, Ladislas Farago, was satisfied with what he saw. Although he thought both McCarthy and Scott had done much of the work in making the film authentic, he believed the director was most responsible for its authenticity. "I see and feel you behind every scene—the Schaffner touch that made this picture," he wrote in a cover letter he sent with a signed copy of his book. Donald E. Baruch, the chief of the motion picture production branch of the Department of Defense's information directorate, took a similar view. Since he oversaw the military's interaction with the film industry, he knew something about war films. "In my opinion," he told McCarthy, "you are to be commended for bringing General Patton to the screen so authentically, realistically and handsomely. Your reverence for the subject has heightened the color and excitement. It should be talked about greatly as it is a picture of many thoughts."[79]

Those who had lost family members in combat also spoke out about the film, and these views were not limited to those grieving from World War II. "How dare anyone use the statement allegedly spoken by General Patton referring to dead 'G.I.s' as 'dumb bastards'?" the mother of a soldier killed in Vietnam told McCarthy. "Has it occurred to any of you at all that you have opened the wounds of many broken hearted families all over the country." The sister of an officer who had died at Kasserine Pass also found this section of the film objectionable. "However they had something besides equipment—they had indomitable courage. I think you can possibly understand my personal reaction to your colossal error."[80]

The film also drew the ire of animal rights activists. In May, the London Daily Mirror ran a story reporting that during film, the crew film killed a horse with dynamite, two mules with poison, and a donkey, which they had clubbed to death. "It is quite deplorable in this day and age that films can be made for the entertainment of the public which involve suffering or death to animals," Trevor Scott, executive director of the International Society for the Protection of Animals, declared. McCarthy never took this issue seriously. News stories on this subject had briefly appeared in London papers during shooting, but nothing had come of them. It is worth noting that these stories were factually in error; the crew had killed only two mules through lethal injection. "From my point of view, I pray that when my time comes I can, without pain, go as quickly and comfortably as the two mules did," McCarthy explained. Richard Zanuck did not take the issues seriously either. "This is a matter of historical fact and I'm sure we can defend it," he wrote at the bottom of a memo.[81]

It was only after Trevor Scott took the issue to the British Board of Film

Censors, which had the power to force the studio to alter the film for release in the United Kingdom, that McCarthy realized the real problem he faced. Globalization required that he abide by the rules of other countries, and at the time, the British were more sensitive to animal rights than their American cousins. Entertainment reporters quickly followed up, asking if animals shown being killed on the screen were real or props. McCarthy confirmed—privately—to the secretary of the board that the crew had killed two mules through lethal injection. His statement that the animals had died painlessly was sufficient for them. Publicly, though, the studio stalled for a month, before confirming—or to be more accurate, clarifying—this report. "Animals were killed, but it was done humanely," McCarthy admitted. "If this man was upset he has my sympathy. But it is the sort of thing that happens in every film." That response was not particularly politic. McCarthy received a letter telling him his attitude was "ugly and repelling." This correspondent added, "That you justify it by claiming 'the animals died painlessly by injection' is indicative of your values."[82]

There was much truth in that observation. During the war, Patton had indeed shot a mule that was blocking the advance of a U.S. column—as was depicted in the film—but there had been no legitimate reason for the crew to destroy two animals. Props could easily have sufficed. That the destruction of these animals became a minor public relations setback for the studio was an indication that society's views on this subject were changing, but also how slowly that adjustment was taking.

Race became another issue involving this film. Ray Martell of the Mexican-American Political Association contacted the studio. Martell was an actor with some extremely limited success in television, and he wanted McCarthy and the Zanucks to cast Americans of Hispanic ancestry in the film. A colleague of North's had also raised this issue with him before shooting started. McCarthy explained that the film was being filmed in Spain and there were hundreds of Spanish-speaking members of the crew. The problem with the film was it was a historical set piece, and no Mexican Americans had been close to George S. Patton Jr. When Richard Zanuck saw McCarthy's response, he wrote, "Dear Frank, This letter will be helpful." Nothing more happened on the matter.[83]

Some people objected to the racial matters that did appear on screen. Richard Vetter, vice president of Dimension 150—the company that manufactured film the studio used in *Patton*—wrote McCarthy, telling him the production was a wonderful work of art. He warned him, however, that

Scott's line about "killing some Japs in the South Pacific" would cost them millions in the Japanese market. This issue also worried the studio's executive in charge of distribution for Japan. McCarthy began checking and reported to both men that the word *Japs* was never uttered in the film. The Patton character did talk about killing Japanese, but he never used any derogatory term.[84] Since there was nothing—literally—to this issue, it died quickly.

Others complained about what was not on the screen. Wilbert Dyer, a cab driver in Columbus, Ohio, got a good deal of media attention when he complained about the depiction in the film of the 761st Tank Battalion, a segregated black unit. On screen, this unit was composed entirely of white soldiers. "I know they were just trying to make a history of Patton and I don't expect them to branch out and make a Negro history, but they shouldn't hide us either." McCarthy responded to the issue with a letter to the editor of certain newspapers. He noted that while the 761st was the only black combat formation under Patton's command, there were only 397 men in the battalion. The total strength of the Third U.S. Army was 250,000. As a result, the battalion constituted 16/100 of 1 percent of the total manpower under Patton's command.[85]

Still, the issue continued to fester. One black veteran of the conflict stated that he had lost a $25 bet that there would be black troops in the film. *Jet* magazine picked up on this issue. Dyer was the main source for this story, and there was no reference to McCarthy or his explanation. "I admire the story and the way it portrayed Patton," Dyer stated, "but it mentions this unit and says they marched over 100 miles to fight and win a major battle, then lets the world believe it was white men who accomplished this."[86]

Nothing happened in the wake of this commentary, and studio executives might have thought the race issue had gone away, but after a year, the National Association for the Advancement of Colored People took up the issue. Leonard H. Carter, the western regional director for the organization, wrote Dennis C. Stanfill, president of the studio, to complain about the absence of the 761st and the role of black Americans in combat in World War II and in Vietnam. "At a time when the percentage of black combat fatalities exceeds the percentage of blacks employed in the civilian population, it is most unfortunate and damaging to have such an otherwise historically accurate document downplay and ignore the important contributions of blacks to the survival of this nation."[87]

Carter's complaint resulted in a meeting between himself and Mc-Carthy. The producer characterized the meeting as "friendly." He explained that there were 192 battalions in the Third Army and that they had avoided mentioning any of these units because they wanted to avoid reaction from veterans about their inclusion or exclusion. The only exception was the 101st Airborne Division, which had been surrounded at Bastogne. McCarthy then produced a copy of the 761st's official history and showed, using its maps, that the unit had been on the northern flank of the Third Army's advance and was not in the southern column that entered the Belgium village. Carter and his legal counsel, Robert Gnaizda, took this explanation in good faith. They still tried to salvage the meeting and asked that Twentieth Century-Fox make a documentary about the 761st that would precede future showings of *Patton*. McCarthy basically said no, it would be too expensive for the studio to make such a film, but he suggested that the NAACP produce this documentary using official U.S. Army footage and then distribute it on their own. His "no" was polite but firm. Carter then asked if the studio would consider establishing a scholarship for the NAACP that would be associated with Patton in some fashion. Mc-Carthy said that he could not answer for the studio. In October, Stanfill sent Carter a $500 check and told him that was all the studio could spare.[88]

A far bigger concern for the studio involved issue of gender rather than race. Would women go to see *Patton*? The movie was a war picture, and that genre normally attracted men in excessive fashion. In addition, there was only one woman with a speaking part in the finished film. Studio executives were concerned. Women were an important segment of the audience in and of themselves, but they also had influence on their husbands and boyfriends. "Women too have been going to see *Patton*," Schaffner remarked. "George Scott's performance attracts them. It has that kind of manliness women haven't seen in years."[89]

Perhaps the group with the most vested interest in this film was, in the end, the Patton family. The general's children had never cooperated with any Hollywood production, and Frank McCarthy had never given up on trying to get them involved in the production or, at a bare minimum, maintaining cordial relations. He invited them to the film's premiere and offered to set up a private showing for them. The family declined both offers.[90] Robert Patton, the general's grandson, later wrote that his parents, aunts, and uncles were unhappy when they heard that the film was getting made, but they were curious to see it when it finally came out. His father, Colonel George S. Patton IV, took him to see a matinee showing at a theater in New York's Times Square. After listening to Scott's opening monologue, Colonel Patton leaned over to his son and whispered, "Sounds nothing like him. My old man had a high voice." Robert Patton had never known his grandfather and felt no personal connection. It was just another film to him, but during the scenes depicting the relief of Bastogne as Scott's character walked among the men of the Third Army, he heard his father weeping.[91]

The reaction of the colonel's sister was no less emotional. "I am looking forward with great interest— + great trepidation—to your movie," Ruth Ellen Totten told McCarthy. She went to see the movie in Boston as just another patron, along with her cousin and a few friends. Totten was trembling in her seat and was prepared to be offended. The film, however, made a real impression on her—but so did the reaction of the audience. There was frequent applause in the theater. When the movie ended, she was sobbing. Two days later, she composed a letter to McCarthy: "I think it is the best movie I have seen since 'Gone with The Wind' and that Mr Scott has done a tour de force as Patton and that it was done in the most subtle and excellent taste, with many many touches that I have to go again to see to fully appreciate."[92]

Totten went further, writing an essay for publication that was widely reprinted in various newspapers. She told the American public that she and her family had fought the making of this film. "We were wrong to this extent; they were more sensitive, more just, and more realistic in their portrayal than any of the contemporary people who portrayed him and judged him. We were right in this respect; if we had not fought so long and so hard to block the motion picture, they might have made it sooner and not have had George Scott for the title role." She explained that Scott had spent time studying her father's mannerisms and personality. "So many of his gestures, particularly, his 'mirthless smile' were so true to life that it gave me quite a start." The actor's work "indicated to us, the family, that he not only liked General Patton, he understood him—which few people did, do, or ever will."[93]

Kass of the *Richmond Times-Dispatch* was "stunned" when she saw that article. "I think you need no other kudo (except, of course, full coffers) to make all your efforts worthwhile," she told McCarthy. "Her reaction is ultimate evidence that everything from your concept, Coppola's script, Franklin's direction and Scott's performance, resulted in integrity."[94]

Richard Zanuck had a similar reaction when he saw Totten's letter. He scribbled a note on it for McCarthy: "I think this is just great, Frank. I assume you've sent a copy to Scott. I've sent DZ a copy. Congrats on finally winning a long battle."[95]

9. The Legacy

Patton did not alter the way films were shot, produced, or distributed, but it had an enormous and powerful legacy nonetheless. Different audiences in the United States were already trying to appropriate the film as their own before, during, and after its release. One of the most influential of these groups was the film industry itself. There is an old saying that imitation is the sincerest form of flattery. Copyright laws not withstanding, many in Hollywood began paying tribute to *Patton*, adopting its story about power for their own purposes in a way that happens to only a few productions. As a result, it is clear that *Patton* is one of the most important films made in the twentieth century.

The first way to measure the legacy of this film is to examine the awards it earned. The film industry at the time recognized the quality of the film. The National Board of Review of Motion Pictures named *Patton* the best picture of 1970. Schaffner won the best director's award for 1970 from the Director's Guild of America. McCarthy accepted the award for him because the director was on set shooting his next film, *Nicholas and Alexandra* (1971). The award from the guild was particularly important because that winner usually—but not always—wins the Oscar for best director as well.[1]

The next big award presentation was the Oscars. The rejection that Scott had suffered from his two previous nominations, however, had convinced him that he wanted nothing to do with the Academy Awards. When he was nominated, he attempted to decline, and when that was not possible, he decided not to attend the presentations. Scott was the feature of a cover story in *Time* magazine—his stature was moving beyond the entertainment industry—but his position toward the awards show seemed to many observers to be costing him his chance at winning an Oscar. McCarthy noticed an air of resentment in Hollywood toward his lead actor.[2]

The awards were presented on April 16, 1971, at the Dorothy Chandler Pavilion in the Music City complex in downtown Los Angeles. The show was broadcast on NBC, and the television cameras showed the celebrities arriving on the red carpet leading into the glass front of the pavilion. Prominently featured in this section of the telecast were Omar Bradley and his wife, Kitty. They were, however, overshadowed by Sally Kellerman, who was nominated in the best supporting actress category for her role as Major Margaret "Hot Lips" Houlihan in M*A*S*H (1970). Kellerman received a good deal of media attention for the dress she wore to the event. She wore a tight peach velvet gown with a U-shaped plunging neckline that exposed her décolletage. "The dress had to have been constructed right on her," a reporter for the Los Angeles Times speculated.

Patton was nominated for ten awards, but the night started off poorly for the film. At first, the evening seemed to favor Patton. Shirley Jones and Harry Belefonte presented in the best sound category. Douglas Williams and Don Bassman won for Patton. As this win was announced, television cameras cut to Bradley, sitting in the audience. Then, despite this promising beginning, things started to go horribly wrong for the film. Genevieve Bujold and James Earl Jones made the presentation for cinematography. After some awkward jokes about the dashiki that Jones was wearing, the two announced that Freddie Young had won for his work in Ryan's Daughter (1970), beating out Koenekamp. Later in the show, Joan Blondell and Glen Campbell gave out the Oscar for original score. Goldsmith lost to Francis Lai's music in Love Story (1970). It was another defeat for Patton, but also another personal setback for Goldsmith. He was now zero for five in Oscar nominations. Alex Weldon then lost special visual effects to A. D. Flowers and L. B. Abbott for their work on Tora! Tora! Tora! (1970).

It looked to be a long night for the cast and crew of Patton, but then Bob Hope and Petula Clark presented the Oscar for art direction. The team that Urie McCleary led on Patton won. McCleary, who spoke for all four, kept his remarks simple: "We thank you."

The Patton onslaught had begun.

Bujold and Walter Matthau then presented the award for film editing. Hugh S. Fowler was the winner. He shook hands with Matthau after reaching the stage and then said: "I do really thank you very, very much for this little beauty."

The next Patton veteran to win was the director himself. Ryan O'Neal along with Janet Gaynor, the first recipient of the best actress award, presented the Oscar in the directing category. Schaffner was still on the set of Nicholas and Alexandra, so Malden accepted on his behalf. The sound was poorly calibrated when the actor stood in front of the podium and micro-

phones. He began to talk and O'Neal generated some laughs from the audience when he placed the trophy on the podium. Malden chuckled at the
miscues of live television, but that was as close as he came to losing his
composure. "Let me say, you couldn't have given it to a better fella. He deserves it. I know. I was there."

Sarah Miles, a nominee for best actress herself, and George Segal presented the award for best original screenplay. After awkwardly reading
jokes from a cue card, she corrected him when he said her name wrong,
and Segal shook his head as she mispronounced the name of the nominees. These miscues actually got more laughs than their scripted jokes.
The winners for this award were Coppola and North. Because Coppola
was busy shooting The Godfather (1972), North spoke alone: "I would hope
that Patton is not just a war picture, I would hope it is a peace picture."

The next category in which a member of the Patton cast and crew was
nominated was best actor. Scott was the front runner, but his attempt to
decline the honor gave this moment more anticipation than normal.
Jones, one of the other nominees, said Scott clearly deserved the win, but
there was no telling, given his personal boycott. Goldie Hawn, who had
won best supporting actress the year before, made the presentation. Before opening the envelope, she explained that the award went to a performance and not an actor. In addition to Scott, the nominees were O'Neal
for Love Story, Jones for The Great White Hope (1970), Jack Nicholson for Five
Easy Pieces (1970), and Melvyn Douglas for I Never Sang for My Father (1970).

Hawn opened the envelope containing the name of the winner, and a
low sound of anticipation rippled through the crowd seated in the Dorothy
Chandler Pavilion. "Oh, my God! It's George C. Scott," she said with a
shocked look of disbelief. Then it turned to one of happiness. The audience exploded with thunderous applause as she smiled. "The murmur before the announcement of George C. Scott told the tale of why everyone
was really there!" Army Archerd, the entertainment and gossip columnist,
observed. McCarthy accepted the award because of Scott's boycott. He was
careful to avoid using the words "thank you."

The final category involving Patton was the award for best picture. The
nominees were Patton, Love Story, Airport, Five Easy Pieces, and M*A*S*H.
Steve McQueen presented this award, and after he introduced each title, a
clip from the film played. The scenes from Patton were of the general demanding that his staff work hard and be prepared to die, and another of
him demanding a prayer for good weather from a chaplain. The television

cameras then cut to Bradley as McCarthy made a comment to him. Both were smiling and beaming. It was their moment.

Then it became McCarthy's moment. *Patton* won, and McCarthy went to the stage alone. "I accept this award cheerfully, under no duress." The audience laughed at that subtle reference to Scott. "With deep obligations and thanks to many, particularly the Zanucks, father and son . . . " Applause filled the auditorium with those words. The Zanucks were in the process of losing control of Twentieth Century-Fox, and his remarks were a nice tribute to his patrons. McCarthy continued: " . . . who gave the *Patton* project their confidence and support during the 20 years that have elapsed since I first proposed it. Thank you." He repeated those last two words over and over, with growing strength each time.[3]

Within days of this event, McCarthy donated his trophy to the George C. Marshall Library at the Virginia Military Institute. It has been displayed there off and on ever since.[4]

Patton not only won honors, large and small; it also made a number of the "all-time best" lists that people often like to put together. These type of rankings are fallacies, but they collectively attest to the power and influence of *Patton*. In 1998, in the wake of the release of *Saving Private Ryan* (1998), film critic Mick LaSalle of the *San Francisco Chronicle* selected the best World War II movies. *Patton* was one of his choices. "George C. Scott's flamboyant performance as the crusty, egomaniacal World War II general is the highlight." A few weeks later, Ron Weiskind and Barbara Vancheri, the critics of the *Pittsburgh Post-Gazette*, put together a list of the best war films ever made. According to the criteria they used, "the movies had to feature soldiers during actual historical wars," there were no westerns or science fiction titles, and the films had to focus primarily on combat and military operations. *Patton* placed first on their list. "Director Franklin Schaffner's film biography captures Patton, a flawed man but an unquestionable hero, in all his complexities."[5]

Such views were also common among the general public. In 2003, the staff of *USAA Magazine*, the official publication of USAA, the insurance agency that serves the military and retired military community, surveyed its membership on their favorite war films of all time. The USAA membership selected seven films, but the staff made no attempt to rank the selections. The seven titles were *The Bridge on the River Kwai*, *The Longest Day*, *Patton*, *Saving Private Ryan*, *We Were Soldiers*, *Twelve O'Clock High* (1949), and *The Deer Hunter* (1978). A short paragraph description of each film and comments from members on the movie was part of this article. "Schaffner's direction of this fascinating personality portrait makes it one of the greatest military movies ever produced."[6]

More significantly, and certainly more attention-getting than these lists, were the actions of the American Film Institute. Starting in 1998, the AFI, like other people and organizations at the end of the century, began putting together lists ranking the greatest individuals, events, or developments of the twentieth century. In the case of the AFI, the centennial of the American motion picture industry also coincided with the move into the twenty-first century. To celebrate this anniversary, the institute got more than 1,500 people in the motion picture industry—actors, writers, directors, producers, cinematographers, editors, executives, critics, and historians—to select the 100 greatest American movies made between 1896 and 1996. The organization made the list public on a CBS television special *AFI's 100 Years . . . 100 Movies*. In the eighty-ninth position was *Patton*. The entire list is provided in Table 9.1.

The AFI then created several other lists, including the best action, comedy, and romance movies of the first hundred years of American film, and sponsored a television special for each one. In 2003, the institute sponsored its sixth television special: *AFI's 100 Years . . . 100 Heroes and Villains*. This special actually featured two different lists: the fifty greatest heroes and the fifty greatest villains. The judges used a criteria that defined a hero as "a character(s) who prevails in extreme circumstances and dramatizes a sense of morality, courage and purpose. Though they may be ambiguous or flawed, they often sacrifice themselves to show humanity at its best." The selection criteria also included the cultural impact of "characters who have a made a mark on American society in matters of style and substance." The historical legacy of "characters who elicit strong reactions across time, enriching America's film heritage while continuing to inspire contemporary artists and audiences" was another consideration of the jury. The character of General George S. Patton Jr. from *Patton* placed twenty-ninth on the roster of heroes. The entire hero list is provided in Table 9.2.[7]

A third way to measure the impact of *Patton* is to look at how it shaped the making of other productions. There is no minimizing the impact it had on the making of *The Godfather* (1972). Coppola was making this film when he won the Academy Award for best screenplay. "I was really almost about to get fired from *The Godfather*," Coppola explained on his *Patton* DVD com-

Table 9.1. List of 100 greatest American movies, 1896–1996

1. Citizen Kane (1941)	38. Double Indemnity (1944)
2. Casablanca (1942)	39. Doctor Zhivago (1965)
3. The Godfather (1972)	40. North By Northwest (1959)
4. Gone with the Wind (1939)	41. West Side Story (1961)
5. Lawrence of Arabia (1962)	42. Rear Window (1954)
6. The Wizard of Oz (1939)	43. King Kong (1933)
7. The Graduate (1967)	44. The Birth of a Nation (1915)
8. On the Waterfront (1954)	45. A Streetcar Named Desire (1951)
9. Schindler's List (1993)	46. A Clockwork Orange (1971)
10. Singin' in the Rain (1952)	47. Taxi Driver (1976)
11. It's a Wonderful Life (1946)	48. Jaws (1975)
12. Sunset Boulevard (1950)	49. Snow White and the Seven Dwarfs
13. The Bridge on The River Kwai (1957)	(1937)
14. Some Like It Hot (1959)	50. Butch Cassidy and the Sundance Kid
15. Star Wars (1977)	(1969)
16. All About Eve (1950)	51. The Philadelphia Story (1940)
17. The African Queen (1951)	52. From Here to Eternity (1953)
18. Psycho (1960)	53. Amadeus (1984)
19. Chinatown (1974)	54. All Quiet on the Western Front (1930)
20. One Flew Over the Cuckoo's Nest (1975)	55. The Sound of Music (1965)
21. The Grapes of Wrath (1940)	56. M*A*S*H (1970)
22. 2001: A Space Odyssey (1968)	57. The Third Man (1949)
23. The Maltese Falcon (1941)	58. Fantasia (1940)
24. Raging Bull (1980)	59. Rebel Without a Cause (1955)
25. E.T. The Extra-Terrestrial (1982)	60. Raiders of the Lost Ark (1981)
26. Dr. Strangelove (1964)	61. Vertigo (1958)
27. Bonnie and Clyde (1967)	62. Tootsie (1982)
28. Apocalypse Now (1979)	63. Stagecoach (1939)
29. Mr. Smith Goes to Washington (1939)	64. Close Encounters of the Third Kind
30. The Treasure of the Sierra Madre (1948)	(1977)
31. Annie Hall (1977)	65. The Silence of the Lambs (1991)
32. The Godfather Part II (1974)	66. Network (1976)
33. High Noon (1952)	67. The Manchurian Candidate (1962)
34. To Kill a Mockingbird (1962)	68. An American in Paris (1951)
35. It Happened One Night (1934)	69. Shane (1953)
36. Midnight Cowboy (1969)	70. The French Connection (1971)
37. The Best Years of Our Lives (1946)	71. Forrest Gump (1994)

72. Ben-Hur (1959)	87. Frankenstein (1931)
73. Wuthering Heights (1939)	88. Easy Rider (1969)
74. The Gold Rush (1925)	**89. Patton (1970)**
75. Dances with Wolves (1990)	90. The Jazz Singer (1927)
76. City Lights (1931)	91. My Fair Lady (1964)
77. American Graffiti (1973)	92. A Place in the Sun (1951)
78. Rocky (1976)	93. The Apartment (1960)
79. The Deer Hunter (1978)	94. Goodfellas (1990)
80. The Wild Bunch (1969)	95. Pulp Fiction (1994)
81. Modern Times (1936)	96. The Searchers (1956)
82. Giant (1956)	97. Bringing Up Baby (1938)
83. Platoon (1986)	98. Unforgiven (1992)
84. Fargo (1996)	99. Guess Who's Coming to Dinner
85. Duck Soup (1933)	(1967)
86. Mutiny on the Bounty (1935)	100. Yankee Doodle Dandy (1942)

Source: American Film Institute.

mentary. He was feuding with Paramount about the scheduling, budget, and casting. "I really think—that to this day—that had I not won that Oscar, for sure I would have been fired off *The Godfather* because it looked that way. And, you know, it is a big thing to win an Oscar. And, um, and uh, they would have been embarrassed to fire me after such a nice, uh, thing."[8]

Seven years later *Patton* helped shape the screenplay of *Apocalypse Now* (1979). John Milius wrote the script to this film along with Coppola. Milius liked Patton's line about war: "I love it. God help me, I do love it so. I love it more than my life." Milius incorporated a similar line when Lieutenant Colonel Bill Kilgore (Robert Duvall) discussed napalm.[9]

The film shaped other productions that had no involvement from *Patton* alumni. In the science fiction television series *Battlestar Galactica* (1978–1979), the writers and producers created the character of Commander Cain, who was played by Lloyd Bridges for a "Patton in Space" episode.[10] The actor René Auberjonois took inspiration from George C. Scott in two roles he played in the *Star Trek* films and television programs. In *Star Trek VI: The Undiscovered Country* (1991), he had an unbilled role playing a marine colonel. Throughout rehearsal sessions, he delivered his lines in a raspy voice, which was a homage to and impersonation of Scott's Patton. Most of his lines ended up getting cut from the final theatrical version, but in *Star Trek: Deep Space Nine* (1993–1999), the third Star Trek television series,

Table 9.2. List of top fifty film heros

1.	Atticus Finch	*To Kill a Mockingbird* (1962)
2.	Indiana Jones	*Raiders of the Lost Ark* (1981)
3.	James Bond	*Dr. No* (1962)
4.	Rick Blaine	*Casablanca* (1942)
5.	Will Kane	*High Noon* (1952)
6.	Clarice Starling	*The Silence of the Lambs* (1991)
7.	Rocky Balboa	*Rocky* (1976)
8.	Ellen Ripley	*Aliens* (1986)
9.	George Bailey	*It's a Wonderful Life* (1946)
10.	T. E. Lawrence	*Lawrence of Arabia* (1962)
11.	Jefferson Smith	*Mr. Smith Goes to Washington* (1939)
12.	Tom Joad	*The Grapes of Wrath* (1940)
13.	Oskar Schindler	*Schindler's List* (1993)
14.	Han Solo	*Star Wars* (1977)
15.	Norma Rae Webster	*Norma Rae* (1979)
16.	Shane	*Shane* (1953)
17.	Harry Callahan	*Dirty Harry* (1971)
18.	Robin Hood	*The Adventures of Robin Hood* (1938)
19.	Virgil Tibbs	*In the Heat of the Night* (1967)
20.	Butch Cassidy and the Sundance Kid	*Butch Cassidy and the Sundance Kid* (1969)
21.	Mahatma Gandhi	*Gandhi* (1982)
22.	Spartacus	*Spartacus* (1960)
23.	Terry Malloy	*On the Waterfront* (1954)
24.	Thelma Dickerson and Louise Sawyer	*Thelma & Louise* (1991)
25.	Lou Gehrig	*The Pride of the Yankees* (1942)
26.	Superman	*Superman* (1978)
27.	Bob Woodward and Carl Bernstein	*All the President's Men* (1976)
28.	Juror #8	*12 Angry Men* (1957)
29.	**General George S. Patton**	**Patton** (1970)
30.	Luke Jackson	*Cool Hand Luke* (1967)
31.	Erin Brockovich	*Erin Brockovich* (2000)
32.	Philip Marlowe	*The Big Sleep* (1946)
33.	Marge Gunderson	*Fargo* (1996)
34.	Tarzan	*Tarzan The Ape Man* (1932)
35.	Alvin York	*Sergeant York* (1941)
36.	Rooster Cogburn	*True Grit* (1969)
37.	Obi-Wan Kenobi	*Star Wars* (1977)

38. The Tramp	*City Lights* (1931)
39. Lassie	*Lassie Come Home* (1943)
40. Frank Serpico	*Serpico* (1973)
41. Arthur Chipping	*Goodbye, Mr. Chips* (1939)
42. Father Edward	*Boys Town* (1938)
43. Moses	*The Ten Commandments* (1956)
44. Jimmy "Popeye" Doyle	*The French Connection* (1971)
45. Zorro	*The Mark of Zorro* (1940)
46. Batman	*Batman* (1989)
47. Karen Silkwood	*Silkwood* (1983)
48. Terminator	*Terminator 2: Judgment Day* (1991)
49. Andrew Beckett	*Philadelphia* (1993)
50. General Maximus Decimus Meridus	*Gladiator* (2000)

Source: American Film Institute.

Auberjonois played a supporting role. His character, Odo, is a grumpy individual with a gruff voice that Auberjonois took in part from his previous role.[11] Mike Sussman, the producer of *Star Trek: Enterprise* (2001–2005), the fifth series in the science fiction franchise, wrote the screenplay to "In a Mirror, Darkly, Part 2" and based one scene on *Patton*. Even though Sussman copied none of Scott's language for a scene with a speech to the troops, he rented a copy of *Patton* to "get inspired."[12]

In the documentary *Bigger, Stronger, Faster: The Side Effects of Being American* (2008), writer/director/narrator Chris Bell actually uses clips from *Patton*. Bell explores the use of steroids in American sports in this film, looking at the experiences of himself and his brothers. Bell includes a section from the *Patton* introduction where Scott's character is discussing how losing is hateful to Americans. The clip is used to show that there is a win-at-all-costs mentality in American society that is not limited to individuals using steroids, and one that Bell questions. "There is a clash in America between doing the right thing, and being the best," Bell states.[13]

A fourth way to measure the influence of this film is to look at how it has been referenced in a host of other films. *Patton* is mentioned repeatedly in other productions. In Spalding Gray's one-man film, *Swimming to Cambodia* (1987), he repeats the stories of Nixon watching Patton "over and over again" as he orders the invasion of Cambodia. In *Defending Your Life* (1991), Daniel Miller (Albert Brooks) imitates Scott's Patton in one scene. In *Forget*

Paris (1995), Debra Winger's Ellen Andrews character mentions the film. In the "'Twas the Night Before Chaos" (December 13, 1994) episode of the series *Home Improvement* (1991–1999), the main character, Tim Taylor (Tim Allen), must deal with a visiting father-in-law who has recently retired from the U.S. Army and is having difficulty making the adjustment. Taylor's father-in-law compensates with an obsession with Patton and *Patton*. There is even a point in the episode where Taylor's mother-in-law imitates Scott's performance. Characters also refer to the film in episodes of *News Radio* (1995–1998), *The West Wing* (1999–2006), *NCIS: Naval Criminal Investigative Service* (2003–present), and *Gilmore Girls* (2000–2007).[14] In the made-for-television movie *Second String* (2002), a National Football League quarterback reminisces about his high school coach using *Patton* as a motivational technique. This effort failed: "Got beat 56–3."

The actor Kelsey Grammer got to deliver the most surreal reference to *Patton* in *An American Carol* (2008). Writer/director David Zucker uses the basic story structure that Charles Dickens developed in *A Christmas Carol* to show an Oscar-winning, left-wing documentary filmmaker who wants to abolish the Fourth of July as a national holiday the error of his ways. Grammer's General George S. Patton appears in the role of the Spirit of Christmas Past. When Grammer first appears on screen, the echoing trumpets of the fanfare from *Patton* play as part of the soundtrack. "You're General George Patton, from the movie?" the filmmaker asks in disbelief. "No, from the United States Army," the general replies.[15]

A number of other films pay tribute to *Patton* by silently lifting scenes from the film. The most popular is the opening in front of the flag. Scenes of this nature appear in *Royal Flash* (1975), *1941* (1979), *Smokey and the Bandit Part 3* (1983), *Superman III* (1983), *Blades* (1989), *The People vs. Larry Flynt* (1996), *Pleasantville* (1998), *Small Soldiers* (1998), *South Park: Bigger Longer and Uncut* (1999), *Spun* (2002), *The Movie Hero* (2003), *Stick It* (2006), and *Avatar* (2009). In *Pleasantville*, a character is standing in front of a giant projection of bowling scores as he rallies his supporters. "Only instead of standing in front of an American flag, I have him standing in front of a bowling scores, 'cause bowling scores are so much more American," writer, producer, and director Gary Ross chuckles on his DVD commentary. "That's their flag." Sampling the music from Patton was another popular fashion. In *Smokey and the Bandit Part 3* director Dick Lowry starts with a reproduction of the opening scene, including camera cuts and close-ups on Jackie Gleason's character, Sheriff Buford T. Justice, in the exact fashion that

Shaffner used. Every references to date to the opening in a television program has been a parody in episodes of *The Tonight Show* (1954–present), *Sanford and Son* (1972–1977), *Punky Brewster* (1984–1988), *The Simpsons* (1989–present), *The Adventures of Brisco County, Jr.* (1993–1994), *Dexter's Laboratory* (1996–2003), *Family Guy* (1999–2002, 2005–present), *Futurama* (1999–2003), and *Sealab 2021* (2000–2005).[16]

More interesting than a laundry list of movies and television programs is an examination of their type. Consider the fact that a parody of the opening scene appears in *Sesame Street Presents Follow That Bird* (1985), *Space Jam* (1996), *Antz* (1998), *Toy Story 2* (1999), *Recess: School's Out* (2001), and *Daddy Day Camp* (2007). All of these are children's movies. The opening scene is obviously not aimed at the little ones that make up the primary audience of these productions, but rather the parents that often end up watching these films with their sons and daughters. The adults watching *Follow that Bird* in 1985 were probably old enough to have watched *Patton* when it was first released, but many of those watching *School's Out* in 2001 might not have even been born in 1970. They would have watched *Patton* many years after its initial release on cable or home video. The fact that these films were made over a nineteen-year period is a tribute to the enduring legacy of that biographical film. These pop cultural references show the long shelf life of *Patton*.[17]

The opening scene is also parodied in the teen oriented movies *The New Guy* (2002), *Jackass 2.5* (2007), and *Van Wilder: Freshman Year* (2009), indicating that either these films attract an audience significantly older than the youth demographic, or that the filmmakers behind these movies believed that the market they were trying to attract knew and understood *Patton*. These scenes were major elements in all three films. In *The New Guy*, reflecting a tendency of many filmmakers to adopt Coppola's dialogue for their projects, the actor D. J. Qualls appears in front of a large U.S. flag, wearing an ill-fitting uniform that is identical to the one Scott wore, right down to the rank insignia and medals. His character is trying to inspire a high school football team: "All this hoo ha about being dead and not wanting to fight and staying out of the game is a load of crap!" He also adds: "American high school students traditionally *love* to fight! All real football players love the sting of battle!"[18]

While the opening scene was a popular section for parody and reference, other parts of the motion picture spoke to filmmakers as well. In 1974, the X-rated animated feature *The Nine Lives of Fritz the Cat* (1974) has a scene where Fritz the Cat hallucinates while smoking marijuana. In one of his lives, he finds himself in Berlin during the last days of the Third Reich being shot at by a blue animated crocodile-like character wearing an American uniform and helmet that bear a striking resemblance to the one Scott wore at the beginning of *Patton*. The crocodile delivers his lines in a raspy voice: "I got that Nazi rat bastard."[19]

Scott and Schaffner were not above making a small reference to *Patton* in another film they made together. In 1977, they teamed up again for a cinematic adaptation of the Ernest Hemingway novel *Islands in the Stream*. The main character is Thomas Hudson (George C. Scott), a world-renowned sculptor living in the Bahamas in 1940. The movie starts with Hudson's three sons from his two previous marriages coming to visit him for the summer. During this vacation, his eldest son tells him he is going to Canada to enlist in the Royal Air Force. During the second third of the movie, Hudson's first wife, Audrey (Claire Bloom), comes to the island to tell him that their son is dead and that she is getting married. The reference to *Patton* is subtle as she tells Hudson that her new husband is a general. In the novel, she indicates that he is in the military but never identifies his rank.[20]

There is also a homage to *Patton* in *Batman* (1989). Toward the end of the film, Batman (Michael Keaton) is in the Batplane, strafing the Joker (Jack Nicholson) in an effort to stop the villain's criminal spree in Gotham City. The Joker stands out in the open and fires on the Batplane with a handgun. This scene is a reproduction of the scene where a German Luftwaffe planes interrupt the meeting General Patton is having in North Africa about the lack of air cover.[21]

The longest and most sustained tribute came from the creative minds behind the animated television series *The Simpsons* (1989–present). An episode called "Bart the General" (February 4, 1990) included a number of direct and indirect references to *Patton*. The story focuses on Bart Simpson's (Nancy Cartwright) confrontation with a schoolyard bully. After being beaten up twice, he turns to Grampa Simpson (Dan Castellaneta) for advice. They go to a military surplus store for advice on strategy where One-Armed Herman (Harry Shearer), the proprietor, tells him, "The key to Springfield has always been Elm Street. The Greeks knew it. The Carthaginians knew it." Tugging at his grandfather's sleeve, Bart says, "Grampa, I think this guy is a little nuts." His grandfather puts his arm around his grandson's shoulder and replies, "Oh, yeah, well General George S. Patton was a little nuts, and this guy is completely out of his mind." Then the echoing trumpets of the *Patton* soundtrack start playing, taking the viewer into and out of the commercial break. When the episode resumes, Bart starts recruiting fellow classmates who are tired of being bullied. With everyone in the group wearing military helmets, Bart has them start practicing military drills, doing calisthenics, and running obstacle courses to prepare for their confrontation with their oppressors. At one point, in a reproduction of the scene where Patton watches his troops advance toward the Germans in the Battle of the Bulge, Bart surveys his soldiers as they march past him with the *Patton* soundtrack playing in the background. The music plays again when Bart shows his troops how to use a water balloon.

A few moments later, there is a homage to the slapping incident. Bart comes up to one of his classmates sitting on a street curb. "What's a matter with you solider?"

"It's my nerves, sir. I just can't stand the barking anymore."

"*Your* nerves!" Bart replies before slapping him. "I won't have cowards in my army."

Grandpa Simpson comes up from behind his grandson and slaps him even harder. "Sorry, Bart. You can push them out of a plane, you can march them off a cliff, you can send them off to die on some god-forsaken rock, but for some reason you can't slap them. Now, apologize to that boy right now."

"Sorry, man."

His soldier's response is short: "That's cool."

Music from *Patton* plays two other times: once when Bart confronts the bully before his troops begin pelting him with water balloons, and later as the show comes to an end and the credits start rolling.

The film *Patton* was parodied again four years later in "Secrets of a Successful Marriage" (May 19, 1994). Homer Simpson (Dan Castellaneta) has taken a job teaching a class at an adult educational annex on how to have a successful marriage. He angers his wife, Marge (Julie Kavner), when he starts sharing personal information about their marriage. To get out of trouble for failing to respect her privacy, Homer begins quoting famous movie quotes from . . . *And Justice For All* (1977) and *A Few Good Men* (1992) about the "system being out of order" and telling her, "You can't handle the truth," before he turns to lines from *Patton*: "Because when you reach over and put your hand into a pile of goo that was your best friend's face,

you'll know what to do." This tactic fails. David Mirkin, the executive produce of the series, notes in the commentary "This is another one of our
mutated, multiple movie reference lines."[22]

Even the Muppets got into the *Patton* reference business. In 1999, the
Jim Henson Company had its puppets make a movie parody calendar.
Each month had a photo of distinctive Muppet characters parodying various movies. Such parodies included Ralph the Dog staring as *The Dogfather*
and Kermit the Frog and Miss Piggy in *Piggy Woman*. The first entry in this
calendar is Rizzo the Rat as *Ratton*. He is standing in front of a U.S. flag in
uniform.[23]

Other productions have paid tribute in smaller ways, lifting dialogue
from *Patton* and adopting it for their own purposes. One of the more popu-
lar ones is the "magnificent bastard" line. This line appears in episodes of
Mystery Science Theater 3000 (1988–1999), *The Simpsons* (1989–present), *The
Critic* (1994), *News Radio* (1995–1998), *Third Rock from the Sun* (1996–2001),
Just Shoot Me (1997–2003), *Battlestar Galactica* (2004–2009), *The King of Kong:
A Fistful of Quarters* (2007), and twice in two *Seinfeld* (1990–1998) episodes.[24]

Other lines of dialogue are peppered throughout other films and television programs. In *Wall Street* (1987), Marvin (John C. McGinley) watches
the price climb up on the electronic ticker, and he quotes Scott's Patton in
abbreviated form: "God, I do love it so." In *Godzilla 2000* (1999), there is a
homage to George C. Scott in the English-language version of this Japanese monster movie. General Takada, played by Takeo Nakahara with Jim
Ishida doing the English-language voice work, explains the expected casualties in his plan to defeat the monster. "Well, I am not saying we wouldn't
get our hair mussed, but I can promise no more than 200, 300 tops." This
line is based on a line that Scott delivers in *Dr. Strangelove*. The homage
continues a few seconds as he discusses his backup plan using a new type
of armor-piercing missile that can penetrate any material. "I guarantee
it'll go through Godzilla like crap through a goose," the general states. In
the second version of the *Battlestar Galactica* (2004–2009) television series,
Richard Hatch, who starred in the 1978–1979 original and who has a supporting role in the remake, plays a character who is outmaneuvered politically by the president and admits defeat. Laura Roslin (Mary McDonnell),
the president, tells Hatch's Tom Zarek that she will not kiss him. "That's a
shame. I shaved very closely in anticipation of being smacked by you,"
Zarek responds.[25]

The music of *Patton* has often been sampled as well. This happened at the end of *Mr. Mom* (1983) so that the film could end on a positive note.[26] Jerry Goldsmith referred back to his previous work in *The 'Burbs* (1989) and then again in *Small Soldiers* (1998).[27] In both cases, he was using the music to portray characters as a bit excessive in their militaristic attitudes and a little buffoonish. This same approach appeared in the low-budget *Lobster Man from Mars* (1989), as well as two films in the *Mystery Science Theater 3000* franchise (1988–1999), *I Accuse My Parents* (1944) and *Boggy Creek II: And the Legend Continues* (1985).[28] *Patton* music appeared in two episodes of *Xena: Warrior Princess* (1995–2001). In both cases, the episode in question was making subtle allusion to the real Patton's belief in reincarnation.[29]

References to the film have even appeared in popular music. In 1998, the Los Angeles–based metal band System of Down released the single "Sugar." The video for this song contained two clear references to *Patton*. First, the band performs in front of a large American flag as green-screen effects allow flames to be superimposed on the white stripes. In addition, there are quick cuts from the band to an actor wearing a U.S. Army uniform similar to the one that Scott wears in the introduction while mouthing the lyrics to the song.[30]

A year later, the punk rock band The Authority used excerpts from Scott's opening monologue. In *On Glory's Side*, Scott's raspy voice proceeds the music. "We are advancing constantly and were not interested in holding on to anything except the enemy. We are going to hold on to him by the nose and we're going to kick him in the ass!" The lyrics of the song continue on in this vein: "I'm never giving up never giving in—I will keep fighting till the end." In another sign that the reality of the historical past and the myth of the fictional film had merged, the band thanks both George C. Scott and General Patton in their liner notes.[31]

Comedians have feasted on *Patton* for three decades. The fact that so much of their work needs to be timely and relevant is another testimony to the enduring power of *Patton*. In 1981, Johnny Carson, the host of *The Tonight Show* (1954–present), did a comedy skit parodying the opening scene from *Patton*. In a gruff voice, he gives his own version of the opening monologue: "All true Americans love the sting of battle. Americans love a winner; will not tolerate a loser. Americans play to win all the time. I wouldn't give a hoot in hell for a person who didn't give it his all to win. Remember, we're a team. We live, eat, sleep as a team. We have the finest food, equipment, the best spirit, the best troops in the world. And I can assure you, you will all do your duty. And I will be proud to lead you wonderful troops into action anytime, anywhere." The camera then pulls back to show that he has been addressing a group of Brownies from a Girl Scout Troop.[32]

Ten years later, on December 14, 1991, Steve Martin hosted the sketch comedy show *Saturday Night Live* (1975–present). When Chris Farley, one of the cast members, is afraid of performing, Martin calls him a coward and slaps him. Dressed in an army uniform and helmet, Martin then goes on a slapping spree behind the sets, calling a number of people cowards as the cameras follow him.[33]

In 1993, comedian turned actor Denis Leary made a music video of his song "I'm an Asshole," which can be seen today on YouTube. In what is basically a commentary on American culture, he sings about his efforts to antagonize others. In the middle of the video, he reproduces the opening scene of *Patton*. He is on a stage with a giant U.S. flag in the background, wearing a U.S. Army riding breeches–style uniform with a polished helmet displaying the four stars of a full general. He delivers a long spoken-word rant in the middle of the song as the camera cuts back and forth between him driving a car and standing on stage in a Pattonlike uniform.[34]

Impressionist David Frye, who made a name for himself in the early 1970s imitating Richard Nixon, released a comedy CD in 1998 entitled *Clinton: An Oral History*. During a series of skits that mocked the sex scandal, impeachment, and trial of President Bill Clinton, Frye includes a performance as George C. Scott's Patton. Somehow the general makes an appearance at a fund-raiser that Jack Nicholson is holding for Clinton. "You are nothing but a gutless draft dodger. That is all you have ever been as far as I'm concerned. You make me puke! You don't deserve to wear that uniform."[35]

On August 23, 2006, Mo Roca did a skit for *The Tonight Show* on the Miss World contest. As an American, he wants Miss USA to win. The camera cuts to a tight shot of Roca standing in front of a U.S. flag in uniform with general's stars on his shoulders and his helmet. He uses the "crap through a goose" line to describe how the two of them will undermine the contestants from other countries.[36]

Given the artistic and commercial success of *Patton*, it was almost inevitable that there would be a sequel. The driving force behind this effort was Scott himself. Some of his motivation was lingering resentment about losing the arguments about the sometimes harsh portrayal of Patton in the theatrical production. "I never felt satisfied, in my own mind," he explained. "I didn't think he'd been done fair to. I thought there was too much blood and guts, grab-the-tank-and-kill-the-Germans, and very little about the complicated character he was." General Patton fascinated George C. Scott. "There is very little written about Patton that I haven't read," he told a *New York Times* reporter. "As a matter of fact, I was reread-ing his memoirs this morning, just for the hell of it. He was an incredible character."[37]

In 1981, he bought an option on Ladislas Farago's *The Last Days of Pat-ton*. Scott wanted to make a theatrical production, but that effort failed be-cause studios executives were still chasing a youth market that was drastically shrinking. No major studio was interested in the project. He fi-nally got the CBS television network to agree to make a television movie. "All I get is junk offered me in film," he remarked. "There aren't good scripts around for a man my age. Films are oriented toward 16- to 25-year-olds. So television has been very helpful to me in the last few years."[38]

He also had financial reasons for wanting to return to his best-known role. He lost a considerable amount of money making *The Savage Is Loose* (1974). The film was a commercial failure, like many others that he made in the early and mid-1970s, and he soon found himself having to take roles for the paycheck they offered.[39]

The story in *The Last Days of Patton* focuses on the general's life between V-E Day and his death in Germany after an auto accident six months later. In 1986, Scott was within a year of Patton's age at his death, but he looks much older because he established the image of Patton associated with his acting seventeen years before. The years between the two productions clearly show on the actor's face and frame.

After a quick scene introducing the viewers to Patton and his wife, the first thirty minutes focus on Patton's troubles in Bavaria as military gover-nor. He refuses to comply with what the film presents as Eisenhower's personal policy of denazification. This section ends with Patton meeting with Eisenhower (Richard Dysart) and losing command of the Third Army. Although others were present in the room when Eisenhower fired his friend, the production only has the two generals present. Dysart's character does refer to a report that Professor Walter L. Dorn of Ohio State University had written. Scott's character dismisses the professor as "prob-ably a communist in disguise," a comment George S. Patton did indeed make. In actuality, Dorn and his superior, Brigadier General Clarence L. Adcock, were in the room with Patton and Eisenhower. Dorn and Adcock were responsible for advancing the idea that Patton was mentally unbalanced, and they had tapped his phones to prove their point. During the meeting, Dorn made an oral presentation that convinced Eisenhower that his old friend was undermining denazification efforts. The presentation in the film has Patton agreeing to comply with Eisenhower's orders to remove Nazis from various civil service positions in Bavaria, but provoking his firing when he mentions his old friend's political ambitions.

"Now, I admire you," Dysart's Eisenhower remarks. "You've got good qualities, but I've got to face facts. You're just no military governor. I believe it would be in your best interests if you gave up command of the Third Army."

"You're relieving me?"

"I am transferring you."

This period in the general's life was covered in the original film, although most of these events transpired off camera. The makers of *The Last Days of Patton* focused their coverage only on events that never made it on screen in the original and avoided events depicted in the theatrical film. The next forty-five minutes of the production have Patton reacting to his "transfer." At a surprise birthday party that his friends and subordinates held for him, he remarks on how one of his oldest friends had betrayed him. He later tells his chief of staff: "Well, it all boils down to one thing. Ike is bitten by the Presidential bug. He doesn't want me rocking the boat. But he will *never* be President. Telling you that right now."

The fatal accident takes place soon after these comments, coming just after the halfway point in the production. Scott, director Delbert Mann, and screenwriter William Luce were exceptionally faithful to the historical record—more so than the filmmakers behind *Patton*. Incidents large and small during the last few days are reproduced with little dramatic license. Events like people stealing the general's clothes as souvenirs; the location and shape of his head wound; the medical advice of British neurosurgeon Brigadier Hugh Cairns to use a traction system with fishhooks inserted under the general's cheekbones; the conversation that Patton had with Colonel Dr. R. Glenn Spurling where the doctor informed him he would never again have any motor function; his wife's banning any visitation from Eisenhower's former chief of staff, Lieutenant General Walter Bedell Smith; the bland comments the doctors made to the press and the wildly inaccurate and optimistic reports in the media about Patton's condition that followed; his last meeting with Paul Harkins; and his death are all reproduced in as accurate a fashion as one can reasonably expect. Some incidents, like the general receiving a glass of whiskey, were based on an old exaggeration that had plagued the factual record for years. His doctors actually arranged for Patton to get alcohol, which he refused but chose instead to share with the staff members who were taking care of him. Such attention to detail is hardly surprising, given the high level of the accuracy in the original. Scott's interest in exploring the character of a dying man was also particularly strong, and the richness of the actual story made for great drama. Perhaps most important of all was the amount of air time that the creative forces behind the television movie had to devote to such a brief period. Real issues could be explored at length and in depth.[40]

Unlike the original theatrical production, the Patton family cooperated with this television movie. Ruth Ellen Totten helped Eva Marie Saint, the actress playing her mother. "She sent me pictures of the scene in Boston when Patton briefly returned home," Saint told reporters. "I was able to see the things she wore. Those photos were priceless. It's wonderful when people are so giving in that way. She didn't know me but she helped me so much."[41]

Despite the assistance, the critical reaction to the production was mixed. Jim Bawden of the *Toronto Star* noted, "Scott is, if anything, better than he was in the movie, a shattered hulk of a man whose body is failing him. It's as remarkable and sustained a performance was we're likely to see on TV this or any year." A reviewer for the *Christian Science Monitor* declared that Scott's performance was worthy of an Emmy Award, calling *The Last Days of Patton* a "classic tragedy." John O'Conner, in an even-handed review for the *New York Times*, noted that roughly half the film had Patton in a hospital bed fighting injuries from a car wreck that ultimately proved fatal. "For the most part, we are confronted with Mr. Scott indulging himself in what must be one of the longest death scenes in entertainment history." Tom Shales, a critic for the *Washington Post*, observed, "Scott seems to be doing a comedian's impression of Scott playing Scott."[42]

The references to *Patton* in other films, television shows, and other media is a testimony to the quality of this film. *Patton* also made it possible for other films to get made like *The Godfather*—imagine what the saga of the Corleones would have been like without Coppola at the helm—even if they contained no direct reference on screen to *Patton*. As good art, it is entirely reasonable to expect that it would influence other artists. That is a testimony to its quality, but in many ways it influenced reality as well—the topic to which this story now turns.

10. The Impact

There many ways to measure the influence of a film. Since 1970, *Patton* has become a part of modern American society. Not only has the film influenced other artistic endeavors, but it has also become an important symbol. Many people—famous and not—thought *Patton* was Patton and have appropriated it for their own purposes. In a nation that is a political construct like the United States, the things that bind are of critical social importance. Film is a form of media with both a mass and a micro audience. The appropriation of *Patton* is a perfect example of this contradictory phenomenon. Individuals were shaping the culture to their own ends, often in ways that contradicted fairly straightforward elements of the Patton story. A good example came from a captain in the U.S. Marine Corps, rather than the U.S. Army, who decided to use *Patton* for the interests of his service even though the film had nothing to do with the Corps. That captain's name: Oliver North.

In 1972, the corps was facing a serious problem. Graduates of the U.S. Naval Academy could choose a commission in either the navy or marines. Starting with the class of 1968, the marines started failing to fill their allotments for academy graduates. This trend continued with each succeeding class. In the fall of 1972, marine headquarters put Charles Krulak, a marine officer on the faculty of the Academy, in charge of recruiting in an effort to make sure that the corps received its quota of Annapolis graduates. A war hero with a chest full of medals and the son of a legendary marine general, Krulak had no idea of how he was going to reverse this trend, which was a by-product of the American experience in Vietnam more than anything else. Then he had an idea and contacted North, a close friend and former deputy under his command during their tour of service in Southeast Asia. North was well known in Annapolis. As a junior at the academy, he won the midshipmen boxing title, and he returned to his alma mater in later years as a guest judge for other bouts. In 1972, he was an instructor at Marine Base Quantico in Virginia, where he ran a summer course that midshipmen from the academy took.

Krulak and North planned a presentation that took place in Mitscher Auditorium. Krulak worked at spreading the word among the midshipmen, getting members from all four classes to attend even if they had only the slightest interest in becoming a marine. The young men grew quiet when the lights went out; only the stage, with a drawn curtain, was lit. Then the music from *Patton* filled the auditorium. The curtain pulled away to reveal a solitary marine officer standing at attention in front of a huge American flag. The audience erupted into applause.

North was wearing the impressive formal dress blue uniform of his service that included a cape, white gloves, and barracks cap; his medals hung from his chest. For the next forty-five minutes, North spoke about the challenges and rewards of serving as a marine officer. Pacing back and forth across the stage in a performance that captivated his audience, he discussed the daunting and demanding task of leading men into combat and being responsible for their safety and well-being.

When the presentation ended, the midshipmen marched out of the auditorium. Their initial reaction augured ill for Krulak. There was little apparent enthusiasm that evening. At Annapolis, a commission in the Marine Corps, particularly during the Vietnam era, lacked the status and prestige of one in the navy. The true measure of that presentation came a month later, when the midshipmen had to make their service selections. North was back at the academy that day to help encourage and welcome those midshipmen who selected the marines. Not only did the marines fill their quota of Annapolis graduates, but for the first time in years, there was a waiting list. Both Krulak and North went on to bigger and better things. Krulak earned the four stars of a general and became commandant of the Marine Corps. North joined the White House staff during the administration of Ronald Reagan, where he became a central figure in the Iran–Contra scandal.[1]

This type of effort would not have surprised Scott. He understood that people often had trouble differentiating between him and Patton. "After 35 years in the business, people still identify me more with Patton than any other character," he remarked in 1986. "Even today, truck drivers and garbagemen and cabdrivers will call out to me on the street, 'Hey, General, how are you doing?'"[2]

Nor were North's actions all that odd. Time and time again, life imitated art. While *Patton* is a work of fiction, McCarthy set out to make a serious exploration of the real Patton's personality. The care and attention that he, Scott, Schaffner, and the Coppola–North team spent on accuracy was unusual by the standards of the film industry. This fidelity to the actual historical record by this fictional representation, though, affected history—which is what McCarthy wanted to do. A search of the holdings of the Library of Congress shows that there were sixteen books written about Patton before the release of the film. One of them was in Dutch. Since the film's release, there have been eighty-six, including four works in French and one in German. More importantly, the number of Patton studies grows larger with each decade. In addition to these works of nonfiction, there are five fictional accounts listed in the library's holdings.[3] Schaffner had hoped this very thing would happen. "I think that this film will excite history's verdict upon Patton. Influence it? I don't know. I think it will open up the verdict, however. I think it'll open up."[4]

The film also initiated a major shift in World War II historiography. Although Coppola wrote his screenplay, drawing on memoir literature, the predominate theme in secondary accounts during for the first twenty years after the war was on cooperation in the Anglo-American alliance. *Patton*, however, called attention to disputes between the Americans and the British. Starting in the 1970s, historians picked up on this idea. The emphasis in studies of U.S.–British relations was on the arguments between the two English-speaking peoples. The declassification of World War II–era documents sustained this view for four decades. Differences were obvious in matters of policy, but students of this conflict have taken these disputes into other areas, including strategy and an evaluation of professional competence. These studies have been first-rate works of scholarship, but they have had a misleading effect on the overall historical view of the past. One scholar has observed that this emphasis ends up distorting the historical record.[5]

Some have even argued that Patton made history. In a documentary that appears on two versions of the *Patton* DVD, director Oliver Stone argues that Nixon invaded Cambodia because of the film. Stone also discusses his efforts to include a clip from *Patton* in his film *Nixon*. Twentieth Century-Fox was willing to allow this usage, provided that Scott agreed. When Stone asked the actor, he said no. Stone claimed guilt was behind Scott's refusal because he knew what he had inspired.[6] The problem with this ar-

gument is that it assumes that military operations are simple undertak-
ings that a commander in chief can initiate on a whim like some Roman
emperor. The invasion of Cambodia was a complex event that required
weeks of preparation. The most authoritative history of it to date makes
no reference to the film.[7]

According to historian Robert Brent Toplin, *Patton* had an even more
profound impact on Nixon than observers realize. He has suggested that
the film had such an influence on Nixon that it initiated a more combative
approach toward his political opponents and the antiwar movement.[8] The
evidence for this argument is weak; it comes primarily from Hugh Sidey's
article and fails to take into account Nixon's own direct comments about
Patton that he made during his interviews with David Frost. Although we
can never know what went through Nixon's mind while watching the film,
there are more persuasive arguments for Nixon's approach to his political
enemies and the factors that initiated the Watergate crisis. In a detailed
study of the administration's approach to the antiwar movement, historian Melvin Small shows that the new president had a honeymoon period
because of differences between factions of the antiwar movement. Despite
timing that worked to their advantage, the administration began very early
on during its stay in the White House to shape news coverage. It was only
when national patience seemed to wane a year into his tenure that Nixon
and his lieutenants began using rougher tactics.[9]

Another factor—one more mundane than a film—is also important in
assessing Nixon's presidency: the men surrounding him. As Stephen Ambrose, who has to date offered the best Nixon biography, has observed, the
people surrounding Nixon—people like H. R. Haldeman, John Ehrlich-
man, John Mitchell, and Chuck Colson—fed his more base political in-
stincts. Of course, these were some of the same people leaking stories to
Hugh Sidey.[10]

Although the evidence is not particularly strong in showing that the
film shaped national politics, it is strong in showing that the military
made concerted efforts to use the film to its advantage. This process
started long before the transformations that home entertainment systems
and computers offered to viewers. Less than a year after the release of the
film, certain commands within the U.S. Army began showing the opening
monologue to new soldiers during basic training. This effort was the work
of Major General Hal Moore, later played by Mel Gibson in the movie *We
Were Soldiers Once* (2002). The film was shown to new inductees in a class

entitled "Achievements and Traditions." McCarthy provided Moore's command with a 16mm print of this scene, and it was shown five times a week. A year later, Moore had to request another copy because constant use had worn out the print. "The United States Army is presently undergoing a transition to build a new sense of pride and esprit de corps among young recruits," a lieutenant from Moore's training center wrote when making the formal request. "We need a tool that he can relate to. The introduction to your renown[ed] movie, *Patton*, we feel, is that tool." The initiative in using the film was limited to the basic training course at Fort Ord, where Moore was in command, but news of the initiative spread within the army, and soon other units were asking for copies as well. McCarthy enthusiastically worked to support these requests.[11]

In a similar vein, a recruiting sergeant contacted the studio. He told the producer that the film was "truly outstanding" and that he wanted to use it as a recruiting tool. To that end, he asked if the publicity department would provide him posters or lobby displays that he could use in his office.[12]

Military interest in the film continued for years afterward. When the United States invaded Panama in 1989, *Patton* went to war. One of the main missions of that operation was to capture General Manuel Noriega, the de facto military dictator of the country. When Noriega found refuge in the diplomatic mission of the Vatican, U.S. soldiers blared music over loudspeakers, including the soundtrack to *Patton*.[13] A little over a year later, *Patton* went to war again, this time in Iraq. Unit commanders played the opening scene of the film to inspire their troops. In addition, other soldiers played the fanfare from *Patton* as their tanks engaged the Republican Guard.[14]

The army has used *Patton* in more mundane ways. The official U.S. military television network in Germany, the Armed Forces Network, runs a number of public service announcements in between their regular programming. The *Patton* fanfare was included in a public service commercial warning soldiers about the dangers of not being with their unit when it is mobilized.[15]

The film has also had an impact in the world of sport. The first instance came in 1973 when the Tulane Green Wave defeated the Louisiana State Tigers 14–0 in a college football game. It was the first time since 1948 that Tulane had beaten LSU. In a time before VCRs, DVDs, and home entertainment systems, the Tulane players played an audio tape of George C. Scott delivering the opening speech. "Right after we got back from the

Maryland game, we went to the dorm, and I put the 'Patton' tape on," Mark Olivari, a Tulane player, explained. "You'd walk down the hall and hear it; just interludes of Tulane–LSU confidence builders. That was kind of a preliminary crescendo. When we came out for the game, everyone was full into it when we hit the field, it was like a spigot was turned on, and all that enthusiasm just poured out. We had no fear."[16]

Patton has also been extremely popular in the National Football League, and with new technological developments, it became easier for people to use Patton despite the passage of time from its initial release. In 1989 and 1990, Bobb McKittrick, the offensive line coach for the San Francisco 49ers, used the film before several key games to inspire his players. Twenty-five years after the release of the film, the advent of VCRs allowed him to actually play the movie. The opening monologue, where Scott's Patton tells the troops that they have the best spirit, the best equipment, and the best men, reflected McKittrick's own views about his team. The clip was a success. The 49ers won their game and went on to a Super Bowl victory. The next year, the players asked McKittrick to show the scene again before a key playoff game against the Los Angeles Rams. "Juxtapose the Rams for the Nazis, and it comes out pretty good," Bruce Collie, an offensive lineman, remarked. He might have been right—the final score: 49ers 30, Rams 3.[17]

In 1993, Joe Gibbs, head coach of the Washington Redskins, used the film in a slightly different way. He spliced parts of the opening with clips from a game his team had won against the Minnesota Vikings earlier in the season. He played his modified version of Patton just before a playoff game against the Vikings. Washington won 24–7. Martin Mayhew, a cornerback for Washington, said afterward, "I liked when he said, 'Let's not talk about dying for our country. Let's make the other dumb bastards die for their country.' I'll remember that."[18]

In 1996, during the inaugural World Cup of hockey, Ron Wilson, who was the head coach of the U.S. team, did the same thing. He interspersed clips of his players' greatest goals, hits, and plays with inspirational scenes from Patton and the Sylvester Stallone movie Rocky (1976). Then, just before the final against Canada, Wilson delivered his own George C. Scott–style speech. Keith Tkachuk, a forward on the U.S. team, was so worked up and excited from that address that he broke a Canadian player's nose fifteen seconds into the game. He later blamed Wilson's speech. In the end, the United States won the game—and the championship.[19]

Three years later, Gary Barnett, head coach of the University of Colorado football team, used the film in a different manner. During the Thursday night team meeting that he used to set the tone for the coming game, Barnett played the opening scene. It was a revelation for the college players, all of whom were born a full decade after the film came out. Few had ever seen *Patton*. They asked for a second showing on Friday.

Barnett obliged. He stood in front of his team in fatigues, boots and helmet with his face blackened. He delivered his own version of the Scott-as-Patton monologue. "You know I feel sorry for David Winbrush, having to come in here and play the Buffaloes." Winbrush was a running back for the University of Kansas Jayhawks who had set records the year before against Colorado. Instead of standing in front of a giant U.S. flag, Barnett had newspaper clippings of Winbush's success the year before as a backdrop.

"I thought it might have been a little hokey at first," linebacker Tyler Gregorak remarked. "But guys were fired up."

His teammate Ben Kelly, a cornerback, agreed. "Just looking around the room, everybody had an intense look on their face."

It might have helped. It certainly did not hurt. Colorado won the game, 51–17.[20]

At Lake Highlands High School in Dallas, head football coach Mike Zoffuto had his team listen to the music of *Patton* before games. One of his players, Phil Dawson, continued this practice when he played college ball at the University of Texas. "In high school, our team would listen to the *Patton* soundtrack," Dawson explained. "Before games, I lie in bed listening to that. It's something I've always done. If it's not broken, why fix it."[21]

Some sportswriters even had some fun with the film. Brian Murphy of the *San Francisco Chronicle* also wrote a column for ESPN.com. In one of his pieces, he complained how Brian Billick, the head coach of the Baltimore Ravens, was overrated. The team had won a Super Bowl under Billick. The coach liked to be portrayed as an offensive genius, which Murphy noted was based on his authorship of a book. Murphy argued that the Ravens' Super Bowl victory was due more to the quality of their defense rather than the offense. "'Billick, you magnificent bastard, I read your book!'" Murphy declared. "And let me tell you, pal: It sucked."[22]

The film did not always go over well. In his memoir of his baseball career, Jim Bouton noted that his manager with the Houston Astros, Harry "The Hat" Walker, liked the film a bit too much. "Like President Nixon, Harry never should have seen that movie. He got it all mixed up with reality." Unlike football, George C. Scott–type speeches played poorly in base-ball.[23]

Patton has also been used time and time again in the world of politics. This use makes sense since politics has often borrowed terms and ideas like "campaign" and "strategy" from the military. In 1990, comedian Robin Williams performed at a fund-raiser for support of John Kerry's re-election to the United States Senate. A reporter for the *Boston Globe* observed: "There was no ending; Williams' ultra-active mind and his rapid delivery are awe-inspiring. He's an AK-47 with a brain." Part of his set included George C. Scott as Patton along with Saddam Hussein, and U.S. Supreme Court Justice David Souter as Mr. Rogers.[24]

In 1999, Billy Tauzin, a member of the U.S. House of Representatives, made a five-minute video in which he appeared dressed as Scott's Patton. The purpose was to maintain party discipline in the Republican caucus before a key vote. The short film was shown at a closed-door meeting. He appeared in the video wearing a helmet, riding boots, and a military uniform with medals while holding a riding crop, and he delivered his remarks in a raspy, Scottlike voice. "It's a not-too-subtle reminder that we're in the fight of our lives," his spokesman said. The taping was secret, but a vote on the floor of the House interrupted the effort. Tauzin got some curious stares as he cast his vote wearing a trench coat over a U.S. Army uniform.[25]

Senator John McCain—a real war hero in no need of theatrical displays—turned to *Patton* as well. During the New Hampshire primary in 2000, he appeared before a giant U.S. flag to give a strong speech on taxes. The speech—and probably the background—went over well with the crowd.[26]

Paul Begala, the Democratic campaign strategist, has been quite fond of using *Patton* references that were actually Patton references. In 2000, he wrote an article on how the campaign of George W. Bush was using the same tactics that Bill Clinton used in 1992 to unseat his father. He ended up quoting Coppola rather than the real Patton. "This is not a case of grudging admiration, not at all like the scene in 'Patton' in which George C. Scott stands in the desert and shouts at Rommel's tanks, 'Rommel, you magnificent bastard, I read your book!' No, while Bush clearly read Clinton's book (or had someone read it to him), he would never call Clinton 'magnificent,' nor would he acknowledge the debt he owes Clinton." He noted with a certain amount of exasperation: "They oughta be paying us royalties."[27]

Eight years later, Begala made reference to *Patton* again during a presidential campaign. In describing the success of the Clinton campaign against that of the senior Bush, he explained that it is better to be in attack mode than in response mode. "I'm a George S. Patton Democrat. He said the purpose of war is not to die for your country. It's make the other guy die for his country." He said the campaign of Barack Obama needed to do the same thing; they needed to be throwing the first punches rather than responding to issues that developed in the campaign.[28]

The other side of the political spectrum gave as good as Begala. After President Obama gave his December 2009 Afghanistan surge speech, commentator Bill O'Reilly found him wanting. He noted that the president did not want to go down in history as a weak leader and doubted that he would withdraw troops according to the rigid time schedule that he had established. "The bigger problem is Mr. Obama's lack of passion for victory. What the nation needed to hear last night was a little General Patton." O'Reilly then played a clip from the opening monologue of *Patton*: "The thought of losing is hateful to Americans." O'Reilly added, "And instead of a resolute Patton, we got a flaccid Barack Obama."[29]

The business community has also adopted *Patton* as its own. In 1995, Nike aired a commercial during Super Bowl XXIX staring Dennis Hopper. The actor appeared in character as NFL referee Stanley Craver. He gave a soliloquy about football standing before a huge Nike flag.[30]

Perhaps the biggest manifestation of *Patton* being more Patton than Patton was Bill Whorton, a former Florida insurance agent who made a living as a Patton impersonator. "That movie changed my life," Whorton explained to a reporter. "I'm pretty normal until I put on the uniform, and then I really do change personalities." The thing to note is that Whorton was doing an impersonation of Scott doing Patton, rather than an impersonation of Patton himself. He used a gravely voice, knowing full well that the actual Patton had a higher-pitched voice, and he often quoted or paraphrased lines from the movie: "We're going to kick the hell out of them all the time, and we're going to go through them like crap through a goose!" he told a West Point alumni chapter gathered to watch an Army–Navy football game. "We're going to cut out their living guts and grease the treads of our tanks! We're going to murder those lousy goats—whatever they are—by the bushel!"

Whorton does his impersonation as a motivational speaker. He enjoys the initial shock of his audience when he begins the Coppola monologue.

"He motivates me," Whorton explained. "He is the person that gets me up in the morning and gets my blood going. As a matter of fact, I even listened to his music this morning to get going." He was, of course, referring to Jerry Goldsmith's film soundtrack, rather than a piece of music that the general would have recognized.[31]

The public often decides how to determine the meaning of the culture product it consumes. To put that point more directly, life can imitate art in ways that often seem surreal. This process started long before the new computer communication technologies gave the audience real power. These sometimes bizarre developments are a testimony to the skill and dedication of the Zanucks, McCarthy, Coppola, North, Schaffner, and Scott. *Patton* became more real than Patton. Few films can claim that power, and it is another indication of the unique status of this movie.

Conclusion

Patton was a great film. It was an important film. The reason is simple: it appealed to simple myths while exposing more complex realities about American society. Those myths and realities are about power. The *Patton* story is all about power—how it is acquired, maintained, used, and lost. In American society, power is primarily a function of merit. Americans also believe that power must serve a greater good.

As far as simple myths go, the film appealed to popular American views about the use of U.S. power in World War II. In this depiction, the Americans have all the military talent while the abilities of others are suspect. The case of Field-Marshal Sir Bernard Montgomery is a perfect example. It also stresses the importance and ability of a single individual. That theme is at the core of the story that appears on screen, and it is a basic ideal of the United States as a democratic society. To that end, the filmmakers portrayed Patton as a man from another time, a "pure warrior," an "anachronism."

The truth is a little more complex. The real George S. Patton Jr. did not become a general accidentally. He had military genius. He was a forward thinker, and he played a key role in the development of the tank as a weapon of war. Nor was he a rebel. He knew how to play the political game in the U.S. Army. His return to the cavalry branch after World War I certainly makes that point. He came to his understanding of the military operations and tactics through a study of history, but that hardly makes him out of place with his peers.

While Patton made a difference in the conflict—there is no gainsaying his importance—what was even more important was his ability to build. He was a trainer, and he translated his military abilities to an entire fighting force. In that sense—and it is touched on briefly in the film—he understood that a team or organization could do powerful things if properly organized and trained.

On that point, this study also exposes complex realties about power in

American society during the middle part of the twentieth century. Every key individual in the making of *Patton* was a self-made man. Acquiring power is difficult and is usually the result of talent and ability. The only exceptions were the real Patton and the younger Zanuck. Even then, that point can only be taken so far. Both enjoyed wealth and family connections, but neither got to his position of importance or stayed there without ability.

A second point is that education is a major factor in achieving that power. Everyone associated with this project had a college education and would not have become influential without the knowledge they acquired in institutions of higher learning: Patton, McCarthy, Coppola, North, Schaffner, Brown, Scott, and the younger Zanuck. (Scott never graduated from the University of Missouri, but he left school only a few units shy of graduation.) Only the elder Zanuck had no form of higher education to his name.

A third factor is that in a democratic society, even the weak or subordinate have power. Although new communication technologies gave viewers more power in the last decade of the twentieth century, it was still possible as early as the 1970s for small groups and demographics to make *Patton* their own—to make Patton a marine, an army soldier, a Republican, a Democrat, or whatever else they wanted or needed him to be. The film was also an opportunity for women, Hispanics, and blacks to exert influence.

The film also highlights the pace and ramifications of technological change in American society. Americans tend to think that technological innovation is synonymous with progress. McCarthy did not think so when he was looking for World War II–era equipment and clothing. More significantly, Twentieth Century-Fox used the Dimension 150 format with little to show for that effort. This system delivered impressive visual images that did well on old-style one-screen theaters or drive-ins, but it was not a system for the smaller screens of the multiplex theaters that were emerging in the 1970s. There was nothing predestined about this development. Multiplex theaters offered in many ways an inferior product that was smaller and less visually impressive than older venues.

The *Patton* story also makes it clear that there is nothing new to the concept of globalization. This term became all the rage in the 1990s, but ideas about internationalization always come to dominate American thinking about world affairs during times when political factors fade in importance. The interconnectedness of great powers and their financial and trade networks is nothing new. This extremely American movie was shot entirely overseas. This interconnected nature allowed for cultural exchanges in both directions. The role of globalization in the making of *Patton* shows that the film industry was not homogenizing world culture on the basis of what they thought played well among Americans, which is a nice way of saying "cultural imperialism." Internationalization is a two-way process. The libel laws of the United Kingdom and sensitivities about the market in West Germany shaped the making of this film even before the cast and crew left Hollywood. The *Patton* company learned from and depended on the technical and organization skills of their Spanish crew too much for that that argument to be plausible.

The study of the globalization process begs another important question: is there a unified American culture? After all, Americans use a language and economic system that were both developed in the United Kingdom, practice several religions that all originated in Asia before being transmitted to North America through Europe, and base their governmental systems on political ideas that the Greeks first pioneered. Americans even use Arabic numbers. Although there are many inputs to American culture, there is clearly a unique set of values and views that developed in North America that is distinctive even from those of other English-speaking nations. In matters of dress, cuisine, education, and entertainment activities, Americans have created something unique for their themselves. One of those things is culture, and the motion picture is an art form that is truly American in nature. Other societies developed plays, history, and literature as art forms, but Americans introduced cinema to the world. *Patton* might have been filmed overseas and utilized many foreigners in both the cast and crew, but it was still distinctively American. Culture often has nebulous boundaries, but it is still something discrete.

We must also examine the popular ideas about the 1960s and 1970s. They are basically wrong. It is easy to argue that the late 1960s and early 1970s was one of the most tumultuous periods in the history of the nation. Americans—so old arguments go—watched society change in profound ways in the wake of the civil rights movement and began to question their foreign policy after their experiences in Vietnam. First, this argument ignores the fact that there were far more difficult times in the life of the nation: the 1860s (the Civil War), the 1870s (Reconstruction) that followed, the 1850s (the secession crisis that provoked the war), the 1810s (the intense domestic opposition to the War of 1812 that came close to provoking a secession crisis and the fallout that destroyed the Federalist Party), or even the 1930s (the Great Depression).

Second, the reception that *Patton* received brings those old arguments into serious question. The United States is a political construct, with only a few ties that bind. One of those is culture. The audience enjoyed the mythical presentation of a strong leader who knew how to use power and offered hope. People—high and low—appropriated *Patton* as their own and in quite distinct ways, but within well-established norms. Americans continued to have faith in the idea of America.

Another popular view is that the 1970s was a period of dreary resignation to a diminished lot in life, and that many people were cynical about the workings of power in America. The reactions to *Patton* show that these descriptions of the 1960s and 1970s fail to stand up under close examination. Regardless of their politics, Americans wanted to believe—and, in fact, did believe—in the mission of the United States. *Patton* showed that Americans had used power in World War II in ways that made the world a better place. They would do so again. That was also a message in *Patton*. The havoc of the era is a historical fact, but it was the sound and fury of fleeting importance rather than a revolutionary challenge to the basic parameters of American society.

A final issue: while *Patton* appealed to the American ideal about the importance of the individual, the making of this film shows that the concept needs to be placed into a certain amount of context. Like General Patton, *Patton* shows that individuals make a difference when they can use their abilities to engage with others. Patton made his real mark when he used his abilities to spread his abilities to the U.S. Seventh and U.S. Third Armies, making them powerful fighting forces.

The same is true with *Patton*. This film never would have been made without Frank McCarthy. There is no qualification in that statement. None whatsoever. He dominated the three phases of film production: preproduction (securing the property, finding the right people), production (supervising logistics, dealing with a difficult lead), and postproduction (music scoring, editing, marketing). But it is also important to note—as McCarthy himself did at the Oscars—that he needed the Zanucks. Nor would it have been as memorable a film without Francis Ford Coppola or George C. Scott. The contributions of Franklin Schaffner, Karl Malden, Jerry Goldsmith, Fred Koenekamp, Francisco Day, and the rest of the crew are also significant. (Several others won Oscars for their work on *Patton*.) Simply put, good leaders never work in a vacuum; they need others to lead.

One last thing: if you have not yet seen *Patton*, do so. It is a good film.

Epilogue

Darryl F. Zanuck

Despite the success of films like *Planet of the Apes, Butch Cassidy and the Sundance Kid* (1969), M*A*S*H, and *Patton,* Twentieth Century-Fox was in financial trouble in 1970. The studio had lost millions—the number is no exaggeration—each on *Doctor Doolittle* (1967), *Star!* (1968), *Hello Dolly!* (1969), and *Tora! Tora! Tora!* (1970). Because of the widespread popularity of television, film no longer had the audience it had had even five years earlier. Productions designed with the market of the early and mid-1960s in mind were trying to find audiences that no longer existed. Films now had to appeal to niche audiences. Richard Zanuck had to initiate layoffs, and he decided to include Geneviève Gilles after her film *Hello-Goodbye* (1970) was a major artistic and commercial disaster. She, however, was the current mistress of the elder Zanuck, and the father was angry at his son for canceling her studio contract. At the same time, Twentieth Century-Fox owed $110 million, and for that predicament, the film legend also blamed his child. He decided to have his revenge, and on December 29, 1970, he arranged for the studio's board to fire Richard. "Nobody was looking at me," the younger Zanuck recalled. "It was like I had the plague or something." He was gone before *Patton* had won its Oscars.

Virginia Zanuck was not one to take the treatment of her son lightly. Many on the board of directors blamed Darryl F. Zanuck for the decline in the value of their stock as much as his son. She owned a hundred thousand shares and signed a proxy giving her votes to those trying to oust her husband. In a complicated battle, the insurgents lost the fight, but only after the board asked Zanuck to resign, which he did. Four months after he had arranged the firing of his son, Zanuck was forced out of the studio that he had created. He was given a two-picture production deal and an annual retainer of $50,000. He never returned.

Without the work that had made him famous, Zanuck's health began to fade, and Gilles began traveling to avoid a difficult situation. Richard Zanuck managed to put the hurt behind him and contacted his father when he heard about his health problems. When Daryl Zanuck was diagnosed with senile dementia, his family intervened and brought him back to California, where he reunited with his wife. The relationship with Gilles ended. Zanuck saw *The Sting* (1973), which his son had produced, and predicted it would win an Oscar. It did. It was the last film of his son's that he saw.

Zanuck lingered in the fog of Alzheimer's until 1979. He was seventy-seven when he died. At his funeral, the theme to *The Longest Day* was played over and over again.[1]

Frank McCarthy

McCarthy briefly dabbled in television, making *Fireball Forward*, a made-for-television movie that was to have been the pilot for a television series. Ben Gazzara played a fictional character modeled after Patton. Edmund North wrote the screenplay, but these graduates of *Patton* were unable to recapture the magic on the small screen. McCarthy oversaw efforts to turn the Sol Stein novel *The Magician* into a film for Twentieth Century-Fox. He wanted Scott to act in the production, but the actor turned him down. "I still think he is the best actor in the world," McCarthy stated. Nothing came of this project, though, and the producer left the studio in 1972 amid the Zanuck turmoil. He briefly worked on a television movie about George C. Marshall with the studio and had North write the screenplay. This effort also went nowhere.

He went to Universal and began work on *MacArthur* (1977). The comparisons between this effort and *Patton* were inevitable. "This movie will bring the controversial MacArthur into focus. We will not editorialize. No sequence will be fabricated. You naturally have to invent some dialogue but this will be an objective portrait. MacArthur was neither Jesus nor the devil. I think this will balance him off," McCarthy explained. He had said similar things about *Patton*, but Coppola, North, and Schaffner had managed to insert points of view into the production.

The resulting film was something less than a success. Director Joseph Sargent wondered if the topic was too politically charged even though more than twenty-five years had passed since the confrontation between the general and President Harry S. Truman. "No more wars, no more generals," he told the *Hollywood Reporter*. "We were shocked at the amount of flak and controversy we received from all corners in making this film." In another review, he stated, "Maybe we're hearing from the Truman apologists in the guise of bad reviews. For that matter, maybe even the raves are merely masking the reviewers' political prejudices and not really evaluating the film on its artistic merits. It's a thought." Indeed, the *Los Angeles Times* found that the *Kansas City Star*, Truman's hometown paper, gave the film a bad review while in Norfolk, where the MacArthur Memorial is located and where the general is buried, the *Virginian-Pilot* gave it a positive evaluation.

Perhaps, but as another thoughtful reviewer in the *Washington Post* noted, the film was not very good; every part of it lacked "ambition, imagination and resources" to tell the story well. Perhaps—but McCarthy also had a budget that got slashed drastically, and he had to replace many foreign locations with venues in and around Los Angeles, like the Long Beach Naval Station and the Pasadena Arboretum.

Whatever the reason, *MacArthur* would be McCarthy's last film. He died in 1986 at the Motion Picture and Television Fund Hospital outside of Los Angeles. He was seventy-four.[2]

George C. Scott

Scott's career was at its peak in the early 1970s, and he knew he owed much of it to *Patton*. "When I won the Oscar it doubled my fees at the very least," he admitted. "And how do I feel about that? Wonderful. I don't see any paradox at all between my feelings about the Oscar and about the money that goes along with it. I think all actors are astonishingly underpaid. If I could make $10 million a minute I would still be underpaid."

His acting career continued almost until the day he died, but he was doing his best work in the early 1970s. He won the Emmy in 1971 for *The Price*, and that same year, he was nominated for another Oscar for *The Hospital*. He told Arthur Hiller, director of *The Hospital*, that he would accept the Oscar if he won. "It was just too much trouble not to accept," he explained about the controversy following his Oscar refusal. It was a moot point. He did not win. He was nominated for another Emmy in 1972 for his work in *Jane Eyre* and in 1974 received a Tony Award nomination for his role in Un-

cle Vanya. "I get a mental vision of the character and I try to project it," he said, explaining his approach to acting.

He also directed during this time, with mixed results. He won an Emmy for his directing work of *The Andersonville Trial* (1970), which was broadcast on public television, but his two motion pictures, *Rage* (1972) and *The Savage Is Loose* (1974), were bombs. Those two projects cost him most of his savings.

His personal life remained chaotic. His marriage with Dewhurst ended. He then married Trish Van Devere in 1972. They had an up-and-down marriage, and during a separation in the early 1980s, he resumed his affair with Karen Truesdell and even proposed to her. The Scott–Van Devere marriage endured, though. When they celebrated their thirteenth wedding anniversary, he declared, "That's the longest I've ever been married. She is, to me, irreplaceable. That doesn't mean we live in idyllic splendor, but we try to cope with our problems, and I certainly could not conceive of being married to anybody but Trish."

In the second half of the 1970s, he made a number of lesser films, and he left motion pictures to concentrate on acting on the stage and television. On the small screen, he played Scrooge in *A Christmas Carol* (1984), Benito Mussolini in *Mussolini: The Untold Story* (1985), and Patton in *The Last Days of Patton.* He took the lead role in *Mr. President*, a television series that lasted only one season. In the mid-1990s, he hit another minipeak. In 1996, he was nominated for a Tony Award for his performance in *Inherit the Wind.* He won the Outer Critics Circle Award for that role. A year later, he won the Golden Globe, Cable Ace, and Emmy Awards for his role as Juror #3 in a remake of *Twelve Angry Men* (1997) for the Showtime cable network. His costar, Jack Lemon, observed of a key moment in which Scott's character breaks down, "It was deeply moving for all of us. It was good as acting gets." Two years later, in 1999, he died from an abdominal aortic aneurysm in Westlake Village, California. He was alone at the time, alienated from his wife and children because of his drinking. He was seventy-one.[3]

Franklin J. Schaffner

The director continued to enjoy artistic and commercial success throughout the 1970s. He directed *Nicholas and Alexandra* (1971), about the last

Russian czar; *Papillon* (1973), which starred Steve McQueen and Dustin Hoffman; and *Islands in the Stream* (1977), which reunited him with Scott. He served as president of the Director's Guild and was on the board of his alma matter, Franklin & Marshall College. In 1977, the school gave him an honorary doctorate and established the Franklin J. Schaffner Library, where he deposited his papers. In 1978, he made *The Boys from Brazil* with Gregory Peck and Laurence Olivier in the lead roles. This film was about the efforts of surviving officials of the Third Reich to clone Adolf Hitler. His films were nominated for twenty-eight Academy Awards. He directed a few other titles after *Boys from Brazil*, but each was smaller and less successful, and then he stopped working in the 1980s as his health began to flag. He died in 1989 at the age of sixty-nine from cancer. His last film, *Welcome Home* (1989), was released four months later. A reviewer for the *San Francisco Chronicle* called it "a regrettable and dreary melodrama."[4]

Edmund H. North

Patton was the last major project in North's writing career, although that was not obvious at the time. In addition to his projects with McCarthy, he wrote briefly for television in the early 1970s, and he shared credit for the film *Meteor* (1979). He died in 1990 from complications after surgery. He was seventy-nine. "There are no words that could be written to describe this man and his contributions to his art, his community and his guild," George Kirgo, president of the Writers Guild West, said when he learned of North's death. On certain occasions, the guild grants an award to one of its members for service and leadership. The award is named after North.[5]

Jerry Goldsmith

When his work on *Patton* ended, the composer still had a productive career ahead of him. He won five Emmy Awards for his television work, producing the themes for shows like *Barnaby Jones* and *Star Trek: The Next Generation*. He garnered eighteen Academy Award nominations in his lifetime, but won only once for his score in *The Omen* (1976). With the centennial of motion pictures, the American Film Institute conducted a ranking of the hundred greatest scores. Goldsmith was listed twice: for *Planet of the Apes* and *Chinatown* (1974). A study that the British Broadcasting Corporation did found that a piece of his music was being played every minute of every day. "That's good for my ego," he said. He died from cancer in 2004. He was seventy-five.[6]

Karl Malden

After shooting on *Patton* ended, Malden continued to enjoy artistic and commercial success, but most of that work came in television rather than film. "I felt that I had started at the bottom in the theater and worked my way up for 20 years, then started at the bottom with bit parts in films and worked my way up for another 20 years," he explained. "I didn't feel like starting at the bottom again." He managed to avoid that situation on the small screen. From 1972 to 1977, he stared as Lieutenant Mike Stone on the television series *The Streets of San Francisco*. The show was key in establishing the career of Michael Douglas. "Karl more than anyone got me to understand that an actor is just one of a whole team that makes a TV series or movie work," Douglas said when accepting the American Film Institute Life Achievement Award. "Thanks to him, I learned about the dichotomy of standing alone in a craft where one must collaborate." Malden was nominated four times for an Emmy while on the television program. He finally won the award in 1984 for his work in *Fatal Vision*, a television miniseries about the true story of Jeffery MacDonald, a doctor and U.S. Army captain who was convicted of killing his pregnant wife and two daughters. Malden may have been more famous—as he jokingly admitted—for his twenty-one-year work in television commercials as a pitchman for American Express traveler's checks. His closing line, "Don't leave home without them," became a national catchphrase.

From 1989 to 1992, he was president of the Academy of Motion Picture Arts and Sciences. He played a key role in the development of the Margaret Herrick Library, one of the few institutions that preserves the archives and artifacts of the film industry. He used his standing to get the Academy to award director Elia Kazan, who had directed him in his Oscar-winning role in *A Streetcar Named Desire*, a lifetime achievement award. The move was controversial because Kazan had named names when he testified before the House Un-American Activities Committee in 1952. "If anyone deserved this honorary award because of his talent and body of work," Malden said, "it was Kazan." He continued to work as well. The actor's last role came in 2000 as a priest in the television program *The West Wing*. Malden was also active in public service. He served on the U.S. Postal Service's Citizens Stamp Advisory Committee and had a Los Angeles area post office named after him. In 2004, he received the Screen Actors Guild's lifetime achievement award. In 2008, he and his wife, Mona, celebrated their seventieth wedding anniversary. He died in his Los Angeles home in 2009. He was ninety-seven years old.[7]

Richard D. Zanuck

The Oscar nominations that Twentieth Century-Fox productions garnered under his nine-year tenure helped the younger Zanuck after his father's coup de studio. "I would walk up and down the beach at Santa Monica, day after day, trying to work out what to do. I'd broken my arse for nine years at Fox and it had all come to this: being sacked by my own father."

He and David Brown went to work for Warner Bros., where his father had worked early in his career, as executive vice president. He was there for only a year and a half before Lew Wasserman recruited him to work at Universal Studios. In 1971, he and Brown formed the Zanuck/Brown Company, which produced films for Universal. While there, he developed *Sugarland Express* (1974), which is memorable for being the first film that Steven Spielberg directed. Zanuck was impressed with Wasserman's support. "That was such a defining moment for me with Lew. I'd never seen it before and have never seen it since—where a guy in charge says, I don't believe in this but I believe in you. GO." That support produced films like *Jaws* (1975), *The Verdict* (1982), and *Cocoon* (1985).

In 1988, he and his wife formed the Zanuck Company. The first film the company released was *Driving Miss Daisy* (1989), which won the Zanucks an Academy Award for best picture in 1990. A year later, the Academy gave him and Brown its Irving G. Thalberg Award. In 1993, the two also received the David O. Selznick Lifetime Achievement Award from the Producers Guild of America. "I was always the youngest person on the set," he observed. "Now I could be the grandfather of a lot of people I'm working with."

Since then, the younger Zanuck has produced other commercial and artistic successes like *Road to Perdition* (2002), and new versions of *Planet of the Apes* (2001) and *Charlie and the Chocolate Factory* (2005). "These days, right now, are the good old days," he said during the making of the Tim Burton film *Alice in Wonderland* (2010). "I've always approached it that way. That's why I'm still working. I'm not the guy who is ready to sit by the pool. I'm too damn busy. I'm not a nostalgia guy. These last few years, working with Tim Burton, it's been the best time I've ever had."[8]

David Brown

Brown was another casualty in the Zanuck coup at Twentieth Century-Fox. "We brought the company from nothing to a cash flow that has never been equaled. Then it was 1929 all over again." As independent producers, he and Zanuck made films like *The Eiger Sanction* (1975) and *MacArthur*. He admitted that neither one of them had planned this success: "Had we not left Fox involuntarily, we would never have chosen to become entrepreneurs."

He traveled back and forth between Los Angeles and New York throughout the 1980s. When he and Zanuck ended their business partnership, he turned *A Few Good Men* (1992), *Kiss the Girls* (1997), *Angela's Ashes* (1999), and *Along Came a Spider* (2001) into films on his own. He also became a theater producer when he received the script to *A Few Good Men*. He later made *Dirty Rotten Scoundrels* and *Sweet Smell of Success* into plays. When he won the Selznick Award with Zanuck just after their partnership ended, he said his reaction was "one of total joy and gratitude for being able to spend a lifetime in the film world." He was quick to add that he was not "suggesting the lifetime has been spent. I'm busier now than when I was 30, so I take this as a mid-lifetime achievement award." He was seventy-six at the time. He died seventeen years later in 2010 from kidney failure. He was ninety-three. "He was the last great gentleman producer," Aaron Sorkin, the playwright of *A Few Good Men*, said. "You're not going to see his kind again."[9]

Francis Ford Coppola

Unlike almost every other person associated with *Patton*, Coppola's career was just beginning, and it was an impressive one. In 1972, he directed *The*

Godfather, a major commercial and artistic success. He won another Oscar for best adapted screenplay. He then made *The Conversation* (1974) and was nominated for the Oscar for best picture and best original screenplay. That motion picture is not that well remembered because it went up against another Coppola-directed film, *The Godfather, Part II* (1974). This film won six Oscars, including three for Coppola: best director, best picture, and best adapted screenplay.

These wins gave Coppola a unique distinction. He was the only individual to ever win three Academy Awards for writing. He was also the only individual to ever script three films that won best picture. "I first thought of myself as a writer, I loved that work," he said. "The writer's work is pivotal to the theater and the motion picture—as a descendent of the theater."

He is best known, though, as a director. He directed twelve actors and actresses to Oscar nominations. In between work on the *Godfather* movies, he produced *American Graffiti* (1973), which his friend George Lucas wrote and directed. The film was nominated for the best picture Oscar. Coppola then directed *Apocalypse Now* (1979), which garnered him another three Academy Award nominations for best director and best picture in addition to one for best adapted screenplay. The production, though, nearly destroyed him. After the film went over budget, he had to invest much of his own money in the effort. "The way we made it, was very much like the way the Americans were in Vietnam. We were in the jungle, there were too many of us, we had access to too much money, too much equipment; and little by little we went insane. I think you can see it in the film."

Afterward, he established Zoetrope Studios and made *One from the Heart* (1982), in which he experimented with using electronic gadgets and new computer technologies. The result was a budget that kept growing and that nearly ruined him. The new studio went bankrupt. "That was a kamikaze attack—I went down in flames by myself." Coppola spent the rest of the decade and the one that followed making movies primarily in an effort to pay off his debts. A number of these films, like *Peggy Sue Got Married* (1986) and *Tucker: The Man and his Dreams* (1988), were artistically and commercially successful but seemed to pale in comparison to his work in the 1970s. He directed *The Godfather, Part III* (1990), which garnered seven Academy Award nominations, including two for Coppola, but the film lost in every category and contributed to a feeling that the film was a dud. "How any film that has grossed more than $70 million to date and is nominated for best picture and best director can be a flop is tough for me to understand," he stated.

Starting in the late 1980s, he kept stating that he was ready to take time off from film to write his own material and make his own films. Most of his income came from the Niebaum-Coppola Winery in St. Helena, California, rather than from his movie work. The winery eventually became one of the top ten in the United States. It was not until 1997, after making *Dracula* (1992), *Jack* (1996), and *The Rainmaker* (1997), that he was able to actually stop making films for a paycheck. "Only now after all these years am I in a position to say—'You know, I'm gonna write something and I'm not going to make another film for a while.'" He was true to his word and did not make another film for a decade. "People think that if you're a well-known filmmaker you can make any film you want. But nobody can do that except maybe Steven Spielberg. You have to make films the studios think they can make money on. In my case I am able to finance my films myself, which was what I've decided to do now." After his seventieth birthday, he said, "I don't have a lot of time left, but I'm so in love with the cinema that I want to learn all about making movies. I just want to write another screenplay and make another movie."[10]

A NOTE ON SOURCES

Doing the research for this book was a slow process. I did the initial research for this book very quickly in two relatively short trips to Lexington, Virginia, in 2000 and 2004, where I examined the papers of Frank McCarthy. I eventually made four trips to Lexington, but I did most of the research quickly, with the assistance of a digital camera that ended up serving as my personal photocopy machine. I took a picture if an item looked like it might be of any use. Only later would I really examine the document to determine its utility. I did not have the camera with me on my first trip and was a little astonished at how quickly I moved through the material on my second.

The McCarthy papers are the bedrock of this study. It is important to note, though, that there are four separate McCarthy collections. One focuses on McCarthy's military career, another documents his work in making *Patton,* and a third his efforts to make *MacArthur.* The final one comprised a set of additional material that supplemented the *Patton* collection. Each collection has its own box numbering system. All four are cited in this book. To differentiate between these four collections and to make it easier for future scholars to find the material I consulted, I have added a description in parentheses to the citations: Papers of Frank McCarthy (Military) or Papers of Frank McCarthy (*Patton*).

These collections are a gold mine of information and data. McCarthy saved almost every scrap of paper associated with the making of this film: focus group polling data, internal studio memos, handwritten notes, early drafts of screenplays with notations, correspondence with the general public, and review upon review of the film.

Oral histories and interviews are another important source of information in this book. They are of fundamental importance when writing film history because written records are often not preserved. I remember attending a conference just after I had finished graduate school and was conversing with a lot of newly minted Ph.D.s and senior Ph.D. candidates—my professional peers. The topic was contemporary documents versus oral histories. The conversation was not as boring as it sounds. We were a bunch of new professionals discussing our craft. The gist of the discussion was that sometimes not everything got into the historical record, and interviews could prove really useful. Others quickly pointed out that memories fade with time, and after-the-fact recollections can often be wrong. I was pretty proud of myself at the time for using a combination of interviews and written records in the writing of my first book. I figured I was hitting a good medium. Oral histories do indeed fill in gaps, and they also often give the historian some colorful quotes. There is always going to be good and bad information. Sifting one from the other is the job of a good historian.

With that point made, I did not conduct any interviews of my own for this book. Attempts to reach Francis Ford Coppola were unproductive, and, while Richard Zanuck offered to make himself available, our schedules never meshed. I, however, relied on several interviews that I found along the way. The Academy of Motion Picture Arts and Sciences sponsored a massive—and I do mean massive—800-page oral history of Karl Malden. Since he had served as president of the Academy, his willingness to participate in a lengthy interview made sense. Twentieth Century-Fox also conducted interviews with George C. Scott, Frank McCarthy, and Franklin Schaffner just before the release of the film. The purpose of these discussions requires some explanation. The studio did not conduct these interviews to provide a record for future historians. In the 1960s, studio public relations departments would conduct these interviews and put them on film, tape, or phonograph and distributed these recordings to radio and television stations. A local reporter in someplace like Austin or Dallas could then pretend to interview a famous actor or director when their film reached Texas. The McCarthy and Schaffner interviews were lengthy and informative, covering a good number of topics. There was also a certain candor—to a point—in these sessions because both men knew that the studio would never allow the release of derogatory information. So they talked as they saw fit. Transcripts of the McCarthy and Schaffner interviews are available in their papers. For some reason, transcripts of Scott's interview do not seem to exist. Portions of his interview, along with those of McCarthy and Schaffner, are available in audio format in Schaffner's papers. Other portions are available in the documentaries available on the 2006 Cinema Classics Collection DVD version of *Patton.*

Oral history purists would contend that the most authoritative way to use an oral history is to listen to the original recording. In this research, I found that not to always be the case. When I could compare the transcripts to available recordings, I found a number of discrepancies. In these situations, the transcript was more reliable. Although there were sometimes small transcription errors in the paper version, none of these small glitches altered the meaning of what was being said. More frequently, the discrepancies between the two versions were significant, and in those situations, I found the transcript more reliable. Words, sentences, and whole paragraphs were missing in the recordings. The audios were often edited to make them more entertaining or to avoid negative matters. Although I have no training in sound editing, after a time, I could tell when cuts had been made. In this study, I have cited both transcripts and audio recording. When the reference is to a recording, the punctuation and spelling are my own based on what I believe represents their meaning.

The advent of the DVD has proven useful to historians. This media format has led to the creation of commentary soundtracks from writers, directors, and cast. Studios have also added other items to DVDs, like documentaries. I have benefited from these additional features immensely and cited them repeatedly. Coppola's commentary on the Cinema Classics Collection DVD of *Patton* proved useful, and I used it as if it were an interview. This recording often had some of the same shortcomings of an oral history; it was clear that his memories had faded over the course of forty years, and not all of his comments were useful.

A word of order is appropriate here: the media format for home entertaining is changing rapidly. When I started the research for this book, videotape dominated the landscape. Now it is DVD, but high-definition television might be the wave of the future, or Blu-ray, or something else. I have attempted to put as much information in the footnotes as possible on how to acquire the items I consulted, but there are clear limits; companies that produce these media often get acquired or go out of business and often do not provide citable information on a consistent basis. Some of the films and television programs cited in this study were viewed in the theater, on VHS, or on DVD, or were broadcast on television or on demand. For example, during the course of this project, I collected four different versions of *Patton:* a VHS version, and three different DVDs. The Cinema Classics Collection edition DVD was exceptionally important, and it has its own place in the bibliography for a reason: it contains far more material than just the film itself.

Finally, if the footnotes and bibliography seem idiosyncratic, it is because they are.

NOTES

Introduction

1. On the audience in Washington, D.C., see the Norfolk *Virginian-Pilot*, March 8, 1970. For McCarthy on Coppola, see Transcript of Seminar at American Film Institute, November 25, 1975, 91, Folder 5, Box 2, Papers of Frank McCarthy (Additional). For Coppola's views, see his commentary on *Patton*, disc 1. (All references to the 1970 film *Patton* refer to the Cinema Classics Collection DVD version, released in 2006.) On shooting the film, see Kim, Schaffner, 257–258. For the reaction of those who actually saw Patton's speech, see Edwin H. Randal, "The General and the Movie," *Army*, September 1971, 19; and Bradley and Blair, *General's Life*, 173. The emphasis in the original Koenekamp quotes are in George J. Mitchell, "The Photography of *Patton*," *American Cinematographer*, August 1970, 738; Koenekamp quoted in *History through the Lens*, a documentary included on the *Patton* DVD release.

2. Coppola commentary, *Patton*, disc 1; Schaffner to Coppala [sic], March 11, 1970, Folder 1, Box, 30, Papers of Franklin J. Schaffner, Franklin & Marshall College, Lancaster, Pa.

3. Kitamura, *Screening Enlightenment*, ix.

4. Much of the early work on this decade was political history and focused on the radical group Students for a Democratic Society. See, for example, Gitlin, *The Sixties*, which is encyclopedic in nature. James Miller offers a collective biography of the early leaders of Students for a Democratic Society who wrote the Port Huron Statement, which was the mission statement or platform of the organization. According to Miller, "The statement is one of the pivotal documents in post-war American history. Its publication was crucial in catapulting SDS to national prominence." Yet as he concedes in a one-page letter, few have ever heard of the document. Miller, *Democracy Is in the Streets*, 13–14. Maurice Isserman studied the roots of the New Left in "*If I Had a Hammer.*" Miller, Isserman, and Allen J. Matusow see liberalism failing to achieve its early goals because of the actions of left-wing radicals. Matusow, *Unraveling of America*. David Caute sees less significance to the movement, arguing, "The long-term impact of the New Left has been 'cultural' in the broad sense. The distinctive challenge of 1968 to the State, the political system, and corporate capitalism was defeated." Caute, *Year of the Barricades*, 462. The problem with this argument is that it ignores the passage and impact of the Civil Rights Act of 1964 and the Voting Rights Act of 1965. Seeing liberalism in the 1960s as a failure is difficult when one considers the importance of that legislation in the context of 189 years of American history.

Several individuals have studied the motivating forces of these radicals. The books of David Burner and Dominick Cavallo indirectly confirm that they were often responding and confronting a successful political order. Burner, in *Making Peace*, argues that the radical movements of the 1960s destroyed the liberal movements, which had greater potential than the radicals for the nation. James J. Farrell, in *Spirit of the Sixties*, explores the motivation of radicalism and is unique among writers of this era in his emphasis on the theological origins of the protesters. He argues that the ideas the SDS pushed originally came from Catholic theology. Cavallo, on the other hand, argues in *Fiction of the Past* that this radicalism was the effort of middle-class youth to live up to American ideals that they believed their parents' generation had failed to honor. Many of these books must be handled with more skepticism than they have received so far. Most of these writers were veterans of the movements they studied, and they offered their readers books that were half history and half memoir. They often have the same tone as the "we were better, but . . ." memoirs that German generals produced after World War II. In the case of these history–memoir hybrids, we need to keep in mind two important facts. First, the SDS was never that large. The Young Americans for Freedom, a conservative group, had more members than the SDS. Andrew, *The Other Side of the Sixties*. In a another example, the Boy Scouts of America, which is neither right nor left, had more members in the 1960s than both groups put together; Macleod, *Building Character*, 292, has a chart documenting Scout membership in 1967. The second thing to keep in mind is that

these SDS-centric studies often adopt a line that the early part of the decade was good, but that the excess of the counterculture and splinter groups in the later part of the decade destroyed the progress they were making and led to a conservative backlash similar to the one in the French Revolution when the Reign of Terror brought about the Thermidorian Reaction. The problem with that approach is the New Left never came close to controlling any of the levers of power—at least, not to compared to the Jacobins. Other voices from this era were more reflective and show that many people understood the conservative nature of American society, an argument made here in certain sections. Two books that are more reflective than the earlier SDS-focused studies include Collier and Horowitz, *Destructive Generation*, and Brokaw, *Boom!* John Morton Blum, realizing that the SDS was never that large or significant, provides a political history that focuses on the White House, Capitol Hill, and the U.S. Supreme Court. He takes his study to the end of the Nixon administration in 1974 rather than ending it artificially on December 31, 1969. He argues that the political debate of this time was about how—but also whether—the federal government should addresses social inadequacies. Blum admits that the liberal Kennedy and Johnson administrations and the Congresses of those years were sloppy in writing and administering the law, which alienated the public. "Nixon did not have to invent his 'silent majority,' his Middle Americans. They were waiting for him." Blum, *Years of Discord*, 479. Gareth Davies, in *From Opportunity to Entitlement*, argues that Democrats suffered a self-inflicted wound when they embraced entitlements as a way of combating poverty. Until then, under Johnson's leadership, they had embraced policies that would create opportunities, but the Vietnam War sapped Johnson's political authority in the party, and the racially charged urban riots of the 1960s convinced other politicians who wanted his position that the times required a more radical solution. This approach was not particularly popular with most voters. G. Calvin Mackenzie and Robert Weisbrot, in *Liberal Hour*, offer a different view. Important changes in American society, including the suburbanization of the nation that broke the power of urban political machines and increased wealth, moved liberal issues to the forefront. Voters were convinced that there was more than enough wealth to go around and that political leadership in Washington, D.C., was no longer beholden to those in their home districts and states who maintained the status quo. In the end, liberals promised too much, which contributed to disillusionment and backlash.

Others have argued that the 1960s were actually a time when the New Right planted the seeds of what would become the Reagan revolution of the 1980s. See Klatch, *Women of the New Right* and *Generation Divided*; Brennan, *Turning Right*; Andrew, *The Other Side of the Sixties*; Schneider, *Cadres for Conservatism*; and McGirr, *Suburban Warriors*. Rick Perlstein in particular, in *Before the Storm*, attributes this seeding to the 1964 presidential election. Although the conservatives lost that contest, Barry Goldwater's efforts set the foundation for the Reagan era of the 1980s. Donald T. Critchlow, in *Conservative Ascendancy*, argues that the

1970s were key; the Right nearly undid itself on several occasions, but it was Liberal failures that allowed their movement to survive. Sean P. Cunningham, in *Cowboy Conservatism*, looks at the role of Texas in this political development, arguing that it was a key battleground, producing one of the last liberal presidents—Lyndon Johnson— and two conservative Republicans— George Bush and George W. Bush. Cunningham has a good point, and a similar study of California, the state that produced Nixon and Reagan, is in order. Laura Kalman, in *Right Star Rising*, takes the story of this political transformation into the 1970s, examining the period between Watergate and the election of Ronald Reagan, a time when Liberals had an opportunity to neutralize the gains of the right. Dominic Sandbrook, in *Mad as Hell*, does the same. Although he sees the 1970s as a continuation of the 1960s, he believes cultural issues, the Vietnam War, and Watergate led to the decline of big-government liberalism in the late 1970s. H. W. Brands, in *Strange Death*, offers an argument that basically supports these views. America, Brands contends, is basically a conservative nation and that the people tolerated a large government during the Cold War when it was necessary to protect them from an outside threat. Watergate and the end of the cold war killed liberalism because these two developments disillusioned people about the government and then ended legitimate reasons to have state intervention in social matters.

The turmoil of the time was social as well as political, and others have examined social movements. They see a lot of change. The feminist movement had more success, according to Alice Echols in *Daring to Be Bad*. Terry Anderson examined feminists and other groups pushing social change. "Whatever one thinks of the sixties," he wrote, "the tumultuous era cracked the cold war culture and the nation experienced a sea change—a significant transformation in politics, society, culture and foreign policy." The rise of Ronald Reagan, Anderson contends, did not reverse these trends. Anderson, *The Movement and the Sixties*, 412–413. Others have offered up a very different take on this decade. Instead of seeing an improvement in social justice, several historians see the 1960s as leading to a balkanization of U.S. society. David Farber and David Steigerwald argue that the United States was more divided in 1970 than it was in 1959; Farber, *Age of Great Dreams*; Steigerwald, *Sixties*. Lizabeth Cohen, in *Consumer's Republic*, sees a similar phenomenon at work in the rise of high mass consumption in the United States. The country broke up into a number of different markets. Studies of Richard Nixon also advance a similar argument. David Greenberg's study of Richard Nixon, *Nixon's Shadow*, lacks a strong central thesis, but each of his chapters is premised on the idea that Nixon was the central figure in American politics in the postwar era—or, to be more accurate, between the 1940s and 1990s. Daniel Frick, in *Reinventing Richard Nixon*, also sees Nixon as being the central political figure of this era and shows how he exposed important social fault lines. Rick Perlstein, in *Nixonland*, blends social and political history together and takes his story into the 1970s. He blames many of the divisions in American society on the divisive

political tactics of Richard Nixon.

These arguments are interesting, but when one considers American history over the long term, events like the American Revolution—which was a civil war—the U.S. Civil War, Reconstruction, and the persistence of immigrant communities that refused to assimilate during the nineteenth and early twentieth centuries, this emphasis on the schisms of the 1960s does not seem that foreign to the American experience, and probably not even as significant as previous divisions. Irwin Unger and Debi Unger, in *Turning Point*, offer an important economic study of this era, which is no small thing. They originally set out to write a history that focused on 1968, which they claim broke the political order. Instead, they provide a history of the entire decade that is particularly good on economics. Many other histories pay little attention to economics, but the state of the economy had the full attention of those who lived through that decade. *Turning Point* makes a valuable contribution to the literature and shows change taking place within established social parameters. James T. Patterson also examines economics as well as politics, foreign policy, and social affairs in *Grand Expectations*, his book on postwar America. This study won the Bancroft Prize, and Patterson takes his account up to 1974 with Nixon's resignation from office. He argues that Americans had grand expectations and believed that they could do anything, but that sense of confidence fell apart in the late 1960s and early 1970s. No book can do everything, and Patterson's coverage of popular entertainment is minimal, although what he does include is quite good. In his own survey of postwar

America, *American Dreams*, H. W. Brands blends together the Patterson and Cohen arguments and makes them his own. However, he emphasizes the dreams—that is, the ideals—that motivated American society. Reflecting his training as a diplomatic historian, his narrative emphasizes political and diplomatic issues. Works on the 1970s are far less numerous. Francis Wheen's book, *Strange Days Indeed*, offers an international account without much of a central argument. Thomas Borstelmann also offers a globalized history in *The 1970s*. He argues that American society became more and less equal during this decade. The American people committed themselves to an inclusiveness in society but not in the economy. Instead, they made stronger commitments to the free market, which guaranteed an unequal settlement. One of the most innovative books examining postwar America is 'Jules Tygiel's *Past Time*. In a series of essays, he examines the interaction of American society with the sport of baseball. He uses baseball as a lens to show how economic issues such as supply and demand, new business practices and professions, communications technologies (the telegraph, newspapers, radio, newsreels, television, the Internet), race, transportation modes, and work patterns changed American society in ways large and small.

5. Mass media, in the form of publications, film, radio, and television, was a major factor in American society throughout the twentieth century. Historians have conceded historical examinations of these media to communication scholars, sociologists, journalists, and film studies specialists.

Mass media history encompasses both fiction and nonfiction and overlaps with other subfields of history like journalism and pop culture. Scholars also tend to specialize on specific media, such as film, television, or publishing. The main issues historians have been exploring have been the power and influence of the media on American society and culture; the influence of the audience to shape media production; and what type of images have they produced. This book will address each of these issues in ways large and small. Scholars of the newspaper have emphasized its role as the first mass media. They have shown how editors and publishers tried to attract as wide a readership as possible, and they have also tracked the development of a professional ethos. See Baldasty, *Commercialization of News*. On the growth of professionalism, see Leonard, *Power of the Press*; and Ritchie, *Press Gallery* and *Reporting from Washington*. Magazines have seen a good deal of historical examination, while radio has not. Much magazine scholarship has focused on the Gilded Age and the Progressive Era, and has focused on issues of gender and class: Schneirov, *Dream of a New Social Order*; Scanlon, *Inarticulate Longings*; Garvey, *The Adman in the Parlor*; Ohmann, *Selling Culture*. For a historical study that emphasizes the social impact of radio, see Hilmes, *Radio Voices*; for one that studies its impact on politics, see Craig, *Fireside Politics*. Other radio historians have explored the business model that was developed and the alternatives that were considered. See Douglas, *Inventing American Broadcasting*; Smulyan, *Selling Radio*.

One of the issues that has dominated journalism history since the 1960s is the news media's relationship with the military. The combative relationship between reporters and the media was nothing new. The literature on this topic is massive, but the best places to begin are Knightley, *First Casualty*, and Hammond, *Reporting Vietnam*. Film was a major form of mass media during the twentieth century, but it is a topic few historians have seriously examined. Robert Sklar, in *Movie-Made America*, looks at the cinema's impact on American mass culture. He argues that film started off as a working-class art form that introduced themes rebelling against the middle-class, native-born social standards of the late nineteenth century. In an effort to garner bigger audiences, filmmakers developed new styles, but the film industry lost much of its creativity in the 1930s and 1940s as production costs soared. Garth Jowett, in *Film*, advances a similar argument. He focuses on the social phenomenon of going to see films. He argues that cinema was a factor in urbanization and that it destroyed regional and social constraints that traditional gatekeepers had maintained. There are many film history studies that address the era of *Patton*. Seth Cagin and Philip Dray, in *Hollywood Films*, see Hollywood as becoming extremely political in the 1970s. They argue that *Patton* was a major example, although there is a danger in attaching too much meaning to any single film. Edward P. Morgan's *What Really Happened to the 1960s* is a study of how the media covered the events of the 1960s at the time and in the decades that followed. He argues that the corporate-owned media outlets presented a distorted version of the events of that era and often hindered the exercise of

democracy. His account is broad and includes journalism and theatrical film. He bases his study on the belief that the very foundations of capitalism contributed in basic ways to the social ills that faced Americans in the 1960s.

That journalists and filmmakers do history poorly is a fairly obvious argument, but it is a bit unfair. They are not trained or expected to investigate the past the in the fashion of scholars and historians. Faulting them for not making a certain argument also seems unfair. That view is political in nature and is one that readers will accept or reject based more on their political beliefs than on the merits of the argument. James L. Baughman, in *Republic of Mass Culture*, explores competing mass media in postwar American and argues that television won, forcing radio, film, newspapers, and periodicals to cater to niche markets to survive. This insightful study provides much background to information in my account here. Popular culture, like mass media, is a subject that historians have largely abdicated to scholars in other fields. This field began as an opportunity for historians to evaluate the attitudes of average individuals instead of the powerful that are often the focus of history and biography. Paul R. Gorman, in *Left Intellectuals*, documents that left-wing scholars looked down on mass culture as something that degraded the whole of society and objected to serious academic studies of the subject. The right, for its part, never thought much could be done about the problem and focused its energies elsewhere. One should not automatically assume that popular culture is the study of television and film. Historians have been far more extensive in their examinations of American pop culture in the nineteenth century than they have been in the twentieth century. Merle Curti, the Pulitzer Prize–winning historian who became president of the American Historical Association, and Michael Denning have studied the dime novels of the Gilded Age and the Progressive Era and their relationship to class identity among laborers. Curti, "Dime Novels"; Denning, *Mechanic Accents*. Joy S. Kasson's book on William "Buffalo Bill" Cody, *Buffalo Bill's Wild West*, shows how his public relations efforts and stage show shaped public understanding of the West. Cody pushed something that amounted to a frontier thesis of his own: that the region was a critical element in American development and identity. Twentieth-century topics have seen far less investigation. Edward Berkowitz, in *Mass Appeal*, argues that pop culture unites Americans more than it divides them. The role of television is one of the major elements of American popular culture in that century, and Lynn Spigel, in *Make Room for TV*, offers one type of analysis of its impact. She examines how television affected home life, from where it was placed in the home as a piece of furniture, to how it changed social patterns. Katherine J. Lehman, in *Those Girls*, offers a different type of assessment of television during the time *Patton* was being filmed and released. She examines the content of programming, studying the portrayal of single women in the 1960s and 1970s. She shows that television was reluctant to accept the unmarried career woman in her twenties or thirties. Another field of cultural history that overlaps with popular culture and mass media is the globalization of

American culture. Unlike these other two fields, historians have made significant contributions to this area of study, but they—like me—have come primarily from the field of diplomatic history. That scholars with this type of training became interested in culture is understandable. The U.S. Department of State often initiated cultural exchanges during the cold war as a way of combating Soviet political and economic influence. An important trailblazing study that focuses on the pre–cold war era is Rosenberg, *Spreading the American Dream*. Another, more recent pre–cold war study is Rydell and Kroes, *Buffalo Bill in Bologna*. Studies of the cold war years include Hixson, *Parting the Curtain*; Gienow-Hecht, *Transmission Impossible*; Goedde, *GIs and Germans*; and Poiger, *Jazz, Rock, and Rebels*. Film has been a major topic in studies of this type; see Jarvie, *Hollywood's Overseas Campaign*; Fehrenbach, *Cinema in Democratizing Germany*; Ulff-Moller, *Hollywood's Film Wars with France*; Trumpbour, *Selling Hollywood*. This scholarship has emphasized U.S. interaction with Europe. For one that has an Asian focus, see Kitamura, *Screening Enlightenment*. It is worth noting that this field is globalized in and of itself: Gienow-Hecht, Poiger, and Goedde are German, Ulff-Moller is Danish, Kitamura is Japanese, and Jarvie is British. Historians have been wrestling with issues such as Americanization (i.e., the extent of the cultural influence of the United States); modernization (i.e., the cultural changes due to economic and industrial development); and globalization (i.e., the cultural integration of various societies, which may or may not be a polite way of saying cultural imperialism). Because many of the scholars who work in this field are American, they make certain assumptions. Most of these studies examine the transmission of American culture overseas and rarely study the reception, rejection, or adaptation that takes place in foreign societies; nor do they examine the effect that foreign cultures have on the United States. Another factor worth considering—because the United States is an immigrant nation—is whether the United States really has its own culture, popular or otherwise. This study of *Patton* will attempt to address all of these issues to one degree or another.

6. LaPorte, *Men Who Would Be King;* Griffin and Masters, *Hit and Run;* Kashner and Schoenberger, *Furious Love.*

7. McAdams, *American War Film,* is a detailed examination of how the war film genre has changed from one era to the other.

8. Feeney, *Nixon at the Movies,* covers much of the same time period that is covered in this book.

9. Randy Roberts and James S. Olson, in their biography, *John Wayne,* manage to show the production process in the film industry, develop the personality of their subject, and explain his importance in American society. Anyone thinking about taking up the art of biography should read this book as a how-to guide. Lawrence H. Suid has explored the civil–military relationship between film studios and the U.S. military in a series of books on war films in *Guts and Glory, Sailing on the Silver Screen,* and *Stars and Stripes on Screen.* Robert Brent Toplin, in *History by Hollywood* and *Reel History,* studies the historical message that theatrical film sends. For a study that focuses on one film, see Hess and

Dabholkar, *Singin' in the Rain.* All of these studies use a combination of resources, including oral histories and written records stored in archives.

10. Hess and Dabholkar found the same thing in trying to use these websites for their book; *Singin' in the Rain,* xi. See also http://www.bls.gov/data/inflation _calculator.htm.

11. Toplin has argued that the film industry often evokes the past far better than historical studies. This argument has merit, but ultimately fiction is fiction, while history is nonfiction. In particular, see Toplin's discussion of *Patton* in *Reel History,* 131–135, and in *History by Hollywood,* 155–178.

Chapter 1. The General

1. Hirshon, *General Patton,* 24–25.

2. D'Este, *Patton,* 320–328; Hirshon, *General Patton,* 106.

3. D'Este, *Patton,* 320–324; Hirshon, *General Patton,* 278.

4. Hirshon, *General Patton,* 214.

5. Ibid., 198.

6. D'Este, *Patton,* 10–15, 64–69, 107.

7. Hirshon, *General Patton,* 58–59.

8. Ibid., 61–63. I have held both weapons; Patton's design is clearly superior.

9. Ibid., 76.

10. D'Este, *Patton,* 161–164, 179–180.

11. Ibid., 164, 179–180, 184.

12. Ibid., 199–201, 205, 208, 272–273; Sheffield and Bourne, *Douglas Haig,* 304.

13. D'Este, *Patton,* 225, 235–327.

14. Ibid., 248–261, 275, 277.

15. Ibid., 295.

16. Ibid., 296–298.

17. Ibid., 298.

18. Ibid., 300–303.

19. Hirshon, *General Patton,* 270.

20. Ibid., 328–329.

21. Ibid., 412.

22. D'Este, *Patton*, 387, 440.

23. Bradley, *Soldier's Story*, 52; Bradley and Blair, *General's Life*, 58–59.

24. D'Este, *Patton*, 443, photo section opposite 371; D'Este, *Eisenhower*, 266–269.

25. Hirshon, *General Patton*, 267, 300; D'Este, *Patton*, 444–445, 511, 591; D'Este, *Eisenhower*, 433–434.

26. Hirshon, *General Patton*, 315.

27. Bradley and Blair, *General's Life*, 98–99, 139–140.

28. Bradley and Blair, *General's Life*, 151.

29. Hirshon, *General Patton*, 331; D'Este, *Patton*, 481.

30. D'Este, *Patton*, 481–482.

31. Danchev and Todman, *War Diaries*, 360–361.

32. D'Este, *Patton*, 523; Hamilton, *Master of the Battlefield*, 310, 313.

33. Bradley, *Soldier's Story*, 427; Lewis, *Omaha Beach*, 158–161; D'Este, *Patton*, 614, 644.

34. D'Este, *Patton*, 504, 515, 527, 530, 531.

35. Ibid., 533, 539.

36. Ibid., 534.

37. Ibid., 534.

38. Ibid., 534.

39. Ibid., 534.

40. Ibid., 534–535.

41. Ibid., 536–537, 540–543.

42. Hirshon, *General Patton*, 424; D'Este, *Patton*, 543–544; Eisenhower, *Crusade in Europe*, 181.

43. D'Este, *Patton*, 546, 550.

44. Ibid., 579–580, 593.

45. Hirshon, *General Patton*, 459–460.

46. D'Este, *Patton*, 590; D'Este, *Eisenhower*, 507–508.

47. D'Este, *Patton*, 590–591; D'Este, *Eisenhower*, 507–509.

48. D'Este, *Patton*, 623.

49. Ibid., 626–643.

50. Ibid., 640, 650–651, 685, 919 fn 32.

51. D'Este, *Eisenhower*, 643–644.

52. Ibid., 644–645.

53. Ibid., 645.

54. Ibid., 645–646.

55. Bradley, *Soldier's Story*, 473.

56. D'Este, *Patton*, 766–775.

57. Ibid., 783–795.

Chapter 2. The Producer

1. Frank McCarthy interview with Jack Hirshberg, July 1969, 1, Papers of Frank McCarthy (*Patton*).

2. Ibid., 2.

3. Ibid., 6–7, 9.

4. Memorandum on the Appointment by the President of Frank McCarthy as Assistant Secretary of State Succeeding Julius C. Holmes, August 21, 1945, Folder 5, Box 3, Papers of Frank McCarthy (Military); McCarthy interview with Hirshberg, 7.

5. McCarthy interview with Hirshberg, 30, 33–34; Remarks by Frank McCarthy, Annual National Convention, Jewish War Veterans of the United States, August 22, 1969, Folder 1, Box 30, Papers of Frank McCarthy (*Patton*).

6. Frank McCarthy Profile, September 1945, Folder 5, Box 3; Roosevelt to Marshall, April 18, 1945, Folder 13, Box 23, Papers of Frank McCarthy (Military).

7. "Frank McCarthy," *Current Biography: Who's News and Why*, 6, no. 9 (September 1945): 34–35; "The 10 Outstanding Young Men of 1945," *Future: The Magazine for Young Men*, January 1946; *Virginia Military Institute Alumni Review* 21, no. 9 (Winter 1946): 2, 22; Citation for Award as Officer of the Most Excellent

Order of the British Empire, September 1945, Folder 12, Box 31, Papers of Frank McCarthy (Military).

8. McCarthy interview with Hirshberg, 4, 10–11, 32–33; New York Times, August 22, 1945.

9. Acheson to Byrnes, September 22, 1945; McCarthy to Byrnes, October 6, 1945; McCarthy to Truman, October 11, 1945; and Truman to McCarthy, October 11, 1945, all in Folder 12, Box 31, Papers of Frank McCarthy (Military); New York Times, October 9, 1945; Washington Times-Herald, October 12, 1945.

10. McCarthy interview with Hirshberg, 17–18.

11. Ibid., 16–19.

12. McCarthy, quoted in Shorris and Bundy, Talking Pictures, 61.

13. Ibid., 60.

14. McAdams, American War Film, 104–116.

15. McCarthy interview with Hirshberg, 14, 28.

16. Karl Malden Oral History, March 18–July 15, 2005, 225, Oral History Program, Margaret Herrick Library, Academy of Motion Picture Arts and Sciences, Beverly Hills, Calif.; Scott interview audio recording, n.d., Box 87, Papers of Franklin J. Schaffner.

17. Transcript of Seminar at American Film Institute, 47, 103.

18. Mosley, Zanuck, 25; Harris, Zanucks, 48; Custen, Twentieth Century's Fox, 59.

19. Custen, Twentieth Century's Fox, 70, 76–77; Mosley, Zanuck, 71, 75, 127.

20. Custen, Twentieth Century's Fox, 70, 76–77; Mosley, Zanuck, 71, 75, 127.

21. Custen, Twentieth Century's Fox, 193–196; Mosley, Zanuck, 131–133, 152–153.

22. Harris, Zanucks, 48.

23. Custen, Twentieth Century's Fox, 257–265; Mosley, Zanuck, 200–207.

24. Suid, Guts and Glory, 261; McCarthy quoted in Tom Baily, "The Patton Story," Soldier, July 1971, 10.

25. Hollywood Reporter, August 19, 1968; Suid, Guts and Glory, 262; McCarthy quoted in Baily, "Patton Story," 8–9, 11; McCarthy interview with Hirshberg, 20.

26. Suid, Guts and Glory, 261; Patton, Pattons, 295; Guthrie to Trilling, October 6, 1953, and October 9, 1953, Folder: Patton Story, Box 27, Papers of Jack L. Warner, Cinema-Television Library, University of Southern California, Los Angeles; McCarthy to Koegel, October 5, 1961, Folder 6, Box 1, Papers of Frank McCarthy (Patton).

27. Guthrie to Trilling, October 9, 1953, Folder: Patton Story, Box 27, Papers of Jack L. Warner, Cinema-Television Library, University of Southern California, Los Angeles.

28. Emphasis in the original. Hirshon, General Patton, 689–691.

29. McCarthy to Zanuck, October 7, 1953, Folder 8, Box 1, Papers of Frank McCarthy (Patton).

30. Baruch to Muto, January 20, 1956, Folder 8, Box 1, Papers of Frank McCarthy (Patton).

31. Hirshon, General Patton, 691.

32. McCarthy to Harkins, July 19, 1955, Folder 11, Box 1, Papers of Frank McCarthy (Patton).

33. Harkins to McCarthy, July 15, 1955; Ayer to Harkins, n.d.; McCarthy to Harkins, July 19, 1955, Folder 6, Box 12, Papers of Frank McCarthy (Patton).

34. Suid, Guts and Glory, 262.

35. McCarthy to Patton, February 8, 1957, Folder 1, Box 1 and McCarthy to Koegel, October 5, 1961, Folder 6, Box 1, Papers of Frank McCarthy (Patton).

36. Date of promotion listed in "Frank McCarthy Patton Movie Collection," George C. Marshall Research Foundation, 3; Memorandum for the Record, June 25, 1959, Folder 6, Box 1, Papers of Frank McCarthy (Patton).

37. Memorandum for the Record, June 25, 1959, and McCarthy to Koegel, October 5, 1961, Folder 6, Box 1, Papers of Frank McCarthy (Patton).

38. The documentary History vs. Hollywood: "Patton," a Rebel Revisited, on disc 2 of the Patton DVD, claims that production ended with Zanuck's departure. McCarthy to Quinn, February 2, 1961, and McCarthy to Levathes, May 4, 1961, Folder 11, Box 1, Papers of Frank McCarthy (Patton).

39. McCarthy to Quinn, February 2, 1961, and McCarthy to Levathes, May 4, 1961, Folder 11, Box 1, Papers of Frank McCarthy (Patton).

40. McCarthy to Koegel, October 5, 1961, Folder 6, Box 1, McCarthy interview with Hirshberg, 40; Memo: Twentieth Century-Fox's request to film on General Patton, July 19, 1961, Folder: Patton, Box 20, Papers of Larry Suid, Georgetown University, Washington, D.C.

41. Memorandum for the Record, July 31, 1961, Folder 11, Box 1, Papers of Frank McCarthy (Patton).

42. Ibid.

43. Twentieth Century-Fox Studio press release, September 5, 1961, Folder 11, Box 1, Papers of Frank McCarthy (Patton).

44. Brown to Skouras, September 11, 1961, Folder 6, Box 1, Papers of Frank McCarthy (Patton).

45. McCarthy to Banning, September 13, 1961, Folder 5, Box 1, Papers of Frank McCarthy (Patton).

46. Spaulding to Sylvester, December 13, 1961, Folder: Patton, Box 20, Papers of Larry Suid.

47. Kalisch to Sylvester, December 21, 1961, Folder: Patton, Box 20, Papers of Larry Suid.

48. McCarthy to Underwood, January 12, 1962, Folder 7, Box 1, Papers of Frank McCarthy (Patton).

49. Niederlehner to Spaulding, February 9, 1962, Folder: Patton, Box 20, Papers of Larry Suid.

50. Hirshon, General Patton, 699; McCarthy interview with Hirshberg, 63.

51. McCarthy to Strauss, August 17, 1961, and Allen to McCarthy, August 24, 1961, Folder 1, Box 2; McCarthy to Baruch, February 5, 1962, Folder 10, Box 1; Robert S. Allen, Patton: A Profile, November 13, 1961, Folder 5, Box 13; McCarthy interview with Hirshberg, 41, 88.

52. McCarthy to Lancaster, December 6, 1961; McCarthy to Strauss, January 8, 1962, Folder 21, Box 1, Papers of Frank McCarthy (Patton).

53. McCarthy to Strauss, January 8, 1962; McCarthy to Brooks, February 28, 1962; McCarthy to Lancaster, March 8, 1962, Folder 21, Box 1, Papers of Frank McCarthy (Patton).

54. Mosley, Zanuck, 322–323, 325–326, 338–339, 348.

55. Ibid., 340–344.

56. Ibid., 340; Harris, Zanucks, 113.

57. McCarthy to Zanuck, August 17, 1962, Folder 12, Box 1, Papers of Frank McCarthy (Patton).

58. McCarthy to Lancaster, September 11, 1962, Folder 21, Box 1, Papers of Frank McCarthy (Patton).

59. McCarthy to Ruth Ellen [Totten], October 1, 1962, Folder 9, Box 1, Papers of Frank McCarthy (Patton).

Chapter 3. The Screenwriter

1. McCarthy to Underwood, December 15, 1964, Folder 12, Box 1, Papers of Frank McCarthy (*Patton*).

2. McCarthy to Michael Wayne, August 27, 1964, Folder 12, Box 1; McCarthy to Darryl Zanuck, February 15, 1965, Folder 5, Box 3, Papers of Frank McCarthy (*Patton*).

3. McCarthy to Underwood, December 15, 1964, Folder 12, Box 1; McCarthy interview with Hirshberg, 64.

4. Zanuck to Brown, December 23, 1964, Folder 7, Box 1, Papers of Frank McCarthy (*Patton*).

5. Brown to Zanuck, January 6, 1965, Folder 7, Box 1, Papers of Frank McCarthy (*Patton*).

6. McCarthy to Zanuck, February 15, 1965, Folder 5, Box 3, Papers of Frank McCarthy (*Patton*).

7. McCarthy interview with Hirshberg, 41; McCarthy to Horton, July 6, 1965, Folder 10, Box 1, Papers of Frank McCarthy (*Patton*).

8. McCarthy to Zanuck, March 30, 1965, Folder 3, Box 2, Papers of Frank McCarthy (*Patton*).

9. Calder Willingham, "Patton: Hero, Monster or Human Being? Basic Story and Point-of-view," n.d., Folder 3, Box 13; Frank McCarthy, Memorandum for the File, March 25, 1965, Folder 12, Box 1, Papers of Frank McCarthy (*Patton*).

10. Fisher to Ferguson, April 8, 1965, Folder 3, Box 2, Papers of Frank McCarthy (*Patton*).

11. McCarthy to Zanuck, April 28, 1965, Folder 3, Box 2, Papers of Frank McCarthy (*Patton*).

12. McCarthy to Zanuck, April 28, 1965, and McCarthy to Zanuck, May 21, 1965, Folder 3, Box 2 Papers of Frank McCarthy (*Patton*).

13. Zanuck notation on McCarthy to Zanuck, May 5, 1965, and Baruch to McDonnell, April 30, 1965, Folder 10, Box 1, Papers of Frank McCarthy (*Patton*).

14. Frank McCarthy, Memorandum for the File, March 25, 1965, Folder 12, Box 1; McCarthy to Zanuck, May 21, 1965, Folder 22, Box 1, Papers of Frank McCarthy (*Patton*).

15. McCarthy to Zanuck, April 6, 1965, and Zanuck notation on McCarthy to Zanuck, April 12, 1965, Folder 3, Box 2, Papers of Frank McCarthy (*Patton*).

16. Pepper to Twentieth Century-Fox Film Corporation, April 8, 1965; Boss to Colby, June 10, 1965; Edwards to Pepper, June 28, 1965, Folder 6, Box 3, Papers of Frank McCarthy (*Patton*); Allen, *Lucky Forward*; Farago, *Patton*. Compare Allen's page 44 to Farago's 30 or Allen's 90 to Farago's 427 or Allen's 85 to Farago's 463. These were the pages that Boss found suspect but fall legitimately under fair use.

17. Willingham to McCarthy, June 24, 1965, Folder 3, Box 2, Papers of Frank McCarthy (*Patton*).

18. Emphasis in the original. Willingham to McCarthy, June 24, 1965, Folder 3, Box 2, Papers of Frank McCarthy (*Patton*).

19. Emphasis in the original. Willingham to McCarthy, June 28, 1965, Folder 3, Box 2, Papers of Frank McCarthy (*Patton*).

20. Zanuck notation on McCarthy to Zanuck, June 30, 1965, Folder 3, Box 2, Papers of Frank McCarthy (*Patton*).

21. Emphasis in the original. Willingham to McCarthy, July 15, 1965, Folder 4, Box 2, Papers of Frank McCarthy (*Patton*).

22. Calder Willingham, "Patton! Screen Treatment," July 12, 1965, Folder

3, Box 13; and Willingham to McCarthy, July 12, 1965 (emphasis in the original), Folder 4, Box 2, Papers of Frank McCarthy (*Patton*).

23. McCarthy Notes, n.d., Folder 5, Box 2, and McCarthy to Zanuck, July 13, 1965, Folder 4, Box 2, Papers of Frank McCarthy (*Patton*).

24. McCarthy to Zanuck, July 13, 1965, Folder 4, Box 2, Papers of Frank McCarthy (*Patton*).

25. McCarthy to Zanuck, July 30, 1965, Folder 6, Box 2, Papers of Frank McCarthy (*Patton*).

26. McCarthy interview audio recording, n.d., Box 87, Papers of Franklin J. Schaffner.

27. Schumacher, *Coppola*, 3, 5, 14–17.

28. Ibid., 19, 36, 37–41.

29. Schumacher, *Coppola*, 42; McCarthy to Zanuck, July 30, 1965, Folder 6, Box 2, Papers of Frank McCarthy (*Patton*).

30. McCarthy to Willingham, August 4, 1965, and Willingham to McCarthy, August 5, 1965, Folder 4, Box 2, Papers of Frank McCarthy (*Patton*).

31. Article Bibliography, Folder 16, Box 3; Book Bibliography, Folder 15, Box 3; McCarthy's notations on "General Bradley as Seen Close Up," *New York Times Magazine*, November 30, 1947, Folder 17, Box 3, and McCarthy notation to Coppola on James M. Gavin, "Two Fighting Generals: Patton and MacArthur," *Atlantic*, February 1965, 58, Folder 14, Box 3, Papers of Frank McCarthy (*Patton*); McCarthy interview audio recording.

32. McCarthy's notations on "General Bradley as Seen Close Up," *New York Times Magazine*, November 30, 1947, Folder 17, Box 3, and McCarthy notation to Coppola on Gavin, "Two Fighting

Generals," 55, Folder 14, Box 3, Papers of Frank McCarthy (*Patton*); McCarthy interview audio recording.

33. McCarthy notation to Coppola on "Excerpt from a letter," n.d., Folder 13, Box 3, Papers of Frank McCarthy (*Patton*).

34. Coppola commentary, *Patton*, disc 1.

35. Schumacher, *Coppola*, 42; McCarthy interview with Hirshberg, 43, 50; Coppola commentary, *Patton*, disc 1.

36. McCarthy to Fisher, November 9, 1965; Fisher to Ferguson, November 12, 1965, Ferguson to McCarthy, December 21, 1965, Folder 6, Box 2; McCarthy interview with Hirshberg, 42, all in Papers of Frank McCarthy (*Patton*).

37. McCarthy to Richard Zanuck, February 14, 1965, Folder 6, Box 2; McCarthy notations on Francis Ford Coppola, *Patton* Rough Draft, n.d., Folder 1, Box 14; McCarthy notations on Coppola, *Patton*, December 27, 1965, 2, Folder 3, Box 14, Papers of Frank McCarthy (*Patton*).

38. McCarthy to Coppola, December 1, 1965, Folder 16, Box 2, Papers of Frank McCarthy (*Patton*).

39. McCarthy notations on Coppola, *Patton*, December 27, 1965, 67, 95, Folder 3, Box 14, Papers of Frank McCarthy (*Patton*).

40. McCarthy to Coppola, November 19, 1965, Folder 16, Box 2; McCarthy notations on Coppola, *Patton*, December 27, 1965, 67, 95, Folder 3, Box 14, Papers of Frank McCarthy (*Patton*).

41. Schumacher, *Coppola*, 42.

42. McCarthy interview with Hirshberg, 42.

43. Zanuck notation on McCarthy to Zanuck, October 6, 1965, Folder 22, Box 1, Papers of Frank McCarthy (*Patton*); Coppola commentary, *Patton*, disc 1.

44. Zanuck to Zanuck, January 27, 1966, Folder 8, Box 2, Papers of Frank McCarthy (*Patton*).

45. This is a reference to the actor John Wayne, who was called Duke on an everyday basis even before he adopted John Wayne as a stage name, and director Henry Hathaway, who directed Wayne in a number of commercially successful films.

46. McCarthy to Richard Zanuck, February 2, 1966, and Zanuck to Zanuck, February 11, 1966, Folder 8, Box 2, Papers of Frank McCarthy (*Patton*).

47. Zanuck notation on McCarthy to Zanuck, February 22, 1965, and Zanuck notation on McCarthy to Zanuck, February 25, 1966, Folder 6, Book 2, Papers of Frank McCarthy (*Patton*).

48. Coppola commentary, *Patton*, disc 1.

Chapter 4. The Director

1. McCarthy to Richard Zanuck, February 2, 1966, and Darryl Zanuck to Frank McCarthy, March 10, 1966, Folder 13, Box 1, Papers of Frank McCarthy (*Patton*).

2. Darryl Zanuck to Frank McCarthy, March 10, 1966, Folder 13, Box 1, Papers of Frank McCarthy (*Patton*).

3. Ibid.

4. Zanuck to Zanuck, December 15, 1965, Folder 22, Box 1, and Zanuck to Zanuck, January 28, 1966, Folder 13, Box 1, Papers of Frank McCarthy (*Patton*).

5. Huston, *Open Book*, 328; Long, *John Huston Interviews*, 109, 172.

6. Huston, *Open Book*, 265–267; Roberts and Olson, *John Wayne*, 436–438.

7. McCarthy notations on Zanuck to Zanuck, December 15, 1965, Folder 22, Box 1, Papers of Frank McCarthy (*Patton*).

8. McCarthy to Richard Zanuck,

February 2, 1966; Harry Sokolov to Richard Zanuck, February 4, 1966; Richard Zanuck to Darryl Zanuck, February 8, 1966; Darryl Zanuck to Richard Zanuck, February 10, 1966; Darryl Zanuck to Richard Zanuck, March 9, 1966, Box 1, Folder 19, Papers of Frank McCarthy (*Patton*).

9. McCarthy to Richard Zanuck, February 2, 1966, Folder 13, Box 1, Papers of Frank McCarthy (*Patton*).

10. McCarthy to Richard Zanuck, March 1, 1966, Folder 20, Box 1, Papers of Frank McCarthy (*Patton*).

11. McCarthy to Ted [last name unknown], June 29, 1945, Box 1, Folder 13; McCarthy, undated writer notes, and McCarthy to Wyler, April 29, 1966, Folder 16, Box 1, Papers of Frank McCarthy (*Patton*).

12. McCarthy to Ted [last name unknown], June 29, 1945, Box 1, Folder 13, Papers of Frank McCarthy (*Patton*).

13. J.R.W., "Preliminary Notes: Patton," April 5, 1967, Folder 7, Box 2, Papers of Frank McCarthy (*Patton*).

14. Herman, *Talent for Trouble*, 440–441; McCarthy to Ted [last name unknown], June 29, 1966, Folder 13, Box 1, Papers of Frank McCarthy (*Patton*).

15. Herman, *Talent for Trouble*, 441; James R. Webb, "Patton: Writer's Working Script," July 26, 1967, in Folder 2, Box 15, Papers of Frank McCarthy (*Patton*).

16. "Wyler on Webb," undated notes, Folder 13, Box 2, Papers of Frank McCarthy (*Patton*).

17. Darryl Zanuck to Brown, September 18, 1967, Folder 19, Box 2, and G. Byron Sage to McCarthy, August 18, 1967, Folder 13, Box 2, Papers of Frank McCarthy (*Patton*).

18. Silent corrections have been made

to the punctuation of McCarthy interview with Hirshberg, 56–57; McCarthy to Webb, October 4, 1967, Folder 4, Box 15, Papers of Frank McCarthy (*Patton*).

19. Herman, *Talent for Trouble*, 449; Buford, *Burt Lancaster*, 262; Richard Zanuck notation on McCarthy to Zanuck, September 24, 1965; McCarthy to Zanuck, February 8, 1966, Folder 22, Box 1, Papers of Frank McCarthy (*Patton*).

20. Undated note, Folder 13, Box 1, Papers of Frank McCarthy (*Patton*).

21. *Guardian*, August 20, 1992; Reagan to McCarthy, March 10, 1970, Folder 14, Box 9, Papers of Frank McCarthy (*Patton*). Reagan apparently expressed interest in playing this role just before being elected governor of California, according to Schaffner. See the *Fort Worth Star-Telegram*, February 25, 1970. McCarthy explained his concerns about Mitchum's weight to a seminar at the American Film Institute in 1975. Transcript of Seminar at American Film Institute, 12–13.

22. Herman, *Talent for Trouble*, 434–435.

23. Ibid., 449.

24. *Boston Herald-Traveler*, March 29, 1970.

25. Herman, *Talent for Trouble*, 449; McCarthy interview with Hirshberg, 56–57.

26. *Boston Herald-Traveler*, March 29, 1970.

27. Ibid.

28. Kim, *Schaffner*, 247.

29. Zanuck quoted in *The Making of "Patton": A Tribute to Franklin J. Schaffner*, on the *Patton* DVD, disc 2; Zanuck quoted in *History through the Lens*.

30. Franklin Schaffner interview with Jack Hirshberg, July 1969, 17, Folder 4,

Box 28B, Papers of Franklin J. Schaffner; *History through the Lens*.

31. Kim, *Schaffner*, 13–14, 17–22.

32. Ibid., 22, 25, 29, 38–39, 44–45.

33. Ibid., 152–153.

34. Ibid.

35. Ibid., 154–155.

36. Ibid., 131.

37. Kim, *Schaffner*, 163–171.

38. Ibid., 175.

39. Ibid., 188–192.

40. Ibid., 192–206.

41. Ibid., 207–220.

42. Kim, *Schaffner*, 223–242.

43. Schaffner quoted in *The Making of "Patton"*; Schaffner interview with Hirshberg, 2, 4.

44. *Los Angeles Herald-Examiner*, July 3, 1970.

45. *Dallas Times Herald*, February 24, 1970.

Chapter 5. The Actor

1. Harbinson, *George C. Scott*, 7, 13, 19; "George C. Scott: Tempering a Terrible Fire," *Time*, March 22, 1971, 65, 68.

2. Harbinson, *George C. Scott*, 15, 17–18; Christina Kirk, "The Real George C. Scott Stands Up," *New York Sunday News*, March 8, 1970, 30.

3. Harbinson, *George C. Scott*, 24; Kirk, "Real George C. Scott," 1.

4. Harbinson, *George C. Scott*, 25–26; "George C. Scott: Tempering a Terrible Fire," 65; Sheward, *Rage and Glory*, 11.

5. Dan Knapp, "What's Eating away at George C. Scott?," *Miami Herald*, March 22, 1970.

6. Judith Michaelson, "George C. Scott on Tape," *New York Post*, March 7, 1970.

7. Harbinson, *George C. Scott*, 30–31; Knapp, "What's Eating Away?"

8. Harbinson, *George C. Scott*, 33–45.
9. Ibid., 47–54.
10. Ibid., 57–58.
11. Ibid., 60–63.
12. Ibid., 80–81.
13. Ibid., 81; Dewhurst and Viola, *Colleen Dewhurst*, 140–141.
14. Emphasis in the original. Christina Kirk, "The Real George C. Scott Stands Up," *New York Sunday News*, March 8, 1970; "George C. Scott: Tempering a Terrible Fire," 64; Probst, *Off Camera*, 80.
15. "George C. Scott: Tempering a Terrible Fire," 66; Harbinson, *George C. Scott*, 82.
16. Kirk, "Real George C. Scott"; "George C. Scott: Tempering a Terrible Fire," 63.
17. Harbinson, *George C. Scott*, 71; Sheward, *Rage and Glory*, 66.
18. Harbinson, *George C. Scott*, 88–106.
19. Sheward, *Rage and Glory*, 103–106.
20. Harbinson, *George C. Scott*, 111; "George C. Scott: Tempering a Terrible Fire," 66.
21. "George C. Scott: Tempering a Terrible Fire," 63–64.
22. Sheward, *Rage and Glory*, 102–105; Baxter, *Stanley Kubrick*, 99, 187, 194.
23. Server, *Gardner*, 202.
24. Gardner, *Ava*, 254.
25. Server, *Gardner*, 442–444; Gardner, *Ava*, 254; Huston, *Open Book*, 328; Long, *John Huston Interviews*, 109, 172.
26. Sheward, *Rage and Glory*, 139; Herman, *Talent for Trouble*, 434–435.
27. McCarthy interview with Hirshberg, 104.
28. Transcript of Seminar at American Film Institute, 59, Folder 5, Box 2. Schaffner interview with Hirshberg, 21; Schaffner quoted in *The Making of "Patton."*
29. Harbinson, *George C. Scott*, 157;

New York Post, March 7, 1970; George C. Scott, "Why 'Patton'?," in *20th Century Informational Guide to the Film "Patton,"* Folder 17, Box 7, Papers of Frank McCarthy (*Patton*).
30. McCarthy interview with Hirshberg, 57.
31. *New York Times*, August 31, 1990.
32. Suid, *Guts and Glory*, 267.
33. Coppola commentary, *Patton*, disc 1.
34. Schaffner interview with Hirshberg, 23.
35. Walter Hartman, "Comparison of Revised Screenplay July 8, 1968, and Second Revised Screenplay, October 24, 1968," October 29, 1968, Folder 12, Box 2; McCarthy to Zanuck and Brown, November 14, 1968, Folder 24, Box 2, Papers of Frank McCarthy (*Patton*).
36. McCarthy to Zanuck and Brown, November 14, 1968, Folder 24, Box 2, Papers of Frank McCarthy (*Patton*).
37. Ibid.
38. Transcript of Seminar at American Film Institute, 30, 87.
39. Ibid., 47, 53, 103.
40. McCarthy to Zanuck and Brown, December 6, 1968; North to McCarthy, December 20, 1968, Folder 19, Box 2, Papers of Frank McCarthy (*Patton*).
41. Harkins notations on Patton, October 24, 1968. Second Revised Screenplay by Francis Ford Coppola and Edmund H. North, Folder 1, Box 16, Papers of Frank McCarthy (*Patton*).
42. McCarthy to Zanuck, Brown, Fisher, Schaffner, and North, December 23, 1968, Folder 19, Box 2, Papers of Frank McCarthy (*Patton*).

Chapter 6. The Field Marshal

1. Nichols, *Ernie's War*, 358.
2. D'Este, *Eisenhower*, 404.

3. Bradley and Blair, *General's Life*, 30–31, 33–34, 132.

4. Ibid., 53, 79.

5. Ibid., 64–73.

6. Ibid., 93–94, 102.

7. Ibid., 57–58, 131–133, 139–140; D'Este, *Patton*, 461.

8. Bradley and Blair, *General's Life*, 98–99, 139–140.

9. Ibid., 57–58, 131–133, 139–140, 156; D'Este, *Patton*, 461.

10. Bradley and Blair, *General's Life*, 151, 159, 171–172, 200.

11. Ibid., 207, 249, 252; Bradley, *Soldier's Story*, 272; Lewis, *Omaha Beach*, 29, 157; Murray and Millett, *War to be Won*, 419.

12. Bradley and Blair, *General's Life*, 252; Bradley, *Soldier's Story*, 272; D'Este, *Patton*, 611.

13. Bolger, "Zero Defects."

14. Patton, *Patton Papers*, 2:434; Lewis, *Omaha Beach*, 162.

15. D'Este, *Eisenhower*, 403; Hamilton, *Monty: Final Years*, 62; Bradley and Blair, *General's Life*, 232.

16. Bradley and Blair, *General's Life*, 440–441, 468.

17. Ibid., 504–505, 553.

18. Nigel Hamilton, *Monty: Final Years*, 797; Bradley and Blair, *General's Life*, 481, 640.

19. Bradley and Blair, *General's Life*, 665–670.

20. Ibid., 665–670; Frank McAdams, review of "The Patton Project: The Making of a Legendary Film," May 18, 2011.

21. McCarthy to Richard Zanuck, February 2, 1966, Folder 19, Box 1, Papers of Frank McCarthy (*Patton*).

22. McCarthy to Richard Zanuck, February 3, 1966, Folder 15, Box 11, Papers of Frank McCarthy (*Patton*).

23. Bradley to McCarthy, May 27, 1966; Bradley to McCarthy, June 20, 1966; Bradley to McCarthy, March 27, 1967, Folder 15, Box 11, Papers of Frank McCarthy (*Patton*).

24. McCarthy to Bradley, October 17, 1967, Folder 15, Box 11, Papers of Frank McCarthy (*Patton*).

25. McCarthy to Zanuck, July 10, 1968, Folder 26, Box 2; Zanuck to Hough, July 15, 1968, Folder 26, Box 2; McCarthy to Zanuck, July 12, 1968, Folder 16, Box 11, Papers of Frank McCarthy (*Patton*).

26. Bradley to McCarthy, July 19, 1968, and McCarthy to Zanuck, July 19, 1968, Folder 16, Box 11, Papers of Frank McCarthy (*Patton*).

27. McCarthy interview with Hirshberg, 53; McCarthy to Zanuck, July 17, 1968, Folder 16, Box 11, Papers of Frank McCarthy (*Patton*).

28. McCarthy to Zanuck, July 17, 1968, Folder 16, Box 11, Papers of Frank McCarthy (*Patton*).

29. Ibid.

30. Brown to Zanuck, July 25, 1968, Folder 17, Box 11; Zanuck to McCarthy, July 19, 1968, Folder 16, Box 11, Papers of Frank McCarthy (*Patton*).

31. McCarthy to Zanuck, July 19, 1968 (letter), and McCarthy to Zanuck (cable), July 19, 1968, Folder 16, Box 11, Papers of Frank McCarthy (*Patton*).

32. Davis to Lastfogel, July 26, 1968, and Davis to Lastfogel, July 29, 1968, Folder 17, Box 11; Eisenberg to Bradley, October 18, 1971, Folder 19, Box 11, Papers of Frank McCarthy (*Patton*).

33. McCarthy to Zanuck, July 30, 1968, Folder 17, Box 11, Papers of Frank McCarthy (*Patton*).

34. Zanuck notation on McCarthy to Zanuck, July 30, 1968, Folder 17, Box 11, Papers of Frank McCarthy (*Patton*).

35. Kim, *Schaffner*, 249; Davis to Lastfogel, July 29, 1968, Folder 17, Box 11, Papers of Frank McCarthy (*Patton*); Schaffner interview with Hirshberg, 27–28.

36. McCarthy to Hough, November 27, 1968, Folder: Patton II, July 3, 1968–December 5, 1968, Box FX-PF-157, Twentieth Century-Fox Film Corporation Production Files, Young Library, University of California at Los Angeles.

37. McCarthy interview with Hirshberg, 53–56.

Chapter 7. The *Patton* Company

1. Carver, "Montgomery," 149.

2. Ibid., 150–151.

3. Ibid.

4. Hamilton, *Monty: Making of a General*, 319–321, 377, 382–384.

5. Carver, "Montgomery," 154–155.

6. Ibid., 157–158.

7. Hamilton, *Monty: Final Years*, 602–604, 785–786, 837, 929–930.

8. Ibid., 798, 887–902.

9. McCarthy interview with Hirshberg, 59–60.

10. Fielding to McCarthy, December 31, 1968, Box 4, Folder 17, Papers of Frank McCarthy (*Patton*).

11. McCarthy to Ferguson, January 10, 1969, Folder 17, Box 4, Papers of Frank McCarthy (*Patton*).

12. Fielding to Ferguson, January 7, 1969, and McCarthy to Ferguson, January 10, 1969, Folder 17, Box 4; Zanuck notation on Ferguson to Zanuck, March 3, 1970, Folder 18, Box 4, Papers of Frank McCarthy (*Patton*).

13. Fielding to Ferguson, January 7, 1969, and McCarthy to Ferguson, January 10, 1969, Folder 17, Box 4; Zanuck notation on Ferguson to Zanuck, March 3, 1970, Folder 18, Box 4, Papers of Frank McCarthy (*Patton*).

14. Zanuck notation on Edwards to Zanuck, March 20, 1970, Folder 18, Box 4, Papers of Frank McCarthy (*Patton*).

15. Ferguson to McCarthy, January 13, 1969, Folder 17, Box 4; McCarthy to Annenberg, April 22, 1970, and Zanuck notation on Edwards to Zanuck, March 20, 1970, Folder 18, Box 4, Papers of Frank McCarthy (*Patton*).

16. McCleary to Smith, October 14, 1968, Folder: Patton II, July 3 1968–December 5, 1968, Box FX-PF-157, Twentieth Century-Fox Film Corporation Production Files.

17. *Houston Post*, February 22, 1970; McCarthy interview with Hirshberg, 24, 51–52.

18. McCarthy interview with Hirshberg, 24, 51–52.

19. Suid, *Guts and Glory*, 256–257.

20. *Washington Daily News*, March 9, 1970.

21. Twentieth Century-Fox Studio press release, September 5, 1961, Folder 11, Box 1; McCarthy to Zanuck, n.d., Folder 4, Box 17, Papers of Frank McCarthy (*Patton*).

22. Schaffner interview with Hirshberg, 24–26.

23. McCarthy interview with Hirshberg, 110.

24. Schaffner interview with Hirshberg, 24.

25. Malden, *When Do I Start?*, 303–304.

26. *Dallas Times Herald*, July 18, 1969; Schaffner interview with Hirshberg, 40.

27. *Washington Daily News*, March 9, 1970; Malden, *When Do I Start?*, 305; *Los Angeles Times*, January 12, 1969; Kim, *Schaffner*, 252; Schaffner interview with Hirshberg, 28–31.

28. *Hollywood Reporter*, April 28, 1969; Kim, *Schaffner*, 255.

29. Calculation by the author based on comments in Schaffner interview with Hirshberg, 26–27.

30. Karl Malden Oral History, 210.

31. Schaffner interview with Hirshberg, 50.

32. *Los Angeles Times*, March 29, 1970; Schaffner interview with Hirshberg, 28, 48; McCarthy interview with Hirshberg, 29, 67. Still photographs taken on the set of the film show that McCarthy was in uniform on occasion and that Schaffner was wearing the headgear of a U.S. Navy admiral.

33. *Los Angeles Times*, March 29, 1970; Schaffner interview with Hirshberg, 28, 48; McCarthy interview with Hirshberg, 29, 67.

34. *Los Angeles Times*, March 29, 1970.

35. Kim, *Schaffner*, 250.

36. Ibid., 250–251; Koenekamp interview in *The Making of "Patton."*

37. Kim, *Schaffner*, 252.

38. Ibid., 253.

39. Ibid.

40. Mitchell, "Photography of *Patton*," 803–804; McCarthy quoted in "Award Winner: Franklin Schaffner," *Action*, May–June 1971, 14; Koenekamp interview in *The Making of "Patton."*

41. Dale Munroe, "Director Franklin Schaffner," *Show*, August 6, 1970, 16; Schaffner and Koenekamp quoted in *The Making of "Patton"*; Schaffner interview with Hirshberg, 33–36.

42. Mitchell, "Photography of *Patton*," 738–739; Koenekamp quoted in *The Making of "Patton."*

43. Mitchell, "Photography of *Patton*," 740.

44. Ibid.

45. Koenekamp quoted in *The Making of "Patton."*

46. McCarthy interview with Hirshberg, 69–70; and Schaffner interview with Hirshberg, 29–30.

47. McCarthy to Zanuck, n.d., Folder 4, Box 17, Papers of Frank McCarthy (*Patton*).

48. Mitchell, "Photography of *Patton*," 741; McCarthy interview with Hirshberg, 69–70; and Schaffner interview with Hirshberg, 40; Schaffner quoted in *The Making of "Patton."*

49. Scott quoted in *The Making of "Patton."*

50. Scott interview audio recording.

51. Scott quoted in *The Making of "Patton."*

52. Scott quoted in *History vs. Hollywood*.

53. Scott quoted in *The Making of "Patton."*

54. *New York Times*, March 29, 1970.

55. *Los Angeles Herald-Examiner*, February 5, 1970.

56. Randal, "The General and the Movie," 18, 20; Sheward, *Rage and Glory*, 181–182; Suid, *Guts and Glory*, 270.

57. McCarthy to Zanuck, March 16, 1969, Folder 26, Box 2, and McCarthy to Zanuck, June 2, 1969, Folder 4, Box 17, Papers of Frank McCarthy (*Patton*); McCarthy to Zanuck March 24, 1969, Folder: Patton Cables from Spain, Box FX-PF-157, Twentieth Century-Fox Film Corporation Production Files.

58. McCarthy quoted in "Award Winner: Franklin Schaffner," 14; McCarthy to Zanuck, March 21, 1969, Folder 4, Box 17, Papers of Frank McCarthy (*Patton*).

59. Sheward, *Rage and Glory*, 181–182.

60. Kim, *Schaffner*, 260; and Schaffner interview with Hirshberg, 22–24; McCarthy to Zanuck, March 21, 1969, Folder 4, Box 17, Papers of Frank McCarthy (*Patton*).

61. Schaffner interview with Hirshberg, 22–24; Suid, *Guts and Glory*, 270.

62. Silent spelling corrections to "Translation of George C. Scott's Tape," January 24, 1975, Folder 6, Box 2, Papers of Frank McCarthy (*MacArthur*).

63. Scott interview audio recording.

64. *New York Times*, March 29, 1970.

65. McCarthy to Zanuck, n.d., and McCarthy to Zanuck, June 2, 1969, Folder 4, Box 17, Papers of Frank McCarthy (*Patton*); Merman to Hough, April 1, 1969, Folder Patton VI, February 13, 1969, to May 29, 1960, Box FX-PF-160, Twentieth Century-Fox Film Corporation Production Files.

66. McCarthy to Zanuck, n.d., and McCarthy to Zanuck, June 2, 1969, Folder 4, Box 17, Papers of Frank McCarthy (*Patton*).

67. Zanuck to McCarthy, n.d., Folder 4, Box 17, Papers of Frank McCarthy (*Patton*).

68. McCarthy to Zanuck, March 31, 1969, and McCarthy to Zanuck, June 2, 1969, Folder 4, Box 17, Papers of Frank McCarthy (*Patton*); McCarthy to Zanuck, March 28, 1969, Folder: Patton Cables from Spain, Box FX-PF-157, Twentieth Century-Fox Film Corporation Production Files.

69. McCarthy to Zanuck, April 1, 1969, Folder: Patton Cables from Spain, Box FX-PF-157, Twentieth Century-Fox Film Corporation Production Files.

70. Karl Malden Oral History, 212–213.

71. Ibid., 212–213.

72. Sheward, *Rage and Glory*, 179–180; McCarthy to Zanuck, n.d., Folder: Patton Cables from Spain, Box FX-PF-157, Twentieth Century-Fox Film Corporation Production Files; McCarthy to Scott,

April 4, 1969, Folder 4, Box 17, Papers of Frank McCarthy (*Patton*).

73. Sheward, *Rage and Glory*, 179–180; McCarthy to Zanuck, n.d., Folder: Patton Cables from Spain, Box FX-PF-157, Twentieth Century-Fox Film Corporation Production Files; McCarthy to Scott, April 4, 1969, Folder 4, Box 17, Papers of Frank McCarthy (*Patton*).

74. "Award Winner: Franklin Schaffner," 15; Hough to Zanuck, June 11, 1969, Folder A-894 Patton, Box FX-PF-159, Twentieth Century-Fox Film Corporation Production Files.

75. "Award Winner: Franklin Schaffner," 15; Schaffner interview with Hirshberg, 35–36.

76. Goldsmith quoted in *The Making of "Patton."*

77. Kim, *Schaffner*, 256; emphasis in the original Zanuck notation on McCarthy to August 8, 1969, Folder: Patton: Blood and Guts V, December 6, 1968–February 12, 1969, Box FX-PF-157, Twentieth Century-Fox Film Corporation Production Files; Goldsmith quoted in *The Making of "Patton."*

78. Kim, *Schaffner*, 256; emphasis in the original; Goldsmith quoted in *The Making of "Patton."*

70. Jerry Goldsmith interview on *Fresh Air*, January 7, 2002, National Public Radio, http://www.npr.org/.

80. McCarthy to Schaffner, September 24, 1969, Folder 4, Box 30, Papers of Franklin J. Schaffner; Goldsmith quoted in *The Making of "Patton."*

81. *Patton*, disc 1.

Chapter 8. The Audience

1. *Variety*, July 20–26, 1998.

2. Hugh Sidey, "'Anybody see *Patton?*'" *Life*, June 19, 1970, 2B.

Kissinger, *White House Years*, 498, 780. For an editorial cartoon, see *Los Angeles Times*, August 24, 1970. For others spreading the Nixon and Patton story, see *Chicago Sun-Times*, June 17, 1970, and the *New York Post*, June 16, 1970; Zanuck to Peck, June 26, 1970, Folder 1, Box 30, Papers of Franklin J. Schaffner.

3. Feeney, *Nixon at the Movies*, 339–358.

4. "War at Home and Abroad," May 19, 1977, *Frost/Nixon: Complete Interviews*, disc 2.

5. Transcript of Seminar at American Film Institute, 90.

6. Haldeman, *Haldeman Diaries*, 58, 106, 147.

7. Richard Zanuck to McCarthy, n.d., Folder 1, Box 30, Papers of Franklin J. Schaffner.

8. Heston to Zanuck, January 23, 1970, Folder 7, Box 30, Papers of Franklin J. Schaffner.

9. Pogostin to Schaffner, May 7, 1970, Folder 8, Box 30, Papers of Franklin J. Schaffner.

10. "'Patton' Takes Off at Box Office after Oscars," Patton File, Core Collection Files, Margaret Herrick Library, Academy of Motion Picture Arts and Sciences, Beverly Hills, Calif.; McCarthy interview with Hirshberg, 22, 97–101.

11. McCarthy's report to Zanuck had significantly different totals, and even then, the math in it is wrong. McCarthy to Zanuck, December 24, 1969, Folder 1, Box 6, Papers of Frank McCarthy (*Patton*). The calculations here are mine and involve some subjective decisions about legibility. A number of individuals failed to self-identify, and others checked more than one box for gender and/or age. Those results were discarded from

these calculations. As a result, others might come to slightly different percentages—but only slightly. Calculations here are based on the entire contents of Box 6. Because there is no way to differentiate between the questionnaires in the one folder or the other, no effort was made to cite the individual documents.

12. "Award Winner: Franklin Schaffner," 15.

13. Hift to Rosenfield, n.d., Folder 1, Box 32B, Papers of Franklin J. Schaffner.

14. McCarthy interview audio recording.

15. Schaffner interview with Hirshberg, 4.

16. Rosenfield to McCarthy, February 11, 1969, Folder 2, Box 7, Papers of Frank McCarthy (*Patton*).

17. *San Francisco Examiner*, February 25, 1970; Schaffner to Zanuck, April 28, 1969, Folder 1, Box 30, Papers of Franklin J. Schaffner.

18. Kim, *Schaffner*, 262.

19. *Philadelphia Inquirer*, February 15, 1970; *San Francisco Examiner*, February 25, 1970; Schaffner interview with Hirshberg, 4.

20. Suid, *Guts and Glory*, 273; Brown, *Let Me Entertain You*, 239; McCarthy interview with Hirshberg, 101; McCarthy to Banning, September 13, 1961, Folder 5, Box 1, Papers of Frank McCarthy (*Patton*).

21. McCarthy interview with Hirshberg, 22; McCarthy to Beetley, November 6, 1969; McCarthy to Zanuck, November 12, 1969, Folder 4; Eisenhower to McCarthy, January 21, 1969, Folder 7, Box 30, Papers of Franklin J. Schaffner.

22. Baughman, *Republic of Mass Culture*, 137–142.

23. *Chicago Today*, March 15, 1970; *Variety*, November 6, 2006; McCarthy to Totten, January 8, 1970, Folder 2, Box 1, Papers of Frank McCarthy (*Patton*).

24. Louis L. Snyder, "Patton: A Salute to a Rebel: A Guide and Commentary for Classroom Discussion," Folder 14, Box 7, Papers of Frank McCarthy (*Patton*).

25. Ibid.

26. Ibid.

27. Hift to Rosenfield, n.d., Folder 1, Box 32B, Papers of Franklin J. Schaffner.

28. Ibid.

29. Ibid.; Rawsthorne to Rosenfield, February 24, 1970, Folder 19, Box 4, Papers of Frank McCarthy (*Patton*); McCarthy to Rosenfield, November 28, 1969, Folder: Patton 7, June 1, 1969–December 30, 1969, Box FX-PF-157, Twentieth Century-Fox Film Corporation Production Files.

30. Hift to Rosenfield, n.d., Folder 1, Box 32B, Papers of Franklin J. Schaffner.

31. *Hollywood Reporter*, January 21, 1970; *Independent Film Journal*, February 4, 1970; *Boxoffice*, January 26, 1970; *Variety* (January 21, 1970), 3, 9.

32. Judith Crist, "Great Scott!," *New York Magazine*, February 9, 1970, 54; Liz Smith, "Beautiful Blood and Guts," *Cosmopolitan*, April 1970, 14; Gene Shalit, "George C. Scott Commands as 'Patton,'" *Look*, April 21, 1970; Pauline Kael, "The Man Who Loved War," *New Yorker*, January 31, 1970, 73–76; Wanda Hale, "'Patton'—Magnificent Monument to a Hero," New York *Daily News*, February 5, 1970.

33. *Chicago Tribune*, March 5, 1970.

34. *Chicago Sun-Times*, March 6, 1970; March 17, 2002.

35. *New York Times*, February 8, 1970.

36. *New York Times*, June 14, 1970.

37. Zanuck to Peck, June 26, 1970, Folder 1, Box 30, Papers of Franklin J. Schaffner.

38. The Peck letter is not included in the correspondence files that Schaffner maintained, but Zanuck quoted from it. Zanuck to Peck, June 29, 1970, Folder 1, Box 30, Papers of Franklin J. Schaffner.

39. Zanuck to Peck, June 29, 1970, Folder 1, Box 30, Papers of Franklin J. Schaffner.

40. Ibid.

41. One of the best reviews published on this film appeared in the *Pittsburgh Post-Gazette*, March 5, 1970.

42. *Milwaukee Journal*, March 4, 1970; *Honolulu Advertiser*, March 16, 1970; *Memphis Press Scimitar*, February 27, 1970; *Hawaii Times*, March 5, 1970; *Hollywood Citizen News*, February 18, 1970; *San Francisco Examiner*, March 4, 1970; *Houston Post*, March 12, 1970; *Ft. Lauderdale News*, March 4, 1970; *Columbus Citizen-Journal*, February 21 and March 3, 1970; *Columbus Sun-Press*, March 5, 1970; *Christian Science Monitor*, February 9, 1970; *Oregon Journal*, March 6, 1970; *Dallas Morning News*, March 5, 1970; *Cleveland Press*, March 5, 1970; *Buffalo Evening News*, March 6, 1970; *New Orleans Times-Picayune*, March 5, 1970; *Portland Oregonian*, March 6, 1970; *Honolulu Advertiser*, March 13, 1970; *Indianapolis News*, March 5, 1970; *Louisville Courier-Journal*, June 25, 1970; *Cincinnati Enquirer*, March 4, 1970; *New York Post*, February 5, 1970; *Minneapolis Star*, March 2, 1970; *Boston Record American*, March 6, 1970; *Boston Sunday Advertiser*, March 8, 1970; *Boston Globe*, March 5, 1970; *Miami Herald*, March 7, 1970; *Louisville Times*, June 25, 1970; *Honolulu Advertiser*, March 13, 1970; *Los Angeles Free Press*, March 13, 1970; *Washington Evening Star*, March 4, 1970; *Seattle Times*, March 8, 1970; *Atlanta*

Journal, March 4 and 6, 1970; Denver Post, March 4, 1970; Newark Evening News, February 5, 1970; Baltimore Daily Record, March 6, 1970; Washington Daily News, March 5, 1970; Dallas Times Herald, March 5, 1970; Buffalo Courier-Express, March 5, 1970; San Francisco Chronicle, March 4, 1970; St. Louis Globe-Democrat, March 7–8, 1970; Pittsburgh Press, March 5, 1970.

43. Seattle Times, March 8, 1970; Columbus Citizen-Journal, March 3, 1970; Portland Oregonian, March 6, 1970; Kansas City Star, March 8, 1970; Baltimore Daily Record, March 6, 1970; Newark Evening News, February 5, 1970.

44. St. Louis Post-Dispatch, May 17, 1970; Atlanta Journal, March 4, 1970; Denver Post, March 4, 1970; Newark Evening News, February 5, 1970; Dallas Times Herald, March 5, 1970; Journal of Commerce, February 4, 1970; Buffalo Evening News, March 6, 1970; New Orleans Times-Picayune, March 5, 1970; Cleveland Press, March 5, 1970; Ft. Lauderdale News, March 4, 1970; Columbus Citizen-Journal, February 21 and March 3, 1970; Columbus Sun-Press, March 5, 1970; Christian Science Monitor, February 9, 1970; Oregon Journal, March 6, 1970; Dallas Morning News, March 5, 1970; Memphis Press Scimitar, February 27, 1970; Miami Beach Reporter, March 5, 1970.

45. Louisville Times, June 25, 1970; Seattle Times, March 8, 1970; Atlanta Journal, March 4, 1970; Dallas Times Herald, March 5, 1970; Philadelphia Evening Bulletin, March 12, 1970; San Francisco Examiner, March 4, 1970; Washington Daily News, March 5, 1970; Boston Globe, March 5, 1970.

46. Los Angeles Free Press, March 13, 1970; Cincinnati Post and Times-Star, March 5, 1970; Newark Evening News, February 5, 1970; Louisville Courier-Journal, June 25, 1970; Pittsburgh Post-Gazette, March 5, 1970; Baltimore Daily Record, March 6, 1970; Seattle Times, March 8, 1970; Louisville Times, June 25, 1970.

47. Portland Catholic Sentinel, March 6, 1970; Salt Lake Tribune, March 5, 1970; Memphis Commercial Appeal, March 3, 1970; Denver Post, March 4, 1970; Salt Lake City Desert News, March 5, 1970.

48. Detroit Free Press, March 31, 1970; Salt Lake City Desert News, February 19, 1970; Memphis Commercial Appeal, March 5, 1970; Stars and Stripes, February 3, 1970; Austin American, July 30, 1970.

49. Catholic Standard and Times, March 12, 1970; Entertainment World, January 23, 1970, 17, 18; Indianapolis Star, March 5, 1970.

50. Minneapolis Star, March 2 and 3, 1970; Detroit Free Press, March 22, 1970; Stars and Stripes, March 5, 1970.

51. Honolulu Advertiser, March 13, 16, 1970.

52. Daily Advance, July 24, 1970; another editorial column focused on the language of the film in Miami Herald, March 11, 1970; New York Daily News, February 5, 1970.

53. Oakland Tribune, March 6, 1970; Philadelphia Daily News, March 12, 1970; Philadelphia Inquirer, March 12, 1970; Washington Post, March 1, 1970; Philadelphia Evening Bulletin, March 12, 1970; Chicago Today, March 5, 1970; Long Island Press, February 5, 1970; Cleveland Plain Dealer, March 5, 1970; Newsday, February 5, 1970.

54. For positive evaluations, see Boston Record American, March 6, 1970; Atlanta Journal, March 4, 1970; Philadelphia Inquirer, March 12, 1970; Memphis Press-Scimitar, February 27, 1970; Hollywood Citizen News, February 18, 1970;

Oregon Journal, March 6, 1970. For negative evaluations, see *Salt Lake Tribune*, March 5, 1970; *Atlanta Journal*, March 6, 1970; *Seattle Times*, March 8, 1970.

55. *Cleveland Press*, March 3, 1970; *Cincinnati Post and Times-Star*, March 5, 1970; *Seattle Times*, March 8, 1970; *Philadelphia Evening Bulletin*, March 12, 1970; *Columbus Citizen-Journal*, March 3, 1970; *St. Louis Post-Dispatch*, March 17, 1970.

56. Baughman, *Republic of Mass Culture*, 137–142.

57. Rutgers University *Gleaner*, February 18, 1970; University of Miami *Hurricane*, March 17, 1970; University of California at Los Angles *Daily Bruin*, March 5, 1970; University of Southern California, Los Angeles, *Daily Trojan*, undated clipping, Folder 10, Box 8, Papers of Frank McCarthy (Patton).

58. *Dallas Times Herald*, March 2, 1970. In another interview, Schaffner says the audience was 600, which is far more plausible, given the theater's seating capacity. *Fort Worth Star-Telegram*, February 25, 1970.

59. *Daily Express*, May 6, 1970.

60. *People*, May 10, 1970; *Daily Telegraph*, May 8, 1970; *Financial Times*, May 8, 1970; *Sunday Telegraph*, May 10, 1970.

61. *Daily Mirror*, May 6, 1970.

62. *Observer*, May 10, 1970; *Daily Express*, May 6, 1970; *Times*, May 8, 1970.

63. *Sunday Times*, May 10, 1970.

64. Zanuck notation on McCarthy to Zanuck, May 6, 1970, Folder 1, Box 30, Papers of Franklin J. Schaffner.

65. *Montreal Star*, March 12, 1970; *Gazette*, March 12, 1970; *Telegram*, February 28, 1970; also see the review in the *Globe and Mail*, March 12, 1970.

66. *Irish Times*, May 4, 1970.

67. *Le Canard Enchaine*, April 29, 1970; *Le Nouvel Observateur*, April 20–26, 1970; *Paris Match*, May 9, 1970; *France Soir*, April 29, 1970; Raguenet to McCarthy, February 20, 1970, Folder 14, Box 9, Papers of Frank McCarthy (Patton).

68. "Press Quotes—PATTON," May 22, 1970, Folder 1, Box 22, Papers of Franklin J. Schaffner.

69. Prince Rainier of Monaco to McCarthy, May 3, 1971, Folder 6, Box 11, Papers of Frank McCarthy (Patton).

70. Nixon to McCarthy, November 8, 1971, Folder 5, Box 11, Papers of Frank McCarthy (Patton).

71. Reagan to McCarthy, March 19, 1970, Folder 14, Box 9, Papers of Frank McCarthy (Patton).

72. Kass to McCarthy, March 24, [1970], Folder 8, Box 12; Jones to McCarthy, April 16, 1971, Folder 1, Box 11; Lawerence to McCarthy March 17, 1971, Folder 16, Box 9, Papers of Frank McCarthy (Patton).

73. *Los Angeles Herald-Examiner*, June 18, 1969.

74. Reeder to McCarthy February 5, 1970, Folder 14, Box 9 and Johnson to McCarthy December 19, 1969, Folder 5, Box 9, Papers of Frank McCarthy (Patton).

75. Bigland to Bradley, May 26, 1970, and de Guingand to Bradley, February 20, 1970, Folder 19, Box 11, Papers of Frank McCarthy (Patton).

76. Bradley to de Guingand, March 7, 1970, Folder 18, Box 11, Papers of Frank McCarthy (Patton).

77. John Eisenhower to McCarthy, August 13, 1968, and John Eisenhower to McCarthy, March 12, 1970, Folder 3, Box 12, Papers of Frank McCarthy (Patton).

78. John Eisenhower to McCarthy, March 12, 1970, and Eisenhower to

McCarthy, September 2, 1969, Folder 3, Box 12, Papers of Frank McCarthy (*Patton*).

79. Farago to Schaffner, May 20, 1970, Folder 9; Baruch to McCarthy, January 6, 1970, Folder 7, Box 30, Papers of Franklin J. Schaffner.

80. Hayes to McCarthy February 14, 1970, Folder 30; Rogers to Studio, July 15, 1970, Folder 16, Box 9, Papers of Frank McCarthy (*Patton*).

81. *Daily Mirror*, May 6, 1970; Zanuck notation on McCarthy to Zanuck, October 19, 1969, Papers of Frank McCarthy (*Patton*).

82. *People*, June 22 1969; Tyler to McCarthy, May 11, 1970, and McCarthy to Trevelyan, May 27, 1970, and De la Torre to McCarthy, July 10, 1970, Folder 3, Box 5, Papers of Frank McCarthy (*Patton*).

83. Zanuck notation on McCarthy to Zanuck, January 10, 1969, Folder 11, Box 12, Papers of Frank McCarthy (*Patton*).

84. Vetter to McCarthy, December 15, 1969; McCarthy to Vetter, December 14, 1969; McCarthy to Raphel, January 9, 1970, Folder 17, Box 12, Papers of Frank McCarthy (*Patton*).

85. *San Francisco Examiner*, June 27, 1970; McCarthy to Stanfill, August 30, 1971, Folder 6, Box 5, Papers of Frank McCarthy (*Patton*).

86. Theophilus Green, "'Patton' Movie Omits Bravery of Black Heroes" *Jet*, September 3, 1970, 14–19; Harper to Twentieth Century-Fox, September 9, 1970, Folder 5, Box 5, Papers of Frank McCarthy (*Patton*).

87. Carter to Stanfill, June 29, 1971, Folder 6, Box 5, Papers of Frank McCarthy (*Patton*).

88. McCarthy to Stanfill, August 30, 1971; Carter to Stanfill, September 22, 1971; Stanfill to Carter, October 12, 1971,

Folder 6, Box 5, Papers of Frank McCarthy (*Patton*).

89. Munroe, "Director Franklin Schaffner," 16.

90. McCarthy to Totten, January 8, 1970, and Totten to McCarthy, January 21, 1970, Folder 2, Box 1, Papers of Frank McCarthy (*Patton*).

91. Patton, *Pattons*, 296–298.

92. Totten to McCarthy, January 1, 1970, and Totten to McCarthy, March 5, 1970, Folder 2, Box 1, Papers of Frank McCarthy (*Patton*); Ruth Patton Totten, "All I could hear was Georgie Patton's Body Lies a-Moulderin," *San Francisco Sunday Examiner and Chronicle*, March 18, 1970.

93. Ruth Patton Totten, "Daughter Thinks 'Patton' Sensitive, Realistic Movie," *Boston Sunday Globe*, March 22, 1970.

94. Kass to McCarthy, March 24, [1970], Folder 8, Box 12, Papers of Frank McCarthy (*Patton*).

95. Zanuck notation on Totten to McCarthy, March 5, 1970, Folder 2, Box 1, Papers of Frank McCarthy (*Patton*).

Chapter 9. The Legacy

1. *Daily Variety*, March 15, 1971.

2. *Daily Variety*, April 16, 1971; *Time*, March 22, 1971.

3. The 43rd annual Academy Awards, April 15, 1971, NBC telecast, recorded to DVD, Film Archive, Mary Pickford Center for Motion Picture Study, Academy of Motion Picture Arts and Sciences, Los Angeles, Calif.; *Daily Variety*, April 16, 1971; *Los Angeles Times*, April 16, 1971; *New York Times*, April 16, 1971; *Time*, April 26, 1971. Stories in the *Los Angeles Times*, *New York Times*, and *Time* all gave considerable attention to Kellerman's wardrobe. The

article in the *New York Times* attributes the remarks about Patton being a "peace picture" to Schaffner, who was not present at the awards show. The telecast clearly shows that it was North who made the comment.

4. McCarthy to Carter, April 29, 1971, Folder 12, Box 11, Papers of Frank McCarthy (*Patton*); Lexington, Va., *News-Gazette*, May 5, 1971. The trophy is on display at the library. It is occasionally put in storage during remodeling.

5. *San Francisco Chronicle*, July 5, 1998; *Pittsburgh Post-Gazette*, July 26, 1998.

6. Mark Soupiset, "The Magnificent Seven," *USAA Magazine*, October 2003, 18–22.

7. These lists are widely available through a number of different sources. In this case, the rosters are from the section of the AFI website devoted to AFI's *100 Years . . . 100 Movies* (http://www.afi.com/tv/movies.asp) and AFI's *100 Years . . . 100 Heroes and Villains* (http://www.afi.com/tv/handv.asp).

8. Francis Ford Coppola, introduction, *Patton*, disc 1.

9. Coppola commentary, *Patton*, disc 1.

10. "The Living Legend," November 26 and December 3, 1978, directed by Vince Edwards, written by Glen A. Larson, *Battlestar Galactica: The Complete Epic Series*, and the episode guide at the SyFi Channel *Galactica* website (http://www.syfy.com).

11. Interview with René Auberjonois, January 1996, http://www.renefiles.com/janinter.html.

12. Mike Sussman audio commentary, "In a Mirror, Darkly, Part 2," *Star Trek: Enterprise: The Complete Fourth Season*, disc 5.

13. Bell, DVD commentary, *Bigger, Stronger, Faster: The Side Effects of Being American* (2008).

14. "'Twas the Night before Chaos" (December 13, 1994), written by Rosalind Moorem, directed by Andy Cadiff, *Home Improvement: The Complete Fourth Season*, disc 2; *Forget Paris* (1995); "Big Day" (April 18, 1995), directed by Alan Myerson, written by Joe Furey, Brad Isaacs, Josh Lieb, and Paul Simms, *News Radio: The Complete First and Second Seasons*, discs 1 and 2; "An Khe" (February 18, 2004), *The West Wing: The Complete Fifth Season*, disc 4; "Tribes" (January 15, 2008), directed by Colin Bucksey, written by Reed Steiger, *NCIS: Naval Criminal Investigative Service: The Fifth Season*, disc 3; "P.S. I Lo . . . " (May 3, 2001), written by Elaine Arata and Joan Binder Weiss, *Gilmore Girls: The Complete First Season*, disc 5; *Second String* (2002).

15. *An American Carol* (2008) Directed by David Zucker. Written by David Zucker, Myrna Sokoloff, and Lewis Friedman. (Universal City: Vivendi Entertainment, 2008)

16. "Cheaters Never Win," written by Barry Vigon, directed by Art Dielhenn, *Punky Brewster—Season Two*, disc 1; "The Simpsons 138th Episode Spectacular" (December 3, 1995), *The Simpsons: The Complete Seventh Season*, disc 2; Gary Ross DVD commentary, *Pleasantville* (1998); Brad T. Gottfred DVD commentary, *The Movie Hero* (2006); "Hell Comes to Quahog" (September 24, 2006), *Family Guy, Volume Five (Season 5, Part 1)*, disc 1; "High Treason, Part 2" (May 20, 1994), directed by Joseph L. Scanlan, written by Tom Chehak and John Wirth, *The Adventures of Brisco County, Jr.: The Complete Series*, disc 7; "Double Trouble" (May 19, 1996), directed by Rob Renzetti and Genndy Tartakovsky, *Dexter's Laboratory: Season One*, disc 1; "Let 'Em Eat Corn" (July 18, 2004), *Sealab 2021—Season 3*,

disc 2; "War is the H-Word" (November 26, 2000), directed by Ron Hugheart, written by Eric Horsed, *Futurama: The Complete Collection*, disc 7; "Sergeant Gork" (March 12, 1976), teleplay by Ted Bergman, *Sanford and Son: The Fifth Season*, disc 3; "The Best of the 70s and 80s," *The Ultimate Carson Collection*, vol. 1.

17. *Sesame Street Presents Follow That Bird* (1985) Directed by Ken Kwapis. Written by Tony Geiss and Judy Freudberg. (Burbank: Warner Home Video, 2002); *Space Jam* (1996) Directed by Joe Pytka. Screenplay by Leo Benvenuti, Steve Rudnick, Timmothy Harris and Herschel Weingrod. (Burbank: Warner Home Video, 1997); *Antz* (1998) Directed by Eric Darnell and Tim Johnson. Written by Todd Alcott, Chris Weitz and Paul Weitz. (Universal City: Dreamworks Animated, 1999); *Toy Story 2* (1999) Directed by John Lasseter. Screenplay by Andrew Stanton, Rita Hsiao, Doug Chamberlin, and Chris Webb. (Emeryville, CA: Disney/Pixar, 2001); *Recess: School's Out* (2001) Directed by Chuck Sheetz. Written by Jonathan Greenberg; and *Daddy Day Camp* (2007) Directed by Fred Savage. Written by Geoff Rodkey and J. David Stern and David N. Weiss. (Culver City: Sony Tristar Pictures 2008)

18. *The New Guy* (2002) Directed by Ed Decter. Written by David Kendall. (Culver City: Sony Pictures, 2002); *Jackass 2.5* (2007) Directed by Jeff Tremaine. (New York: MTV Studios, 2007); *Van Wilder: Freshman Year* (Paramount Studios, 2009) Directed by Harvey Glazer. Screenplay by Todd McCullough

19. *The Nine Lives of Fritz the Cat* (1974) Directed by Robert Taylor. Written by Fred Halliday, Eric Monte, and Robert Taylor. (Century City: MGM, 2001)

20. *Islands in the Stream* (1977) Directed by Franklin J. Schaffner. Written by Denne Bart Petitclerc. (Hollywood: Paramount, 2005)

21. *Batman* (1989) Directed by Tim Burton. Written by Sam Hamm and Warren Skaaren. (Burbank: Warner Home Video, 2009)

22. "Bart the General" (February 4, 1990), *The Simpsons: Season 1*, disc 1; "Secrets of a Successful Marriage" (May 19, 1994), *The Simpsons: The Complete Fifth Season*, disc 4.

23. Muppet Movie Parody 1999 Calendar section with photos on http://muppet.wikia.com

24. "The Joy of Sect" (February 8, 1998), *The Simpsons: The Complete Ninth Season*, disc 2; "Dr. Jay" (June 29, 1994), directed by Dan Jeup, written by Jon Vitti, *The Critic: The Complete Series*, disc 2; "The Cane" (December 12, 1995), directed by Alan Myerson, written by Brad Isaacs, *News Radio: The Complete First and Second Seasons*, discs 1 and 2 (Culver City, Calif.: Sony Pictures Television, 2005); "Superstitious Dick" (March 2, 1999), *3rd Rock from the Sun*, directed by Terry Hughes, screenplay by Greg Mettler, http://www.3rdrock.com; "Rivals in Romance" (July 19, 2003), directed by Pamela Fryman, written by Steven Levitan and David Hemingson, *Just Shoot Me*; "The Hand of God" (March 11, 2005), directed by Jeff Woolnough, written by David Weddle and Bradley Thompson, *Battlestar Galactica: The Complete Series*; *Mr. Awesome Guide to Girls* (1989), excerpt in *The King of Kong: A Fistful of Quarters* (2008); "The Bottle Deposit, Part 1" (May 2, 1996), directed by Andy Ackerman, written by Gregg Kavet and Andy Robin, *Seinfeld—Season 7*, disc 4; "The Millennium" (May 1, 1997), directed by Andy Ackerman, written by

232

Jennifer Crittenden, *Seinfeld—Season 8*, disc 4; *I Accuse My Parents* (original release 1944; *Mystery Science Theater 3000* commentary September 4, 1993).

25. "Colonial Day" (March 18, 2005), directed by Jonas Pate, written by Carla Robinson, *Battlestar Galactica: The Complete Series*, disc 4 (Universal City, Calif.: Universal, 2009).

26. *Mr. Mom* (1983) Directed by Stan Dragoti. Written by John Hughes. (Century City: MGM, 2000)

27. *The 'Burbs* (1989) Directed by Joe Dante. Written by Dana Olsen. (Universal City: Universal Studios, 1999)

28. *Lobster Man from Mars* (1989) Directed by Stanley Sheff. Screenplay by Bob Greenberg. (Santa Monica: Lions Gate, 2004)

29. "Destiny" (January 12, 1997), directed by Robert Tapert, written by Steven L. Sears, R. J. Stewart, and Robert Tapert, *Xena: Warrior Princess—Season 2*, disc 3; "Déjà Vu All Over Again" (May 17, 1999), directed by Renee O'Connor, screenplay by R. J. Stewart, *Xena: Warrior Princess—Season 4*, disc 8; *Mystery Science Theater 3000* commentary for *I Accuse My Parents* (1944), September 4, 1993, and for *Boggy Creek II: And the Legend Continues* (1985), May 9, 1999, *Mystery Science Theater 3000*, vol. 5, disc 1.

30. System of a Down, "Sugar" Music Video, viewed on http://www.youtube .com.

31. The Authority, *On Glory's Side* (Long Beach, CA: Outsider Records, 1999)

32. "The Best of the 70s and 80s," *The Ultimate Carson Collection*, vol. 1.

33. *Saturday Night Live*, December 14, 1991.

34. Dennis Leary, "I'm an Asshole," video viewed on http://www.youtube.com

35. David Frye, *Clinton: An Oral History* (Seattle: Gag Media CD, 1998)

36. *The Tonight Show*, National Broadcast Company television network, August 23. 2006.

37. *New York Times*, October 31, 1985, and August 13, 1986.

38. *New York Times*, August 13, 1986.

39. *Washington Post*, October 5, 1980.

40. D'Este, *Patton*, 770–804.

41. *Toronto Star*, September 6, 1986.

42. *Toronto Star*, September 12, 1986; *Christian Science Monitor*, September 12, 1986; *New York Times*, September 12, 1986; *Washington Post*, September 13, 1986.

Chapter 10. The Impact

1. Timberg, *Nightingale's Song*, 73–76, 149, 199–200.

2. *New York Times*, August 13, 1986.

3. I performed the search at the Library of Congress catalog website.

4. Schaffner interview audio recording, no date, Box 87, Papers of Franklin J. Schaffner, Franklin & Marshall College, Lancaster, Pa.

5. Hathaway, review of *Britain . . .* , by Matthew Jones, 1448–1449.

6. Oliver Stone quoted in *History vs. Hollywood: Patton: A Rebel Revisited*, disc 2 of the *Patton* Cinema Classics Collection DVD.

7. Shaw, *Cambodia Campaign*.

8. Toplin, *History by Hollywood*, 173–175.

9. Small, "Containing Domestic Enemies," 130–151.

10. Ambrose, *Nixon*, 624–625.

11. Miller to McCarthy, November 27, 1970; McCarthy to Myers, February 15, 1972; McCarthy to Myers, January 26, 1972; McCarthy to Moore, January 25,

1972, Folder 11, Box 12, Papers of Frank McCarthy (*Patton*).

12. Doty to Public Relations Department, Twentieth Century-Fox, March 26, 1971, Folder 2, Box 12, Papers of Frank McCarthy (*Patton*).

13. *The Making of Patton: A Tribute to Franklin J. Schaffner*, disc 2, Patton Cinema Classics Collection DVD.

14. Ibid.

15. I saw this announcement on AFN *Sports* in Stuttgart, Germany, on Tuesday, June 8, 2004.

16. *New Orleans Times-Picayune*, December 1, 1998.

17. *San Francisco Chronicle*, January 17, 1990.

18. *USA Today*, January 7, 1993.

19. *Ottawa Citizen*, May 13, 1998.

20. *Rocky Mountain News*, September 19, 1999.

21. *Dallas Morning News*, October 6, 1994; *Austin American-Statesman*, September 21, 1995.

22. Brian Murphy, "Meet the In-laws," http://espn.go.com/page2/s/ murphy/011126.html.

23. Bouton, *I'm Glad*, 52.

24. *Boston Globe*, October 24, 1990.

25. *New Orleans Times-Picayune*, June 17, 1999.

26. *Milwaukee Journal Sentinel*, February 13, 2000.

27. Paul Begala, "Monkey See . . . How the Bush Campaign Copies Clinton's," *Washington Monthly*, September 2000, 14.

28. *Charlie Rose Show*, September 11, 2008.

29. *O'Reilly Factor*, December 2, 2009.

30. *San Francisco Chronicle*, January 27, 1995.

31. *Tampa Tribune*, December 24, 1996.

Epilogue

1. Baughman, *Republic of Mass Culture*, 137–142; Mosley, *Zanuck*, 382–390; Harris, *Zanucks*, 134; Custen, *Twentieth Century's Fox*, 368–369.

2. McAdams, *American War Film*, 213; *Richmond Times Dispatch*, November 11, 1971, and December 3, 1986; *New York Times*, December 4, 1986; *Hollywood Reporter*, August 8, 1977; *Washington Post*, August 5, 1977; *Los Angeles Times*, August 21, 1977; Edmund H. North, *Marshal: Man of War—Man of Peace*, October 29, 1974, Folder 17, Box 9, Papers of Frank McCarthy (*MacArthur*).

3. *Boston Globe*, September 24, 1999; *Atlanta Journal and Constitution*, September 24, 1999; *Washington Post*, September 24, 1999; *New York Times*, October 31, 1985; Sheward, *Rage and Glory*, 301–302, 342–343, 368–369.

4. *New York Times*, July 3, 1989; *San Francisco Chronicle*, November 4, 1989.

5. *Los Angeles Times*, August 30, 1990; *Daily Variety*, February 18, 2003.

6. *New York Times*, July 23, 2004; PR Newswire, September 24, 2005.

7. *Daily Variety*, July 2, 2009; *Washington Post*, July 2, 2009; *New York Times*, July 2, 2009.

8. *New York Times*, December 23, 2003; *Sunday Telegraph*, January 20, 2008; *Los Angeles Times*, February 2 and April 11, 2010; Bruck, *When Hollywood Had a King*, 342.

9. *Los Angeles Times*, February 2, 2010; *Washington Post*, February 3, 2010; *New York Times*, February 2, 2010.

10. *New York Times*, July 24, 1988, and June 7, 2009; *Variety*, January 12–18, 1998, 152; *Houston Chronicle*, November 23, 1997; *Chicago Sun-Times*, November 23, 1997; *Daily Telegraph*, November 23, 2007; Schumacher, *Coppola*, 436.

BIBLIOGRAPHY

Archives
Academy of Motion Picture Arts and Sciences
    Margaret Herrick Library, Beverly Hills, Calif., Core Collection Files
    Mary Pickford Center for Motion Picture Study, Los Angeles, Calif., Film Archive
Georgetown University, Washington, D.C.
    Lauinger Library
        Papers of Larry Suid
Franklin & Marshall College, Lancaster, Pa.
    Shadek-Fackenthal Library
        Papers of Franklin Schaffner
University of California, Los Angeles
    Young Library
        Twentieth Century-Fox Film Corporation Production Files
University of Southern California, Los Angeles
    Cinema-Television Library
        Papers of Jack L. Warner
Virginia Military Institute, Lexington, Va.
    George C. Marshall Research Library
        Papers of Frank McCarthy (Additional)
        Papers of Frank McCarthy (Military)
        Papers of Frank McCarthy (*Patton*)
        Papers of Frank McCarthy (*MacArthur*)

Oral Histories
Karl Malden by Academy of Motion Picture Arts and Sciences
Frank McCarthy by Twentieth Century-Fox
Franklin Schaffner by Twentieth Century-Fox
George C. Scott by Twentieth Century-Fox

Websites
American Film Institute, http://www.afi.com
ESPN, http://espn.go.com
LexisNexis Database, http://www.lexisnexis.com

Library of Congress, http://www.loc.gov
Muppet Wiki, http://muppet.wikia.com
The René Auberjonois Internet Link, http://www.renefiles.com
3rd Rock from the Sun website, http://www.3rdrock.com
SyFy Channel, http://www.syfy.com
U.S. Bureau of Labor Statistics, http://data.bls.gov/cgi-bin/cpicalc.pl
YouTube, http://www.youtube.com

Newspapers and Magazines

United States

Action	Daily Variety
American Cinematographer	Dallas Morning News
Army	Dallas Times Herald
Atlanta Journal	Entertainment World
Atlanta Journal and Constitution	Fort Worth Star-Telegram
Atlantic	Ft. Lauderdale News
Austin American	Future: Magazine for Young Men
Austin American-Statesman	Hawaii Times
Baltimore Daily Record	Hollywood Citizen News
Boston Globe	Hollywood Reporter
Boston Herald Traveler	Honolulu Advertiser
Boston Sunday Advertiser	Houston Chronicle
Boston Record American	Houston Post
Boston Sunday Globe	Independent Film Journal
Boxoffice	Indianapolis Star
Buffalo Courier-Express	Jet
Buffalo Evening News	Journal of Commerce
Catholic Standard and Times	Kansas City Star
Chicago Today	Life
Chicago Sun-Times	Lexington, Va., News-Gazette
Chicago Tribune	Long Island Press
Christian Science Monitor	Look
Cincinnati Enquirer	Los Angeles Free Press
Cincinnati Post and Times-Star	Los Angeles Herald-Examiner
Cleveland Plain Dealer	Los Angeles Times
Cleveland Press	Louisville Courier-Journal
Columbus Citizen-Journal	Louisville Times
Columbus Sun-Press	Memphis Commercial Appeal
Cosmopolitan	Memphis Press-Scimitar
Current Biography: Who's News and Why	Miami Beach Reporter
Denver Post	Miami Herald
Detroit Free Press	Milwaukee Journal
Elizabeth City, N.C., Daily Advance	Milwaukee Journal Sentinel

Minneapolis Star
New Orleans Times-Picayune
New York Daily News
New York Magazine
New York Post
New York Sunday News
New York Times
New York Times Magazine
New Yorker
Newark Evening News
Newsday
Norfolk Virginian-Pilot
Oakland Tribune
Oregon Journal
Philadelphia Daily News
Philadelphia Evening Bulletin
Philadelphia Inquirer
Pittsburgh Post-Gazette
Pittsburgh Press
Portland Catholic Sentinel
Portland Oregonian
Richmond Times Dispatch
Rocky Mountain News

Salt Lake City Desert News
Salt Lake Tribune
San Francisco Chronicle
San Francisco Examiner
San Francisco Sunday Examiner and Chronicle
Seattle Times
Show
Soldier
St. Louis Globe-Democrat
St. Louis Post-Dispatch
Stars and Stripes
Tampa Tribune
Time
USAA Magazine
USA Today
Wall Street Journal
Washington Daily News
Washington Evening Star
Washington Monthly
Washington Post
Washington Times-Herald
Variety
Virginia Military Institute Alumni Review

College
Rutgers University, Gleaner
University of California at Los Angles, Daily Bruin

The University of Miami, Hurricane
University of Southern California, Daily Trojan

Foreign
Canada
Globe and Mail
Montreal Star

Ottawa Citizen
Toronto Star

France
Le Canard Enchaine
Le Nouvel Observateur

Paris Match

Ireland
Irish Times

United Kingdom
Daily Express
Financial Times

Guardian
Daily Express

Daily Mirror   Sunday Telegraph
Daily Telegraph   Sunday Times
Observer   Times
People   Telegram

Films

An American Carol. Directed by David Zucker. Written by David Zucker, Myrna Sokoloff, and Lewis Friedman. Universal City: Vivendi Entertainment, 2008.

Antz. Directed by Eric Darnell and Tim Johnson. Written by Todd Alcott, Chris Weitz, and Paul Weitz. 1998; Universal City, Calif.: Dreamworks Animated, 1999.

Avatar. Directed and written by James Cameron. 2009; Century City, Calif.: Twentieth Century Fox, 2010.

Batman. Directed by Tim Burton. Written by Sam Hamm and Warren Skaaren. 1989; Burbank, Calif.: Warner Home Video, 2009.

Bigger, Stronger, Faster: The Side Effects of Being American. Directed by Christopher Bell. Written by Christopher Bell, Alexander Buono, and Tamsin Rawady. New York: Magnolia Home Entertainment, 2008.

Blades. Troma Triple B-Header. 1989; New York: Troma Entertainment, 2004.

The 'Burbs. Directed by Joe Dante. Written by Dana Olsen. 1989; Universal City, Calif.: Universal Studios, 1999.

Daddy Day Camp. Directed by Fred Savage. Written by Geoff Rodkey, J. David Stern, and David N. Weiss. 2007; Culver City, Calif.: Sony Tristar Pictures, 2008.

Defending Your Life. Directed and written by Albert Brooks. 1991; Burbank, Calif.: Warner Home Video, 2001.

Forget Paris. Directed by Billy Crystal. Written by Billy Crystal, Lowell Ganz, and Babaloo Mandel. 1995; Atlanta: Turner Home Entertainment, 2000.

Godzilla 2000. Directed by Takao Okawara. Written by Hiroshi Kashiwabara and Wataru Mimura. Uncredited English translation by Michael Schlessinger. 1999; Culver City, Calif.: Sony Pictures Home Entertainment, 2000.

History through the Lens: "Patton": A Rebel Revisited. Documentary on Cinema Classics Collection DVD of Patton. Beverly Hills: Twentieth Century Fox Home Entertainment, 2006.

Islands in the Stream. Directed by Franklin J. Schaffner. Written by Denne Bart Petitclerc. 1977; Hollywood, Calif.: Paramount, 2005.

Jackass 2.5. Directed by Jeff Tremaine. New York: MTV Studios, 2007.

The King of Kong: A Fistful of Quarters. Los Angeles: New Line Home Entertainment, 2008.

Lobster Man from Mars. Directed by Stanley Sheff. Screenplay by Bob Greenberg. 1989; Santa Monica, Calif.: Lions Gate, 2004.

The Making of "Patton": A Tribute to Franklin J. Schaffner. Documentary. Directed by Michael M. Arick. 1997; included on the 1999 DVD release of Patton.

Mr. Mom. Directed by Stan Dragoti. Written by John Hughes. 1983; Century City, Calif.: MGM, 2000.

The Movie Hero. Directed and written by Brad T. Gottfred. Troy, Mich.: Starz/Anchor Bay, 2006.

The New Guy. Directed by Ed Decter. Written by David Kendall. Culver City, Calif.: Sony Pictures, 2002.

The Nine Lives of Fritz the Cat. Directed by Robert Taylor. Written by Fred Halliday, Eric Monte, and Robert Taylor. 1974; Century City, Calif.: MGM, 2001.

1941. Directed by Steven Spielberg. Written by Robert Zemeckis and Bob Gale. 1979; Universal City, Calif.: Universal Studios, 1999.

Patton. Directed by Franklin J. Schaffner. Written by Francis Ford Coppola and Edmund II. North. Cinema Classics Collection. 1970; Beverly Hills: Twentieth Century Fox Home Entertainment, 2006.

The People vs. Larry Flynt. Directed by Milos Forman. Written by Scott Alexander and Larry Karaszewski. 1996; Culver City, Calif.: Sony Pictures, 1997.

Pleasantville. Directed and written by Gary Ross. 1998; Los Angeles: New Line Home Video, 2004.

Recess: School's Out. Directed by Chuck Sheetz. Written by Jonathan Greenberg. Walt Disney Pictures, 2001.

Royal Flash. Directed by Richard Lester. Written by George MacDonlad Fraser. 1975; Fox, 2007.

Sesame Street Presents Follow That Bird. Directed by Ken Kwapis. Written by Tony Geiss and Judy Freudberg. 1985; Burbank, Calif.: Warner Home Video, 2002.

Small Soldiers. Directed by Joe Dante. Written by Gavin Scott, Adam Rifkin, Ted Elliott, and Terry Rossio. Universal City: Calif.: Dreamworks Video, 1998.

Smokey and the Bandit, Part 3. Directed by Dick Lowry. Written by Stuart Birnbaum and David Dashev. 1983; Universal City, Calif.: Universal Studios, 2004.

South Park: Bigger Longer and Uncut. Directed by Trey Parker. Written by Trey Parker and Matt Stone. Hollywood, Calif.: Paramount, 1999.

Space Jam. Directed by Joe Pytka. Screenplay by Leo Benvenuti, Steve Rudnick, Timmothy Harris, and Herschel Weingrod. 1996; Burbank, Calif.: Warner Home Video, 1997.

Spun. Directed by Jonas Åkerlund. Written by Will De Los Santos and Creighton Vero. 2002; Culver City, Calif.: Sony Pictures, 2003.

Superman III. Directed by Richard Lester. Written by David and Leslie Newman. 1983; Burbank, Calif.: Warner Home Video, 2001.

Stick It. Directed and written by Jessica Bendinger. Burbank, Calif.: Buena Vista, 2006.

Swimming to Cambodia. Directed by Jonathan Demme. Written by Spalding Gray. 1987.

Toy Story 2. Directed by John Lasseter. Screenplay by Andrew Stanton, Rita Hsiao, Doug Chamberlin, and Chris Webb. 1999; Emeryville, Calif.: Disney/Pixar, 2001.

Van Wilder: Freshman Year. Directed by Harvey Glazer. Screenplay by Todd McCullough. Hollywood, Calif.: Paramount Studios, 2009.

Wall Street. Directed by Oliver Stone. Written by Stanley Weisner and Oliver Stone. 1987; Century City, Calif.: Twentieth Century Fox, 2000.

Television DVDs

The Adventures of Brisco County, Jr.: The Complete Series. Burbank, Calif.: Warner Bros., 2006.

Battlestar Galactica: The Complete Epic Series. Universal City, Calif.: Universal DVD, 2004.

Battlestar Galactica: The Complete Series. Universal City, Calif.: Universal, 2009.

The Critic: The Complete Series. Los Angeles: Columbia TriStar Home Entertainment, 2004.

Dexter's Laboratory: Season One. Atlanta: Cartoon Network, 2010.

Family Guy, Volume Five (Season 5, Part 1). Century City, Calif.: Twentieth Century Fox, 2007.

Frost/Nixon: Complete Interviews. Liberation Entertainment, 2009.

Futurama: The Complete Collection. Century City, Calif.: Fox Film Corporation, 2009.

Gilmore Girls: The Complete First Season. WB Television Network, 2004.

Home Improvement: The Complete Fourth Season. Burbank, Calif.: Buena Vista Home Entertainment, 2006.

The Last Days of Patton. 1986; Cherry Hill, N.J.: TGG Direct, 2003.

Mystery Science Theater 3000: I Accuse My Parents. Los Angeles: Rhino Home Video, 1996. Original film released 1944.

Mystery Science Theater 3000: Boggy Creek II: And the Legend Continues. Los Angeles: Rhino Home Video, 2004. Original film released 1985.

NCIS: Naval Criminal Investigative Service: The Fifth Season. Studio City: CBS Studios, 2008.

News Radio: The Complete First and Second Seasons. Culver City, Calif.: Sony Pictures Television, 2005.

Punky Brewster—Season Two. Culver City, Calif.: Sony Music Entertainment, 2005.

Sanford and Son: The Fifth Season. Culver City, Calif.: Sony Pictures Home Entertainment, 2004.

Sealab 2021—Season 3. Burbank, Calif.: Warner Home Video, 2005.

Second String. Directed by Robert Liebermann. Written by Tom Flynn. Atlanta: Turner Home Entertainment, 2003.

Seinfeld—Season 7. Culver City, Calif.: Sony Pictures Television, 2006.

Seinfeld—Season 8. Culver City, Calif.: Sony Pictures Television, 2007.

The Simpsons: Season 1. Century City, Calif.: Fox Home Entertainment, 2001.

The Simpsons: The Complete Fifth Season. Century City, Calif.: Fox Home Entertainment, 2005.

The Simpsons: The Complete Seventh Season. Century City, Calif.: Fox Home Entertainment, 2005.

The Simpsons: The Complete Ninth Season. Century City, Calif.: Fox Home Entertainment, 2006.

Star Trek: Enterprise: The Complete Fourth Season. Hollywood, Calif.: Paramount Pictures, 2005.

The West Wing: The Complete Fifth Season. Burbank, Calif.: Warner Home Video, 2005.

The Ultimate Carson Collection. Santa Monica, Calif.: Carson Productions Group, 2001.

Xena: Warrior Princess—Season 2. Troy, Mich.: Starz/Anchor Bay, 2003.

Xena: Warrior Princess—Season 4. Troy, Mich.: Starz/Anchor Bay, 2004.

Broadcast Television

Just Shoot Me, July 19, 2003.
Saturday Night Live, December 14, 1991.
The Tonight Show, August 23, 2006.

Audio Compact Discs

The Authority. *On Glory's Side*. Long Beach, Calif.: Outsider Records, 1999.
Frye, David. *Clinton: An Oral History*. Seattle: Gag Media CD, 1998.

Unpublished Material

George C. Marshall Research Foundation, "Frank McCarthy Patton Movie Collection."
Frank McAdams, review of "The Patton Project: The Making of a Legendary Film," May 18, 2011.

Works Cited

Allen, Robert S. *Lucky Forward: The History of Patton's Third Army*. New York: Vanguard Press, 1947.
Ambrose, Stephen E. *Nixon: The Education of a Politician, 1913–1962*. New York: Simon & Schuster, 1987.
Anderson, Terry. *The Movement and the Sixties*. New York: Oxford University Press, 1995.
Andrew III, John A. *The Other Side of the Sixties: Young Americans for Freedom and the Rise of Conservative Politics*. Piscataway, N.J.: Rutgers University Press, 1997.
Baldasty, Gerald. *The Commercialization of News in the Nineteenth Century*. Madison: University of Wisconsin Press, 1992.
Baughman, James L. *The Republic of Mass Culture: Journalism, Filmmaking, and Broadcasting in America since 1941*. Baltimore: Johns Hopkins University Press, 1992.
Baxter, John. *Stanley Kubrick: A Biography*. New York: Carroll & Graff, 1997.
Berkowitz, Edward. *Mass Appeal: The Formative Age of the Movies, Radio, and TV*. New York: Cambridge University Press, 2010.
Blum, John Morton. *Years of Discord: American Politics and Society, 1961–1974*. New York: Norton, 1991.
Bolger, Daniel P. "Zero Defects: Command Climate in the First U.S. Army, 1944–1945," *Military Review* 71 (May 1991): 61–73.
Borstelmann, Thomas. *The 1970s: A New Global History from Civil Rights to Economic Inequality*. Princeton, N.J.: Princeton University Press, 2011.
Bouton, Jim. *I'm Glad You Didn't Take It Personally*. Edited by Leonard Shecter. New York: William Morrow, 1971.
Bradley, Omar N. *A Soldier's Story*. New York: Holt, 1951.
Bradley, Omar N., and Clay Blair. *A General's Life: An Autobiography*. New York: Simon & Schuster, 1983.
Brands, H. W. *American Dreams: The United States since 1945*. New York: Penguin, 2010.

————. *The Strange Death of American Liberalism*. New Haven, Conn.: Yale University Press, 2001.

Brennan, Mary. *Turning Right in the Sixties: The Conservative Capture of the GOP*. Chapel Hill: University of North Carolina Press, 1995.

Brokaw, Tom. *Boom! Voices of the Sixties Personal Reflections on the '60s and Today*. New York: Random House, 2007.

Brown, David. *Let Me Entertain You*. New York: William Morrow, 1990.

Bruck, Connie. *When Hollywood Had a King: The Reign of Lew Wasserman, Who Leveraged Talent into Power and Influence*. New York: Random House, 2003.

Buford, Kate. *Burt Lancaster: An American Life*. New York: Da Capo Press, 2001.

Burner, David. *Making Peace with the 60s*. Princeton, N.J.: Princeton University Press, 1996.

Cagin, Seth, and Phillip Dray. *Hollywood Films of the Seventies*. New York: Harper and Row, 1984.

Carver, Michael. "Montgomery." In *Churchill's Generals*, edited by John Keegan, 148–165. London: Weidenfeld & Nicolson, 1991.

Caute, David. *The Year of the Barricades: A Journey through 1968*. New York: Harper and Row, 1988.

Cavallo, Dominick. *A Fiction of the Past: The Sixties in American History*. New York: St. Martin's Press, 1999.

Cohen, Lizabeth. *A Consumer's Republic: The Politics of Mass Consumption in Postwar America*. New York: Knopf, 2003.

Collier, Peter, and David Horowitz. *Destructive Generation: Second Thoughts about the '60s*. New York: Free Press, 1996.

Craig, Douglas B. *Fireside Politics: Radio and Political Culture in the United States, 1920–1940*. Baltimore: Johns Hopkins University Press, 2000.

Critchlow, Donald T. *The Conservative Ascendancy: How the GOP Right Made Political History*. Cambridge, Mass.: Harvard University Press, 2007.

Cunningham, Sean P. *Cowboy Conservatism: Texas and the Rise of the Modern Right*. Lexington: University Press of Kentucky, 2010.

Curti, Merle. "Dime Novels and the American Tradition." *Yale Review* 26 (1937): 761–778.

Custen, George. *Twentieth Century's Fox: Darryl F. Zanuck and the Culture of Hollywood*. New York: Basic Books, 1997.

D'Este, Carlo. *Eisenhower: A Soldier's Life*. New York: Henry Holt, 2002.

————. *Patton: A Genius for War*. New York: HarperCollins, 1995.

Danchev, Alex, and Daniel Todman, eds. *War Diaries, 1939–1945*. London: Weidenfeld & Nicolson, 2001.

Davies, Gareth. *From Opportunity to Entitlement: The Transformation and Decline of Great Society Liberalism*. Lawrence: University Press of Kansas, 1996.

Denning, Michael. *Mechanic Accents, Dime Novels and Working-class Culture in America*. New York: Methuen, 1987.

Dewhurst, Colleen, and Tom Viola. *Colleen Dewhurst: Her Autobiography*. New York: Lisa Drew/Scribner, 1997.

Douglas, Susan. *Inventing American Broadcasting, 1899–1902*. Baltimore: Johns Hopkins University Press, 1987.

Echols, Alice. *Daring to Be Bad: Radical Feminism in America, 1967–1975*. Minneapolis: University of Minnesota Press, 1989.

Eisenhower, Dwight D. *Crusade in Europe*. Garden City, N.Y.: Doubleday, 1948.

Farago, Ladislas. *Patton: Ordeal and Triumph*. New York: Ivan Obolensky, 1963.

Farber, David. *The Age of Great Dreams: America in the 1960's*. New York: Hill & Wang, 1994.

Farrell, James J. *The Spirit of the Sixties: The Making of Postwar Radicalism*. New York: Routledge, 1997.

Feeney, Mark. *Nixon at the Movies*. Chicago: University of Chicago Press, 2004.

Fehrenbach, Heide. *Cinema in Democratizing Germany: Reconstructing National Identity after Hitler*. Chapel Hill: University of North Carolina Press, 1995.

Frick, Daniel. *Reinventing Richard Nixon: A Cultural History of an American Obsession*. Lawrence: University Press of Kansas, 2008.

Gardner, Ava. *Ava: My Story*. New York: Bantam Books, 1990.

Garvey, Ellen Gruber. *The Adman in the Parlor: Magazines and the Gendering of Consumer Culture, 1880s to 1920s*. New York: Oxford University Press, 1996.

Gienow-Hecht, Jessica. *Transmission Impossible: American Journalists and Cultural Diplomacy, 1945–1955*. Baton Rouge: Louisiana State University Press, 1999.

Gitlin, Todd. *The Sixties: Years of Hope, Days of Rage*. New York: Bantam, 1987.

Goedde, Petra. *GIs and Germans: Culture, Gender, and Foreign Relations, 1945–1949*. New Haven, Conn.: Yale University Press, 2003.

Gorman, Paul R. *Left Intellectuals and Popular Culture in Twentieth-Century America*. Chapel Hill: University of North Carolina Press, 1996.

Greenberg, David. *Nixon's Shadow: The History of an Image*. New York: Norton, 2003.

Griffin, Nancy, and Kim Masters. *Hit and Run: How Jon Peters and Peter Gruber Took Sony for a Ride in Hollywood*. New York: Simon & Schuster, 1997.

Haldeman, H. R. *The Haldeman Diaries: Inside the Nixon White House*. New York: G. P. Putnam's Sons, 1994.

Hamilton, Nigel. *Master of the Battlefield: Monty's War Years, 1942–1944*. New York: McGraw-Hill, 1983.

———. *Monty: Final Years of the Field-Marshal, 1944–1976*. New York: McGraw-Hill, 1987.

———. *Monty: The Making of a General, 1887–1942*. New York: McGraw-Hill, 1981.

Hammond, William M. *Reporting Vietnam: Media and Military at War*. Lawrence: University Press of Kansas, 1998.

Harbinson, Allen. *George C. Scott: The Man, the Actor, and the Legend*. New York: Pinnacle Books, 1977.

Harris, Marlys J. *The Zanucks of Hollywood: The Dark Legacy of an American Dynasty*. New York: Crown Publishers, 1989.

Hathaway, Robert M. Review of *Britain, the United States and the Mediterranean War, 1842–44*, by Matthew Jones. *American Historical Review* 102, no. 5 (December 1997): 1448–1449.

Herman, Jan. A Talent for Trouble: The Life of Hollywood's Most Acclaimed Director, William Wyler. New York: G. P. Putnam's Sons, 1995.

Hess, Earl J., and Pratibha A. Dabholkar. "Singin' in the Rain": The Making of an American Masterpiece. Lawrence: University Press of Kansas, 2009.

Hilmes, Michele. Radio Voices: American Broadcasting, 1922–1952. Minneapolis: University of Minnesota Press, 1997.

Hirshon, Stanley P. General Patton: A Soldier's Life. New York: HarperCollins 2002.

Hixson, Walter L. Parting the Curtain: Propaganda, Culture, and the Cold War, 1945–1961. New York: St. Martin's Press, 1997.

Huston, John. An Open Book. New York: Alfred A. Knopf, 1980.

Isserman, Maurice. If I Had a Hammer: The Death of the Old Left and the Birth of the New Left. New York: Basic Books, 1987.

Jarvie, Ian. Hollywood's Overseas Campaign: The North Atlantic Film Trade, 1920–1950. New York: Cambridge University Press, 1992.

Jowett, Garth. Film: The Democratic Art. Boston: Little, Brown, 1976.

Kalman, Laura. Right Star Rising: A New Politics, 1974–1980. New York: Norton, 2010.

Kashner, Sam, and Nancy Schoenberger. Furious Love: Elizabeth Taylor, Richard Burton, and the Marriage of the Century. New York: Harper, 2010.

Kasson, Joy S. Buffalo Bill's Wild West: Celebrity, Memory, and Popular History. New York: Hill & Wang, 2000.

Kim, Erwin. Franklin J. Schaffner. Metuchen, N.J.: Scarecrow Press, 1985.

Kissinger, Henry. White House Years. Boston: Little, Brown, 1979.

Kitamura, Hiroshi. Screening Enlightenment: Hollywood and the Cultural Reconstruction of Defeated Japan. Ithaca, N.Y.: Cornell University Press, 2010.

Klatch, Rebecca E. A Generation Divided: The New Left, the New Right, and the 1960s. Berkley: University of California Press, 1999.

———. Women of the New Right. Philadelphia: Temple University Press, 1987.

Knightley, Philip. The First Casualty: From the Crimea to Vietnam: The War Correspondent as Hero, Propagandist, and Myth Maker. New York: Harcourt, 1975.

LaPorte, Nicole. The Men Who Would Be King: An Almost Epic Tale of Moguls, Movies and a Company Called Dreamworks. New York: Houghton Mifflin, 2010.

Lehman, Katherine J. Those Girls: Single Women in Sixties and Seventies Popular Culture. Lawrence: University Press of Kansas, 2011.

Leonard, Thomas C. The Power of the Press: The Birth of American Political Reporting. New York: Oxford University Press, 1986.

Lewis, Adrian R. Omaha Beach: A Flawed Victory. Chapel Hill: University of North Carolina Press, 2001.

Long, Robert Emmet. John Huston Interviews. Jackson: University of Mississippi Press, 2001.

Mackenzie, G. Calvin, and Robert Weisbrot. The Liberal Hour: Washington and the Politics of Change in the 1960s. New York: Penguin, 2008.

Macleod, David I. Building Character in the American Boy: The Boy Scouts, YMCA, and Their Forerunners, 1870–1920. Madison: University of Wisconsin Press, 1983.

Malden, Karl, with Carla Malden. *When Do I Start? A Memoir.* New York: Simon & Schuster, 1997.

Matusow, Allen J. *The Unraveling of America: A History of Liberalism in the 1960s.* New York: HarperPerennial, 1983.

McAdams, Frank. *The American War Film: History and Hollywood.* Westport, Conn.: Praeger, 2002.

McGirr, Lisa. *Suburban Warriors: The Origins of the New American Right.* Princeton, N.J.: Princeton University Press, 2001.

Miller, James. *"Democracy Is in the Streets": From Port Huron to the Siege of Chicago.* New York: Simon & Schuster, 1987.

Morgan, Edward P. *What Really Happened to the 1960s: How Mass Media Culture Failed American Democracy.* Lawrence: University Press of Kansas, 2010.

Mosley, Leonard. *Zanuck: The Rise and Fall of Hollywood's Last Tycoon.* Boston: Little, Brown, 1984.

Murray, Williamson, and Allan R. Millett. *A War to be Won: Fighting the Second World War.* Cambridge, Mass.: Harvard University Press, 2000.

Nichols, David, ed. *Ernie's War: The Best of Ernie Pyle's World War II Dispatches.* New York: Simon & Schuster, 1986.

Ohmann, Richard. *Selling Culture: Magazines, Markets, and Class at the Turn of the Century.* New York: Verso, 1996.

Patterson, James T. *Grand Expectations: The United States, 1945–1974.* New York: Oxford University Press, 1996.

Patton, George S. *The Patton Papers.* Vol. 2. Edited by Martin Blumenson. Boston: Houghton Mifflin, 1974.

Patton, Robert H. *The Pattons: A Personal History of an American Family.* Washington, D.C.: Brassey's, 1994.

Perlstein, Rick. *Before the Storm: Barry Goldwater and the Unmaking of the American Consensus.* New York: Hill & Wang, 2001.

———. *Nixonland: The Rise of a President and the Fracturing of America.* New York: Scribner, 2008.

Poiger, Uta G. *Jazz, Rock, and Rebels: Cold War Politics and American Culture in a Divided Germany.* Berkeley: University of California Press, 2000.

Probst, Leonard. *Off Camera: Leveling about Themselves.* New York: Stein and Day, 1975.

Riehl, Karen Truesdell. *Love and Madness: My Private Years with George C. Scott.* Alpine, Calif.: Sands Publishing, 2003.

Ritchie, Donald A. *Press Gallery: Congress and the Washington Correspondents.* Cambridge, Mass.: Harvard University Press, 1991.

———. *Reporting from Washington: The History of the Washington Press Corps.* New York: Oxford University Press, 2005.

Roberts, Randy, and James S. Olson. *John Wayne: American.* New York: The Free Press, 1995.

Rosenberg, Emily S. *Spreading the American Dream: American Economic and Cultural Expansion, 1890–1945.* New York: Hill & Wang, 1981.

Rydell, Robert W., and Rob Kroes. Buffalo Bill in Bologna: The Americanization of the World, 1869–1922. Chicago: University of Chicago Press, 2005.

Sandbrook, Dominic. Mad as Hell: The Crisis of the 1970s and the Rise of the Populist Right. New York: Knopf, 2011.

Scanlon, Jennifer. Inarticulate Longings: "The Ladies' Home Journal," Gender, and the Promise of Consumer Culture. New York: Routledge, 1995.

Schneider, Gregory L. Cadres for Conservatism: Young Americans for Freedom and the Rise of the Contemporary Right. New York: New York University Press, 1999.

Schneirov, Matthew. The Dream of a New Social Order: Popular Magazines in America, 1893–1914. New York: Columbia University Press, 1994.

Schumacher, Michael. Francis Ford Coppola: A Filmmaker's Life. New York: Crown Publishers, 1999.

Server, Lee. Ava Gardner: "Love Is Nothing." New York: St. Martin's Press, 2006.

Shaw, John M. The Cambodia Campaign: The 1970 Offensive and America's Vietnam War. Lawrence: University Press of Kansas, 2005.

Sheffield, Gary, and John Bourne, eds. Douglas Haig: War Diaries and Letters, 1914–1918. London: Weidenfeld & Nicolson, 2005.

Sheward, David. Rage and Glory: The Volatile Life and Career of George C. Scott. New York: Applause Theatre and Cinema Books, 2008.

Shorris, Sylvia, and Marion Abbott Bundy. Talking Pictures with the People Who Made Them. New York: The New Press, 1994.

Sklar, Robert. Movie-Made America. New York: Random House, 1975.

Small, Melvin. "Containing Domestic Enemies: Richard Nixon and the War at Home." In Shadow on the White House: Presidents and the Vietnam War, 1945–1975, edited by David Anderson, 130–151. Lawrence: University Press of Kansas, 1993.

Smulyan, Susan. Selling Radio. Washington, D.C.: Smithsonian Institution Press, 1994.

Spigel, Lynn. Make Room for TV: Television and the Family Ideal in Postwar America. Chicago: University of Chicago Press, 1992.

Steigerwald, David. The Sixties and the End of Modern America. New York: St. Martin's Press, 1995.

Suid, Lawrence H. Guts and Glory: The Making of the American Military Image in Film. 2nd ed. Lexington: University Press of Kentucky, 2002.

———. Sailing on the Silver Screen: Hollywood and the U.S. Navy. Annapolis: Naval Institute Press, 1996.

———. Stars and Stripes on Screen: A Comprehensive Guide to Portrayals of American Military on Film. Lanham, Md.: Scarecrow Press, 2005.

Timberg, Robert. The Nightingale's Song. New York: Simon & Schuster, 1995.

Toplin, Robert Brent. History by Hollywood: The Use and Abuse of the American Past. Urbana: University of Illinois Press, 1996.

———. Reel History: In Defense of Hollywood. Lawrence: University Press of Kansas, 2002.

Trumpbour, John. Selling Hollywood to the World: U.S. and European Struggles for Mastery of the Global Film Industry, 1920–1950. New York: Cambridge University Press, 2002.

Tygiel, Jules. Past Time: Baseball as History. New York: Oxford University Press, 2001.

Ulff-Moller, Jens. *Hollywood's Film Wars with France: Film-Trade Diplomacy and the Emergence of the French Film Quota Policy.* Rochester, N.Y.: University of Rochester Press, 2001.

Unger, Irwin, and Debi Unger. *Turning Point: 1968.* New York: Charles Scribner's Sons, 1988.

Wheen, Francis. *Strange Days Indeed: The 1970s: The Golden Days of Paranoia.* New York: Public Affairs, 2010.

INDEX